THE MONTREAL CANADIENS

D'ARCY JENISH

THE MONTREAL CANADIENS

100 YEARS OF GLORY

DOUBLEDAY
CANADA

LIBRARY AND ARCHIVES CANADA CATALOGUING IN PUBLICATION

Jenish, D'Arcy, 1952-
   The Montreal Canadiens : 100 years of glory / D'Arcy Jenish ; foreword by Bob Gainey.

Includes bibliographical references and index.
ISBN 978-0-385-66324-3

   1. Montreal Canadiens (Hockey team)—History. 2. Montreal Canadiens (Hockey team)—Biography. I. Title.

GV848.M6J45 2008   796.962'640971428   C2008-903735-9

Jacket images: Derik Murray/Hockey Hall of Fame
Printed and bound in the USA

Published in Canada by
Doubleday Canada, a division of
Random House of Canada Limited

Visit Random House of Canada Limited's website: www.randomhouse.ca

BVG   10   9   8   7   6   5   4   3   2   1

To the memory of my mother and father.

CONTENTS

INTRODUCTION
BY BOB GAINEY

"You can't go back, but you can go there again."
These are the words that pushed me from decision-making to decision on
a beautiful spring day in May 2003. As I turned my car into the long
driveway at our home on Stony Lake, forty kilometres northeast of
Peterborough, I knew I would be the next general manager of the Club
de Hockey Canadien.

A few days later, on June 3, 2003, a press conference was held at the
Bell Centre, home of the Canadiens, to introduce me in my new role.

The questions from the herd of journalists came at slap-shot speed.
Cameras clicked and flashed even faster. Many of the questions I didn't
have answers for . . . yet. Would coach Claude Julien be returning? What
would I do with player contracts? Who were the prospects in the system?
How did I explain the dismal season the Habs had just completed, missing
the playoffs?

There was one answer I did have, to a question which came both subtly
and directly: Why would I agree to take this position? The team was a
disaster. The fans were enraged. The media were on the warpath. The
future looked dismal. Why put myself in this unenviable position?

The answer was easy and, to me, crystal clear; In Montreal, the Canadiens *matter*! In Quebec, the Canadiens *matter*! In Canada, the Canadiens *matter*!

All of that only made the general manager's job more challenging, a point captured by Terry Mosher, also known as Aislin, celebrated editorial cartoonist of the Montreal *Gazette*. In the next day's paper, Mosher depicted me standing behind the podium at the press conference being asked, "Do think you can walk on water?" Answer: see page viii!

The Montreal Canadiens mattered to me. And I knew how important, how vital and how deeply rooted they were in the culture and history of Montrealers, Quebecers, Canadians and others.

I had learned these lessons early in my playing days. In September of 1973, I began what would be a sixteen-year career with the Habs. I recall a situation about a year later, while looking for a dentist office early one morning in the borough of Verdun. Hoping to ask for directions, I walked into a café filled with diners enjoying breakfast. The entire place went completely silent. Nobody moved. Every person there recognized me. And all of us were in shock—they because I was there, and I at the realization they knew me. I got my directions and left, relieved, as quickly as I could.

I was reminded of the importance of the Montreal Canadiens in many ways and many places, like the time I was in Helsinki, Finland, playing with Team Canada. Walking incognito (I believed) along a downtown street, I was approached from the opposite direction by a person who made eye contact and then asked in heavily-accented English: "What happened to the Canadiens in the playoffs?" There is no escape from Montreal fans!

Loyalty to the Canadiens tends to run deep and long, as I learned from my old friend Richard Halford of New York City. A year ago, he called to let me know it was the fiftieth anniversary, to the day, of the game he saw with his father at Madison Square Garden between the Canadiens and Rangers. He got Rocket Richard's autograph after the game and has been a fervent Canadiens fan ever since.

From my rookie season thrity-five years ago, I have been in contact, directly or indirectly, with much of the Canadiens' history. In that time, I met many former players and staff. I was curious about their careers and put a lot of questions to Blake, Richard, Bouchard, Curry, Pollock,

Mahovlich, Laperrière, Bowman and others. They were generous with their replies. Their memories let me touch, hear and see the reality of their lives with the Habs back to the 1930s.

In this centennial history, D'Arcy Jenish gets it right. He pushes aside the cobwebs of memory. He has sanded and scraped away the layers of time. He has resisted the fluffy, romantic versions which have become common, and delivered us the nitty-gritty, real-deal story—the good, and the not so good. I can tell you this because I know.

The Canadiens will be 100 years old on December 4, 2009. The story of the team runs parallel to, and often intersects with, the history of Canada. They are one and the same. Les Canadiens have been parts of the lives of our great-grandparents, our grandparents, our parents and ourselves. May long life be the hallmark of this great Canadian, Quebec, Montreal institution. May not only our children, but grandchildren and great-grandchildren, have the opportunity to learn about, watch and understand why the Habs are such an important part of our collective history and culture.

Bonne Anniversaire centième Club de Hockey Canadien! Many, many, more to come!

PROLOGUE
THIS IS HOCKEYTOWN

OTHER CITIES MAY LAY CLAIM TO THE TITLE, says Pierre Boivin during an animated discussion in his corner office on the seventh floor of the Bell Centre, home of the Montreal Canadiens. Then, with a sweep of his arm, he gestures at the city beyond his windows. "Make no mistake about it, *this* is Hockeytown."

Montreal is Hockeytown by dint of history and the citizenry's enduring passion for the sport. It is where a raw and ragged game—shinny played on the icebound creeks and rivers and lakes of a wintry nation—came indoors and became hockey, the world's first arena sport. It is where the first rules were written, where the first team was formed—the McGill University Redmen in 1877—and where the sport's most hallowed prize, the Stanley Cup, has come to rest thirty-nine times since it was first awarded in 1893, a prize captured by the Canadiens, Maroons, Wanderers, Shamrocks, Victorias and the Winged Wheelers of the Montreal Amateur Athletic Association.

In the 1890s, when the sport was young and the Stanley Cup brand new, the Winged Wheelers, Victorias and Shamrocks and their rabid followers were hockey's hottest rivals. A few decades later, in the Roaring

Twenties and Dirty Thirties, English Montreal had its team, the Maroons, and French Montreal had its standard-bearer, the Canadiens, and games between them produced war both on the ice and in the stands.

For seven decades now, ever since the demise of the Maroons, Montreal's sporting public has worshipped at one altar, that of the Canadiens, and the passage of time has done nothing to diminish the ardour of the citizenry. "When we win on Saturday night, you get on the subway Monday morning and three-quarters of the people are smiling," says Boivin, president and CEO of the Canadiens. "If we lose a couple and Toronto's ahead by a point, Montrealers are very unhappy. If we don't make the playoffs, spring is hell. To some degree, the city's productivity is influenced by the team's performance. Hockey is part of what makes this city tick."

And yet, in the first years of the current century, hockey in Montreal was in jeopardy. Le Club de Hockey Canadien was grievously ill and in danger of folding. The team was mediocre and missing the playoffs more often than not. Attendance was declining. Financial losses were mounting. Furthermore, there appeared to be no way out. The Canadiens were damned by circumstances beyond their control. Player salaries had risen to untenable levels, owing to the free-spending ways of wealthier rivals, most of them in the United States. The Canadiens, like the five other NHL teams based in this country, were paying their athletes in U.S. dollars but earning their revenues in a domestic dollar worth about twenty-five percent less. On top of all this, the Canadiens were saddled with over eight million dollars per year in municipal taxes, whereas the league average was less than a million per team.

"We were losing a ton of money year in, year out," Boivin recalls. "There was no way we could make money because of structural economic and competitive disadvantages. We had no hope of surviving."

The Canadiens and their Colorado-based owner, George N. Gillett Jr., solidly supported the lockout of the players that cost the NHL its entire 2004–05 season. The NHL Players' Association eventually capitulated and accepted a new collective bargaining agreement with a yearly salary cap, initially set at $39 million (U.S.) per team. This drastic measure trimmed the Canadiens' payroll by about $12 million annually and helped save the franchise.

"Toronto was the only Canadian club that could have survived long-term and been competitive under the old regime," Boivin adds. "We would have seen the relocation or the demise of the other five teams, and Montreal was no exception."

Hockey returned to the city in the fall of 2005. The Canadiens played their first home game against the Ottawa Senators on the evening of October 10, a Tuesday. About ninety minutes before the puck dropped, the main doors of the Bell Centre opened and a crowd several hundred strong surged into the lobby. Boivin was there to welcome them. So were Gillett and general manager Bob Gainey and former players Henri Richard, Yvan Cournoyer and Réjean Houle. By game time, they had greeted several thousand people, a slice of the sellout crowd of 21,273.

The return of the NHL was cause for jubilation in the city that gave birth to the game. The league's financial foundation had been restored and the future of its oldest and greatest franchise seemed assured. And the Canadiens had something else to celebrate: the one-hundredth anniversary of Le Club de Hockey Canadien—formed on December 4, 1909.

That fall, the Canadiens launched their centennial celebrations. The first significant public event occurred prior to a Saturday night game on November 12, when the Canadiens retired jersey number twelve. Left winger Dickie Moore, a two-time scoring champion, wore that sweater from 1951 to 1963, and right winger Yvan Cournoyer from 1964 to 1979. In the run-up to 2009, the team also retired numbers worn by Bernard Geoffrion (five), Serge Savard (eighteen), Ken Dryden (twenty-nine), Larry Robinson (nineteen) and Gainey (twenty-three). These joined numbers already taken out of circulation to honour Jacques Plante (one), Doug Harvey (two), Jean Béliveau (four), Howie Morenz (seven), Maurice Richard (nine), Guy Lafleur (ten) and Henri Richard (sixteen).

Two major events were planned for the centennial year. The league awarded Montreal the 2009 All-Star Game and scheduled the contest for January 25, the one-hundredth anniversary of the first match to go into the books as part of the Canadiens' official record. The league also named Montreal as host of the 2009 Entry Draft.

Amid this prolonged centenary, a remarkable transformation was taking place. Gillett, who was seen as an interloper when he acquired the club and its building in January 2001, was proving to be a good owner, and he was winning the respect of Montrealers. Boivin and his executive group were overhauling the Canadiens' business organization, while Gainey and his staff in the hockey department were rebuilding the team through trades, free-agent signings and, above all, the draft.

As the Canadiens completed their ninty-ninth season, these efforts were beginning to yield results. Le Club de Hockey Canadien had reclaimed its status as one of the best in the sport. The Canadiens were contenders again, and another Stanley Cup—a twenty-fifth for the team and a fortieth for the city—seemed a distinct possibility.

PREFACE
A TEAM LIKE NO OTHER

WHEN WE THINK OF THE MONTREAL CANADIENS, we think of many things, some obvious, some less so. There's the Stanley Cup, of course, which was awarded to the Canadiens for championships won in 1916 and 1924, in 1930 and '31, in 1944, '46 and '53, in fifteen of twenty-three seasons between 1956 and 1979, in 1986 and again in 1993. We think of longevity, because the Canadiens have been playing for a hundred years, longer than any professional hockey team.

We think of the gods of hockey: Plante in goal, Harvey and Robinson on defence, the Rocket, Béliveau and Lafleur for the offence. And a host of lesser deities: the Pocket Rocket, Boom Boom Geoffrion, Cournoyer and Moore; Dryden, Savard and Gainey. Stars from the edge of living memory: Elmer Lach, Butch Bouchard, Ken Reardon and Bill Durnan. Stars from an era beyond memory: Newsy Lalonde, Aurel Joliat and George Hainsworth, the Cleghorns, Didier Pitre and Jack Laviolette. And those who went from the rink to hospital beds to their graves: Bad Joe Hall in 1919, Georges Vézina in 1926 and Howie Morenz in 1937.

We think of stern and demanding coaches: Dick Irvin, Toe Blake and Scotty Bowman, each of whom was the best of his day. Shrewd managers:

I

Tommy Gorman, Frank Selke and Sam Pollock, who ran the team for a total of thirty-nine years and won eighteen Stanley Cups. Owners who spanned the spectrum from aristocratic to flamboyant: George N. Gillett Jr. and the Bronfmans; the Molsons and Senator Donat Raymond; Ernest Savard, Colonel Maurice Forget and their partners in the depths of the Great Depression; Léo Dandurand, Joseph Cattarinich and Louis Létourneau (the three musketeers of the 1920s and early 1930s); George Kennedy, who named the team, created the logo, guided the Canadiens to their first Cup, led them into the NHL, died prematurely in 1921 and fell into obscurity; and Ambrose O'Brien, one of the founders, the original financier and the nominal proprietor for the first twelve months.

We think of a team that has had five homes: the Jubilee Rink, deep in the city's French-speaking east end; the Westmount Arena, Montreal's premier hockey venue until fire devoured all but its brick walls in January 1918; the Mount Royal Arena, which replaced the Westmount; the Forum, which was erected on the site of an outdoor roller skating rink of the same name and was the most famous hockey stadium in the world by the time the Canadiens played their final game there on March 11, 1996; and the Bell Centre, which, with its seating capacity of 21,273 is the biggest arena in North America, and which acquired a heart, according to the French-language journalists who cover the team, on the night of April 9, 2002, when Canadiens captain Saku Koivu skated onto the ice after six months of chemotherapy treatments for cancer and received an eight-minute standing ovation from the fans.

We think of the team's ardent followers, once a small tribe of working-class, French-speaking east-end Montrealers who embraced the *bleu, blanc, rouge* as their own and nicknamed them *l'équipe des habitants*—team of the habitants—in early 1914 amid the cataclysmic conflict now known as World War I. A small tribe that created a chant to cheer on their team: "*Halte-là! Halte-là! Halte-là! Les Canadiens sont là,*" which can be translated as "Hold it! Hold it! Hold it! The Canadiens are here." The tribe followed the Canadiens from rink to rink, a journey that began at the Jubilee and ended at the Forum, where management reserved a section for them—the fifty-cent-a-ticket bleachers behind the wire at the north end of the building—

where they sat, shoulder to shoulder, packed as tightly as sardines in a tin. They became known as the Millionaires, and they stuck with the team through the Roaring Twenties and the Great Depression and World War II, through victory and defeat, through near-bankruptcy and resurrection until Selke arrived after the war, ripped out their bleachers, put in seats and priced them beyond the means of the Millionaires.

By then, Montrealers of every stripe—French and English, wealthy and poor—had embraced the team. By then, play-by-play radio broadcasts and the arrival of the Rocket had created fans in every nook and cranny of the province of Quebec, and soon television would make new followers of those in every province of the Dominion who admired the unparalleled speed, flair, finesse and artistry of Les Canadiens de Montreal—the single exception being in anglo, Protestant, Leaf-obsessed Ontario.

Through all these changes, the fans have been as passionate and demanding as any in sport. For years, they vented their anger at opponents and officials by littering the ice with hats, toe rubbers, programs, pop bottles and pennies—a disruptive and dangerous practice stopped by Selke. But neither the prim, proper, teetotalling manager nor anyone else—not the Forum ushers and not the Montreal police—could control the fans on the evening of March 17, 1955, the evening they exploded and rioted to protest the suspension that ended the Rocket's season.

Time has tested the fans. They have witnessed only two Stanley Cups in the past thirty years. Yet they remain faithful. Since the fall of 2005, they have filled every seat in the Bell Centre for every game and set league attendance records. The fans have stuck with their team because in Montreal, hockey is embedded in the psyche of the citizenry and the fibre of the culture. *La ville est hockey,* as the team's marketing slogan puts it. The city is hockey. The game is played and then it is discussed. Win or lose, there is no place for the players to hide. But they can escape. They can demand a trade, or play out their contracts and become free agents. So there has been a diaspora, a steady exodus of pampered and muscular millionaires from a hockey hotbed to somnolent southern markets where the game is often an afterthought.

The fans are one part of this equation. The media form another. For at least six months each year, the Canadiens are *the* sports story in Montreal.

In the off-season, they are just another story, but a story nonetheless. A pack of journalists thirty, forty, fifty strong watches every practice and covers every game. The players live in a fishbowl, and when they perform poorly, they end up in a frying pan. The organization is questioned daily, and no one is exempt—not the general manager, not the coach, not the third-line checker or the fourth-string rookie.

This is nothing new. For most nights over the past century, the press box has been full. Once, newspapermen filled every seat. They represented the *Star*, the *Herald*, *The Gazette* and the *Standard; La Presse, Le Devoir, La Patrie, Le Canada, Le Petit Journal, Montréal-Matin* and, more recently, *Le Journal de Montréal*. Some of the journalists started as young men and were still at it in their old age. The *Herald*'s Elmer Ferguson covered the team from 1917 till 1967; Red Fisher of *The Gazette* for over half a century starting in 1955. On the French side, some have made careers of covering the Canadiens: Zotique Lespérance, Jacques Beauchamp and, more recently, Yvon Pedneault—who started with *La Presse* in the early 1970s before becoming the colour man with the all-sports channel Réseau des Sports—and Bertrand Raymond of *Le Journal de Montréal*, who has also been at it for four decades.

Long ago, the newspapermen had to make room for the guys from radio and then television. Some of the broadcasters achieved fame as voices of the Canadiens: Danny Gallivan in English, René Lecavalier in French. These days, there are website reporters and occasionally journalists from Russia, Finland and elsewhere, come to write about their compatriots skating for the Canadiens.

The beat reporters have produced an enormous record in two languages, but their work is quickly consumed, sent to the archives and forgotten. The story of the Canadiens survives in a small library of books published over the past half century, player biographies and ghostwritten autobiographies, picture books for the coffee table, short histories and year-by-year reference works, and at least two titles of lasting renown: *The Hockey Sweater*, Roch Carrier's tale for children, and *The Game*, Ken Dryden's insider account of the 1970s Canadiens.

So much has been written by so many that there is a tendency to wonder: What's missing? What more can be said? The history of the Canadiens is like an old house that has seen too many coats of paint. In the telling and retelling, much of the story's original sparkle and freshness have been lost. This volume is an attempt to recapture the spirit and excitement of events as they unfolded. It rests on the assumption that history is never more exhilarating than the day it happens. Therefore, the book is based almost entirely on a reading of the vast record of the French- and English-speaking journalists who have covered the team. It is built around the prominent personalities—on and off the ice—the turning points and the dramatic moments.

It examines the history of the Canadiens from the moment of conception to the present day. It is the culmination of a four-year journey through archives and libraries, through reel after reel of microfilm containing the work of men who rode the trains and planes with the team, who fraternized with the players off the ice, who dined with the coaches when they were on the road. On many occasions, I have felt like the homeowner who lifts the shag carpet in the living room or the linoleum in the kitchen and finds something remarkable hidden underneath.

This book will challenge the conventional notions about the formation of the Canadiens. It will demonstrate what a miracle it was that the organization survived its first winter, let alone its first century. It will shed new light on the founders of the team, how it acquired its name and how the Canadiens came to be called the Habitants. It will bring overlooked figures out of the shadows, correct misconceptions about others and portray the team's great players as they once were—talented, doubt-filled young men struggling to make it in the big time.

Hockey, like other pro sports, does not exist in a vacuum. It is shaped by the larger events and the society around it, and a history of the Montreal Canadiens should take account of the world beyond the rink. When we think of this team, what comes immediately to mind is all those Stanley Cups. But the most remarkable thing about the Canadiens is that they have survived through war and peace, prosperity and recession, two world wars and a worldwide depression, cataclysms that caused competitors—the Montreal Wanderers, the original Ottawa Senators, the Montreal Maroons and the New York Americans—to buckle and fold.

When the Canadiens began playing, there were horses and wagons in our streets. The automobile was a novelty. The passenger train was the fastest means of transportation and the telegraph was the most efficient means of communication. The world was a different place, and hockey a very different game.

It was played by seven men a side—-the seventh being the rover—and each played the entire sixty minutes unless injury, exhaustion or misconduct sent them to the sidelines. A game consisted of two thirty-minute halves and was played on sheet of dull, grey, natural ice with no painted lines or other markings. A scorekeeper at the penalty box recorded who was winning and losing. A judge of play kept track of time with a pocket watch, and goal judges seated in the stands behind the net raised their arms to signal a goal.

The fans smoked during games and gambled openly on the outcomes. Arena operators oversold their buildings for important contests, since there were no official seating capacities. Spectators filled the aisles and sat in the rafters. Sportswriters and telegraphers created play-by-play accounts that were sent across the country, mere minutes behind the play, via wires strung alongside the transcontinental railway.

This was hockey when the Canadiens were founded in smoky hotel rooms in downtown Montreal, late in the autumn of 1909, amid the heat of a long-forgotten war between the leading professional clubs of the day. . . .

1909–1910
A HAPHAZARD START

AMBROSE O'BRIEN had been hanging around the lobby of the Windsor Hotel all evening, seated in a deep, comfortable leather chair one minute, up pacing the next, all the while trying to be patient and pleasant with everyone he met despite the knot in his gut, a tightness brought on by anger rather than anxiety.

The eight-storey stone-and-brick hotel—Montreal's grandest—was busy that night, a Thursday, the 25th of November, 1909. Guests arrived from Windsor Station, the Canadian Pacific Railway terminal located below the lip of the hill at the end of Peel Street. The hockey men strolled in, club by club—the officers of the Ottawa Senators, the Quebec Bulldogs and the two Montreal teams, the Wanderers and the Shamrocks. They always met at the Windsor, and on this occasion they had come for the annual pre-season meeting of the Eastern Canada Hockey Association. A pack of sportswriters awaited the start of the proceedings and the anticipated dust-up between the Stanley Cup champion Senators and the three-time champion Wanderers, who had been feuding for weeks. And clustered here and there were delegations who had come to apply for ECHA franchises: two from Montreal, a third from Cornwall, Ontario, and O'Brien on behalf of his hometown team, the Renfrew Creamery Kings.

He had arrived early, at 5:30 p.m., intending to corner some of the hockey men and make the case for the Kings, who were named for Renfrew's dairy, which produced the best milk products in the Upper Ottawa Valley. They had been the strongest team in the valley league three years running, but the two trustees of the Stanley Cup had denied them the opportunity to challenge the Cup holders. So the Kings decided to pursue their ambitions by joining the ECHA, where the top professionals competed.

O'Brien, twenty-four, was well-dressed and self-assured and hoped for a fair hearing. Instead, he suffered the sting of big-city condescension. Seeing the Ottawa delegates, Dave Mulligan and Percy Butler, enter the hotel, he intercepted them on the way to the dining room. They hadn't time to sit down, so O'Brien quickly made his pitch. Mulligan and Butler looked at each other and laughed. "Oh, Renfrew," one said, then threw his shoulders back and his chest out and strutted to dinner.

O'Brien was furious. How could they presume that the size of your town was any measure of your ability? Hadn't small, remote Kenora, a spit of a place amid the forests and lakes of northwestern Ontario, produced the swift and tenacious Thistles, who twice challenged the Ottawa Silver Seven for the Cup? Hadn't the Thistles thrilled hockey fans across the Dominion when they wrested the Cup from the Wanderers in January 1907?

And what about his father, Michael John O'Brien? There was proof, if any were needed, that where you came from or how you got started were no impediments to success. M.J., as everyone called him, was an Irish immigrant. He had grown up in rural Nova Scotia, had gone to work at fifteen and begun to make his fortune building railways in Nova Scotia and Ontario. Now, at age fifty-eight, M.J. was sole owner of the O'Brien mine, one of twenty-two silver producers around the rough-and-tumble town of Cobalt in the Timiskaming District, three hundred miles northwest of Montreal on the Ontario–Quebec border. Cobalt silver was producing eye-popping profits and making millionaires of a few lucky men, and M.J. was one of them. He could easily have purchased every hockey club in the country if he were so inclined—which he wasn't, though he did lend financial support to the Creamery Kings, as well as teams in Cobalt and the nearby mining town of Haileybury.

Pacing the lobby of the Windsor that evening, Ambrose O'Brien had time to brood—and to contemplate what he would do to Ottawa, given the opportunity. The hockey meeting began in Room 135 at 9:30 p.m. About a dozen men attended, and they had a full agenda. Salaries had to be capped because unfettered competition for talent was driving costs through the roof. Expansion was on the table—the four-team league needed at least two more clubs, a longer schedule and the revenue the additional games would generate. But the fight between the Senators and the Wanderers took precedence.

The Wanderers had a new owner, the ambitious promoter Patrick J. Doran, who had built the Jubilee Rink on Ste-Catherine Street, two miles east of St-Laurent Boulevard, the divide between English and French Montreal. Doran had decreed that the Wanderers would play home games in his rink, but Ottawa objected. Apart from its location, the Jubilee was too small for big-time hockey. It could hold only 3,500 people.

Ottawa insisted on the Westmount Arena, Montreal's premier hockey venue. It was located at the corner of Ste-Catherine and Wood Avenue, a mile and a half *west* of St-Laurent Boulevard. The Arena had nine rows of seats and could accommodate more than seven thousand spectators, thus producing bigger gate receipts, which were shared with visiting teams.

Money wasn't the only issue, though. Senators supporters often travelled by train to Montreal for big games. The Arena had a spacious, well-heated lobby, so there was no standing outside to buy tickets on cold, winter nights. Fans could rent small rugs to place on the benches for warmth and comfort. The bandstand was big enough for an orchestra of thirty to provide halftime entertainment and to play "God Save the King" at the end of a game. And the Arena had been renovated in 1908, its dressing rooms enlarged and shower baths installed, which allowed the Ottawa players, who were the reigning Stanley Cup champions, to wash away the sweat of a game and ride back to the capital in style.

The Senators, Shamrocks and Bulldogs had conspired to break the deadlock, and they sprang their trap at the meeting. They voted to disband the ECHA and form a new loop called the Canadian Hockey Association—

without the Wanderers. Surprised and stung, Wanderer representatives Fred Strachan, Dickie Boon and Jimmy Gardner stomped out of the room, slammed the door behind them and headed for the lobby, followed by the pack of reporters.

O'Brien, as he later told his father's biographers, Scott and Astrid Young, was seated when the Wanderer men charged downstairs. He was struck by Gardner's flushed and contorted face, and his language—the most profane and imaginative outburst of obscenities O'Brien had ever heard. Gardner headed for the front door, but was restrained by Boon and Strachan, which was no easy task. Gardner was a feisty individual who had scrapped and badgered his way through seven seasons of senior hockey and had the scars to prove it. When at last he agreed to stay, Gardner took a seat next to O'Brien and said: "Say, you O'Briens have other hockey teams up north, haven't you? In Haileybury and Cobalt?"

"We help support hockey teams up there," O'Brien replied.

"Ambrose, why don't you and I form a league?" Gardner said. "You've got Haileybury, Cobalt and Renfrew. We have the Wanderers. And I think if a team of all Frenchmen was formed in Montreal, it would be a real draw. We could give it a French-Canadian name . . ."

And then he stopped. He could hear the scratching of pencils on paper. He looked up. The sportswriters, scribbling furiously, stared back. Gardner had said too much. His comments would make the next day's papers. He gave the reporters a cold, hard glare that sent them back upstairs to eavesdrop on the meeting in Room 135.

Then, Gardner drew the other three toward him and, in a low, conspiratorial voice, he said, "We'll call this team les Canadiens."

The idea of creating a French-Canadian team was a good one, but it did not originate with Gardner. The newspapers had reported several times that fall that the ECHA would award a French-Canadian franchise. Economics, not egalitarianism, drove the officers of the leading clubs. Salaries were spiralling to unsustainable levels. The clubs could not agree on rules to control the movement of players, nor could they resist the urge to throw big money at the best pros. Sometimes they even raided each other's rosters in mid-season. The game needed a larger fan base, and the logical place to turn was Montreal's French-speaking community. At the time, the city had a population of about 465,000, one-third of them English, the balance French, but the French were barely represented in competitive hockey. English-speaking Montrealers of all stripes had their teams, initially formed from the membership of social and athletic clubs. The Winged Wheelers of the Montreal Amateur Athletic Association represented those of British descent. The Shamrocks were the Irish team. The Victorias were made up of Montrealers of Scottish descent. As the game grew in popularity, recreational leagues were organized and teams drawn from the city's hotels, banks, department stores, railways and other workplaces.

French-speaking Montrealers were much slower to embrace the game. For one thing, facilities were scarce. In 1895, there were eight indoor rinks in the city's English-speaking quarters, but only one in the French districts. The other reason was cultural. Where the English formed athletic clubs, their French counterparts gathered in social clubs to dine, dance and fraternize.

In 1896, however, some prominent French Montrealers formed an organization, modelled on the MAAA, to promote participation in team sports such as lacrosse, baseball, football and hockey. The club was called L'Association Athlétique d'Amateurs le National, and it created the first French-Canadian hockey team, recruiting students from several classical colleges. They had learned the game from Irish boys who attended the same schools, though the Irish took their classes separately and in English. The Nationals also fielded a senior lacrosse team, which won the Dominion championship in 1898. In that year, another group of French Montrealers formed L'Association Athlétique d'Amateurs le Montagnard to stimulate team sport.

By the turn of the century, French-speaking Montreal boasted three arenas, and participation in hockey was increasing. The Nationals and Montagnards entered an intermediate circuit in 1901, and the Nationals joined the newly formed senior-level Federal Amateur Hockey League in 1904. One year later, the Montagnards tried their luck at senior hockey. By 1907, both had dropped out, and for the next two seasons French Montreal was represented in senior hockey only by the few players who caught on with the Shamrocks or the Wanderers.

That changed on the evening of November 25, 1909. The newly formed Canadian Hockey Association awarded a franchise to the Nationals, and the Wanderers' as-yet-unnamed league would have a rival French-Canadian entry.

O'Brien and the officers of the Wanderers decided to hold their founding meeting on Thursday, December 2, 1909, and all agreed to work as discreetly as possible, so as to avoid giving anything away to the competition. O'Brien went north to line up financial backers in Renfrew, Cobalt and Haileybury; the Wanderers sent a representative to Toronto to offer a franchise to a syndicate that was trying to build a new arena there, while Gardner continued to denounce the duplicity of the Senators and their allies. "We were made the subject of one of the most contemptible deals ever pulled off in the annals of sport in this or any other city," he wrote in the *Montreal Star*.

Delegations from the Wanderers, Renfrew, Cobalt and Haileybury attended the inaugural meeting, and they named their new entity the National Hockey Association of Canada, for which they were roundly scorned. "In its tentative state the league is easily the most pretentious organization that has yet been attempted by the hockey clubs in Canada," declared the next day's *Gazette*. "It will be an expensive combination in some respects, but it was stated last night that the men behind it had the money and were willing to back their teams freely."

Two nights later, the NHA clubs met again, this time in Room 129 of the Windsor. Down the hall and around the corner, in Room 135, the CHA reps were also meeting. The latter had convened to draw up a schedule, but afterward refused to release a copy to the reporters who had hovered in the corridor from mid-afternoon till 10:30 p.m. The officers of the NHA showed no such reserve. They emerged and made three announcements. Their league would have a French-Canadian team called le Canadien (a name that immediately became plural in newspaper reports). They had hired Jack Laviolette, one of the fastest skaters in the game, to assemble the team and also to be a player. Lastly, Cobalt's representative, Tommy Hare, an

O'Brien employee, would deposit five thousand dollars in a Montreal bank on Monday morning to guarantee the operating expenses and player salaries for the French team.

The English-language papers devoted most of their Monday sports pages to news of the latest developments. "Efforts to bring to a sharp conclusion the war among the professional hockey clubs failed and the two leagues formed within the past ten days settled down to what promises to be a bitter fight for supremacy," *The Gazette* noted. Mostly, the journalists lamented the folly of the hockey men. Montrealers would be expected to support five professional teams and at least two amateur senior teams. All told, they would play forty-seven home games, compared with twenty-four the previous winter—"a bill of hockey that will make the most ardent fan gasp," one reporter noted.

The French-language press, meanwhile, barely acknowledged the story. UN NOUVEAU CLUB CANADIEN, the headline in *La Presse* read. The new organization was Le Club de Hockey le Canadien—not to be confused with Le Club Athlétique Canadien, formed in 1905 to encourage French-Canadian participation in sports and to promote wrestling matches and other sporting events. The paper ran six inches of copy, below the fold, and an oval-shaped thumbnail photo of Laviolette in a turtleneck sweater—undoubtedly a team uniform—with his hair parted smartly down the middle and a hint of a smile on his full, angular face.

Laviolette had been christened Jean-Baptiste, but he grew up as Jack in the staunchly Loyalist town of Belleville, Ontario, and later in Valleyfield, Quebec, at the western tip of the province. He played lacrosse all summer and hockey all winter and was good enough at both to move from small-town to big-city teams and from commercial to senior hockey. He spent the 1904 season playing in Montreal and the next three in Sault Ste. Marie, Michigan, with a team called the Indians, in the U.S.–based International Hockey League, the game's first all-pro loop. Then he returned to Montreal and spent two years playing senior hockey and lacrosse and running a drinking establishment called Jack's Cage, a popular hangout on Notre Dame Street.

With the Canadiens, Laviolette was managing a team for the first time, and he had to move quickly. He had just a month till the opening game, and only a few days before the first cold snap, the first dash of wintry weather that would allow the rinks to freeze over and the players to start practising. That happened at mid-month, and by December 16 ice time was hard to come by at the Arena and the Jubilee. Both sheets, marred by thin patches and high spots, were in use from mid-afternoon till late evening, including Christmas Eve. Juniors, intermediates and seniors, amateurs and pros, and teams from schools, colleges and the commercial leagues all took turns tuning up for the 1910 season.

Laviolette faced two challenges as he assembled his starting seven. They would have to be better than the Nationals if they were to be the team of French Montreal, and they would have to be able to skate a full sixty minutes against two of the strongest clubs in the land: the proud and strapping Wanderers, a perennial powerhouse, and the astonishing Renfrew Creamery Kings, who were soon to become known in the newspapers as the Millionaires, thanks to the free spending of the O'Briens. Ambrose and M.J. spent the entire month of December, and a smidgen of their silver fortune, attempting to plunder the lineup of the Cup-holding Senators and, when that effort proved largely unsuccessful, recruiting other top pros by offering outlandish salaries.

The officers of the National Hockey Association had given the Canadiens one significant advantage: they had agreed to forgo signing French-Canadian players until Laviolette had completed his roster. There were two skaters Laviolette wanted badly, and the Nationals were after them, too. The first was his old friend Didier Pitre.

Pitre and Laviolette had played together as boys in Valleyfield and as adults in Montreal and the International league. In his travels, Pitre had acquired the nickname Cannonball. He had thick wrists and powerful legs, and his weight occasionally blossomed to two hundred pounds, but he was surprisingly quick and nimble on skates. He played defence and liked to carry the puck; his dashes down the ice often ended with a blistering snap of his wrists and a bullet-like shot that intimidated the poorly padded goaltenders, splintered the end boards or missed the mark entirely and sent the spectators diving for safety.

Though physically powerful, he had a gentlemanly temperament. "Many played brutally, but Pitre was not one of them," Montreal *Herald* sports editor Elmer Ferguson wrote many years later of the player he had watched as a child. "It is doubtful if the big, good-natured Frenchman ever did a mean or unsportsmanlike thing in his whole career." A French-Canadian journalist would later write: "Pitre was a very loyal player with a generous heart. The fans liked his lively character, his engaging repartee, his extraordinary drive and the unbelievable speed of his rushes."

Pitre spent the summer and fall of 1909 working for his brother-in-law, who operated an automobile service station in Sault Ste. Marie, Ontario. In early December he received a telegram from Laviolette outlining, in a few clipped phrases, the situation in Montreal: "New league formed. New Canadien team formed. Big money available. Come to Montreal."

Pitre quit his job, bought a one-way ticket and boarded the first eastbound train. At North Bay, a representative of the Montreal Nationals met Pitre's train and joined the player in his compartment. The emissary told him about the new Canadian Hockey Association. He told him that the Nationals had been awarded a franchise and that the team would represent French Montreal. He offered one hundred dollars a week for a ten-week season, and Pitre, assuming that this was the team Laviolette had mentioned in his telegram, signed on the spot. He discovered his mistake during a stopover in Ottawa. There on the platform stood Laviolette, waiting for the train. Laviolette explained that he was with the Canadiens, the other French-Canadian team, that he would be playing one of the defence positions and that he wanted Pitre as his partner. Pitre could not say no to a friend of such long standing, and he signed with the Canadiens.

The Nationals cried foul and launched a legal action for breach of contract. The case went to court on January 4, 1910, the day before the Canadiens' season opener, and a justice of the peace granted an injunction prohibiting Pitre from playing. Twenty-four hours later, a lawyer for the Canadiens appeared before a single judge of the Court of Appeal and argued that the Nationals had misled Pitre by saying that Laviolette would be coaching their team. The lawyer also reasoned that a player could not be forced to compete for a team against his will. The judge agreed and lifted the injunction.

The second player of French-Canadian descent whom the Canadiens and Nationals both coveted was Édouard Lalonde, the son of a Cornwall, Ontario, shoemaker. Lalonde, who spoke only a few words of French despite his heritage, was a star in hockey and lacrosse and was one of the few individuals in Canada who earned a living as a professional athlete. He weighed 168 pounds, had a fiery temperament and was a prolific scorer.

Lalonde was known as Newsy, a nickname he had acquired after working as a child apprentice in the pressroom of the *Cornwall Freeholder*. By age seventeen, he was playing senior hockey for Cornwall, and the following season he joined the senior team in Woodstock, Ontario. He turned pro in 1907 with Sault Ste. Marie, Ontario's IHL squad, the Algonquins, and earned thirty-five dollars a week. Lalonde arrived on the train half an hour before the opening game of the season against the Soo, Michigan, Indians. He hadn't eaten all day, but dressed anyway and scored two goals. Afterward, the Indians offered Lalonde fifty dollars a week, the Algonquins matched the offer, and Lalonde stayed put.

Before joining the Canadiens, Lalonde played two seasons with the Toronto Arenas of the Ontario Professional Hockey League, which was known as the trolley league because players travelled by electric train to contests in Brantford, Guelph, Waterloo and Berlin (renamed Kitchener after World War I). In his first year, Lalonde played nine of twelve games, scored twenty-nine goals and won the scoring championship. The following winter, he missed four of fifteen games because of injuries and finished second with twenty-four goals.

Lalonde came to terms with Laviolette on December 14, 1909, after a brief negotiation conducted by telegraph, and arrived in Montreal the following day for a pre-season skate with his new teammates. Laviolette, meanwhile, announced to the press that his roster was complete and that the Canadiens would begin training in earnest for their opening game on January 5, 1910, against the Cobalt Silver Kings.

———

The Silver Kings were a hastily assembled, no-name bunch. They had practised just twice, and Montreal fans were familiar with only two of the
players—Steve Vair and Walter Smaill, both ex-Wanderers lured north by
big salaries. The Kings were starting a three-game road trip that included
matches against the Wanderers and Renfrew. They wore smart, new blue
sweaters trimmed with red and grey stripes at the waist and shoulders and
the name Cobalt tucked inside an egg-shaped C. The Canadiens wore solid
blue sweaters with a large, elliptical C superimposed on a white horizontal
bar. White pants and red socks completed the uniform. These were the
colours of English- and French-Canadians: the blue, white and red of the
Union Jack and the *bleu, blanc, rouge* of *le tricolore,* the flag of France, which
often flew at parades and other public events in Quebec.

At 8:45 p.m., following a fifteen-minute warmup, the bell sounded to
start the game and the players took their positions. Joe Cattarinich, a
prominent Montreal lacrosse player but a newcomer to professional
hockey, guarded the Canadiens' net. Laviolette, playing point, lined up fifteen feet in front of him. Pitre, the cover point, stood in front of
Laviolette, leaving a another fifteen-foot gap, and Lalonde, the rover,
positioned himself about the same distance from Pitre. The forwards—
left winger George Poulin, centreman Ed Decarie and right winger Art
Bernier—lined up opposite their Cobalt counterparts.

No one knew what to expect of these two teams. Not the men in the
makeshift press box representing *The Gazette,* the *Montreal Star, La Presse,*
La Patrie and a sprinkling of other papers. Not the staff and management of
the Jubilee, who were hosting their first senior-level game. And not the
spectators, most of whom arrived shortly before game time and formed a
noisy, jostling crowd pressed against the main entrance on Ste-Catherine
Street and halfway around the building, all of them eager to buy their tickets and to get in from the cold.

They filled the front-row boxes and the four rows of benches along
both sides and one end of the ice surface. They lined the rails of the
standing-room sections behind the benches. The reporters estimated that
the building could accommodate 3,500 and guessed that there were over
three thousand present that night. "A surprisingly large number journeyed

from the West End to see the game," one journalist wrote, "but the bulk of the gathering was undoubtedly drawn from the French-Canadien population of the East End of the city."

By all accounts they witnessed a whirlwind of a game. Newsy Lalonde opened the scoring three minutes in, following a solo sprint down the ice. He slipped past the Cobalt defenders, fell to the ice before he could shoot and scored from his knees. Lalonde assisted on the Canadiens' second goal and put in another to give his side a three–one lead after thirty minutes.

Early in the second half, he left the game with a sprained ankle. Cobalt dropped a man and the teams played six aside. The Kings tied the score at three, then went ahead by one, but the Canadiens pulled even. The visitors put another pair past Cattarinich, and that should have settled the matter, but Bernier and Laviolette each scored with under two minutes remaining, and the score stood at six apiece when the bell rang.

The game had all the speed and intensity of a season-ending finale or even a Stanley Cup match, according to the press-box observers. The fans smoked throughout the contest, and toward the end they watched through a thick haze that hovered over the ice. A female spectator, the mother of one of the players, suffered a painful gash when struck across the nose and cheek by an errant stick. The players left the ice sporting an assortment of cuts, nicks, fat lips and blackened eyes. The band began playing "God Save the King," and four to five hundred fans made for the exits before the two on-ice officials declared that the outcome would be decided in overtime.

Those spectators who left regretted their hasty departure. Cobalt took control and repeatedly pinned the Canadiens in their own end. The Kings showered shots at the Montreal net, but Cattarinich held them off and made two dazzling saves that ended a Cobalt siege and gave his teammates a lift. They took possession, charged down the ice, and Poulin scored at five minutes and twenty-five seconds to make the final score seven–six.

"It was a wild hurrah from start to finish," the next day's *Gazette* concluded, "with a scene of tremendous enthusiasm at the finish to mark the first victory of the all-star French-Canadian team."

———

The Canadiens did not play again for two weeks, and between games another upheaval shook the hockey world. The dire predictions of the newspapermen proved accurate. The clubs had flooded the market. There was not enough talent to stock Montreal's five professional teams and not enough fans to support them. The opening games of the NHA season were close, hard-fought contests; those of the CHA were mostly lamentable. On January 11, a Tuesday, the Shamrocks beat the Nationals seventeen to eight and a *Montreal Star* reporter wrote: "In stoney silence, the games [goals] piled up. To say that the attendance was sparse would be kindly. To say it was almost invisible would be near the literal truth. The game was like free trade—too jug handled to be interesting or profitable."

The following day, the Shamrocks and the Senators abandoned their CHA partners and initiated merger talks with the NHA. By Friday, the negotiations had advanced far enough to schedule a meeting. On Sunday afternoon, January 15, in Room 135 at the Windsor—the "famous old room," in the words of one journalist—the hockey men gathered. Each NHA club had a representative present, though Ambrose O'Brien spoke for both Renfrew and the Canadiens.

The Shamrocks and Senators submitted written applications, without conditions, and these were accepted immediately. All parties turned their attention to the schedule and spent four hours drafting one for an expanded seven-team league. Two representatives of the Nationals also attended. Everyone assumed the Nationals would acquire the Canadiens from O'Brien and merge the two teams.

This was the logical course to follow. The AAAN was fourteen years old, it had a healthy membership of French-speaking Montrealers and it continued to field a senior lacrosse team each summer. But the sale of the Canadiens faltered on two points. First, O'Brien insisted that the Nationals honour his contract with Patrick Doran, under which the French-Canadian team was to play at the Jubilee for three seasons. The Nationals maintained that they had a contract with the Arena and couldn't make money if their team were based at the Jubilee. O'Brien's asking price also proved too steep. The Nationals would have to assume the club's existing debt of $1,400, in addition to player contracts worth $6,200.

"It is unfortunate how these events have turned out," proclaimed *La Patrie*, which billed itself as the people's paper. "But we must not blame the directors of the Nationals who, in this affair, have acted with much prudence and wisdom."

By chance, the Canadiens had survived the merger. By default, they would represent French Montreal in professional hockey. Yet they remained an orphan of a team, with an uninterested absentee owner and little or no support in the community.

O'Brien had the pleasure of watching both his teams on the evening of January 19, when the Canadiens visited Renfrew to play the Creamery Kings. There was no question as to where his allegiance lay. He wanted the Kings to win the Stanley Cup to spite Ottawa, of course, but also to boost Renfrew's prospects. A Dominion hockey championship would distinguish his hometown from all the other ambitious little farming and lumbering and mining communities sprouting across the country. And he had spared no expense to pursue his dream. O'Brien and his father, M.J., had signed some of the biggest stars in the game, had made headlines in the country's leading newspapers and had made a shambles of the economics of hockey.

The O'Briens began on December 7 with a brazen attempt to snatch four members of the Ottawa Senators just as the reigning champions were reassembling to begin their pre-season training. Creamery King executive George Martel intercepted Albert "Dubbie" Kerr and Marty Walsh aboard a Brockville–Ottawa train and took the players to Ottawa's Windsor Hotel for interviews with M.J., who promptly offered each man $1,200 for the twelve-game season and jobs in Renfrew paying one thousand, two hundred dollars a year. The next day's *Ottawa Citizen* called the offers "bewildering," because the O'Briens were offering much more more than either had ever earned before. Kerr and Walsh could have lived for five to six years on that kind of money, according to the paper. Yet they hesitated. They were being asked to desert one of the best organizations in the game, and a city second only to Montreal as a hockey centre. They would do it, they told the O'Briens, if Renfrew signed fellow Senators Fred Lake and Fred Taylor.

This caused a day of frantic negotiations. M.J. remained at the Windsor, while Ambrose and Martel huddled with the players at Hurd and Company, a sporting goods store at 191 Sparks Street. Senators executives gathered just down the street at the business premises of Llewellyn Bate, who owned a string of Ottawa grocery stores. The auction lasted three hours. Messengers raced back and forth with offers and counteroffers. At one point, M.J. told the players, "You go to the Ottawas and tell them to make their best proposition and whatever they offer you, even if it is ten thousand, we will raise them."

The Senators only went as high as two thousand dollars per player. The O'Briens finally bid $2,700 each for Kerr and Walsh, and three thousand each for Lake and Taylor. They were also prepared to grant two-year deals worth five thousand. They produced certified cheques for the full amounts and, when that failed to persuade, they put cash on the table. But loyalty prevailed over lucre. Taylor turned down Renfrew first, and the others followed.

M.J. and Ambrose quickly rebounded. They next went after Lester Patrick, former captain of the Wanderers, and his brother Frank, both of whom were working in their father's lumber business in Nelson, British Columbia. Three other eastern clubs were also interested, even though Lester had already signed with the Edmonton Eskimos for their upcoming Stanley Cup challenge series against the Senators. Negotiations were conducted by telegraph. All told, the Patricks received twenty-six proposals over a two-week period. The talks culminated in a day of escalating bidding, primarily for Lester. The Wanderers offered $1,200. The Senators topped that with two thousand. But the O'Briens prevailed, and their bid put hockey on the front pages of leading newspapers.

"The Creamery town backers have landed the biggest fish in the hockey pool," the *Ottawa Citizen* declared on December 13. "Both men have pledged their services to the club for the season, in return for which the Renfrew magnates will separate themselves from six thousand dollars, each of the Patrick boys receiving $3,000. They will draw from Renfrew the biggest stipend ever received by hockey players."

But Ambrose and his father weren't finished. They received word a few days later that Taylor, the Ottawa cover point and one of the game's top attractions, might be available after all. He was a colourful player who had a showman's personality and had acquired the nickname Cyclone. After three pro seasons in the International league, he had joined the Senators in 1908 and made an immediate impression with the team and its fans. "He's better than any of us," conceded the veteran Alf Smith. "He's so goddamned fast it's impossible to keep up with him."

The Cyclone earned five hundred dollars a season with Ottawa and $420 per year as a junior clerk in the railway lands branch of the federal Department of the Interior. At the time of the O'Brien raid, he was bucking for a promotion. Senators executives had lobbied on his behalf, and several prominent members of Parliament had even arranged a special examination for him. But the department would not move, so Taylor decided to apply additional pressure. He began negotiating with the O'Briens. He sat out the Senators' pre-season training sessions and became the story on the Ottawa sports pages. Would he show for tonight's practice? Had he signed with Renfrew? These questions preoccupied the team and its fans for nearly two weeks. On December 18, an *Ottawa Citizen* reporter described a day of perplexing talks. Larry Gilmour, the only local player on the Creamery Kings, told the *Citizen:* "Taylor is going to Renfrew with us this afternoon. We have his contract and have a position waiting for him. There is no doubt that we have him at last."

"Taylor is not going to Renfrew," Llewellyn Bate declared. "You can bet on that. He will be out to practise with the Ottawas tonight."

Taylor, a shrewd negotiator who was good at playing one side against the other, added to the confusion. "Yes, I have signed a Renfrew contract," he said, "but there is . . . a proviso attached to it. It is not a binding contract."

"Have you settled finally with either the Ottawa or the Renfrew club?" the journalist asked.

"No."

"Are you going out to practice tonight?"

"Yes."

"In Ottawa or Renfrew?"

"With the Stanley Cup holders."

The uncertainty ended on December 28, when Taylor jumped to Renfrew for a total of $5,250. He would be paid three thousand for playing hockey, he would receive a thousand as a performance bond and he would be given a job paying $1,250, all of which made him one of the highest-paid athletes in North America.

Taylor's colleagues in the railways lands branch held a going-away party on January 3 and presented him with a suitcase. His former teammates bade him farewell by telling him he would be welcome to attend their Stanley Cup banquet in the spring. Taylor responded by saying the banquet would take place at M.J. O'Brien's new hotel in Renfrew.

A crowd of 1,500 packed Renfrew's arena on January 19 for the game between the Canadiens and the Creamery Kings, whom the newspapers were now calling "the Millionaires." Three times in the first half, the Montrealers took the lead; on each occasion, Renfrew quickly pulled even, and the teams went to their dressing rooms tied at three after thirty minutes.

Again, Lalonde was the Canadiens' best player. He scored twice and assisted on a third goal and fought a running battle with Lester Patrick. He and Patrick were both penalized three times, and they resumed hostilities following the break. As the *Montreal Star* reported, "Patrick cut Lalonde's head open with a swing of his stick and as soon as the Renfrew leader got back in play Lalonde got him with a wicked cross check that sent the famous rover into the air as though shot from a cannon."

The Millionaires dominated the second half, scoring six straight goals before Lalonde batted a loose puck into a wide-open net with Renfrew goalie Bert Lindsay caught out of position. Final score: Renfrew nine, Canadiens four.

The Renfrew game set a season-long pattern for the Canadiens. They had established themselves as the fastest team in the league. They came at their opponents like a whirlwind, but invariably faded as the contest progressed. They lost their next three games, beat Haileybury nine–five on February 7 and then dropped six straight to fall from contention. Meanwhile, O'Brien's high-priced stars worked their way back into the race over the next three weeks to set up a dramatic showdown with the powerful and unbeaten Ottawa Senators.

———

The big game between Ottawa and Renfrew was played in the capital on Saturday, February 12. Earlier that week, Taylor had spent an afternoon at the *Ottawa Citizen* chatting with the sports reporters and his former teammate Percy Lesueur, goaltender for the Senators. In the course of the conversation, Taylor boasted that he would put one past Lesueur after skating backward through the entire Ottawa team. The newspaper reported the remark, and it caused a stir. An indignant Senator fan phoned the *Citizen* to announce that he would wager a hundred dollars that Taylor wouldn't score. He placed the money with the owner of the King Edward Hotel, and another fan put a hundred down on Taylor.

Others were shelling out big money for tickets. Seventy-five-cent reserved seats were selling for up to six dollars. Demand for standing room, as well as rush seats, was unprecedented. On game day, fans began lining up at four o'clock. By six, the lineup stretched for two blocks, and by 7:30 it was four blocks long. "A fierce scramble for seats ensued once the doors were thrown open," a journalist noted, though police officers managed to maintain order.

Fans lined the standing-room sections three and four deep. Every beam and rafter was filled. Dozens of men peered through windows on the roof, which were thrown open to clear the building of tobacco smoke. Two hundred and fifty Renfrew fans sat in the northeast corner, and a hundred from Brockville sat together elsewhere. All told, over seven thousand people— Ottawa's largest crowd ever—packed the building.

The teams took their warmups shortly before the 8:30 start. The moment Taylor appeared, fans began chanting, "Here he comes, here he comes." They hurled lemons, oranges and other objects, including a whisky flask. Taylor did not score that night—skating forward *or* backward—but he and the rest of the Millionaires played brilliant hockey, and so did the Senators.

Lester Patrick tied the game at five apiece with minutes to go, and the teams played two five-minute overtime periods. Ottawa scored three times, and the partisan crowd erupted. "Hats were thrown in the air, ribbons, muffs and flags waved and tossed about," the *Citizen* reported, "and when referee Russell Bowie blew his whistle for the last time the crowd swarmed pell-mell down on the ice, the Ottawa players getting a great ovation as they disappeared into their dressing room."

Those unable to attend the game kept abreast of the play via telegraph and telephone. The *Citizen* placed a telegraph operator at rinkside and he sent out a running account, which was transmitted to the newspaper's offices several blocks away over a wire strung especially for the occasion. The newsroom telephones rang all evening and till 2:30 the following morning. Calls came from Renfrew, Perth, Almonte, Arnprior, Buckingham and Pembroke—not to mention Ottawa.

Four days after this stirring contest, the Canadiens made a strange move. They released Newsy Lalonde, their top scorer and only consistent offensive threat. Lalonde had played seven games in the colours of the Canadiens and accounted for eighteen of the team's forty-two goals. Montreal hockey fans quickly discerned that Ambrose O'Brien was behind the decision. His Millionaires were approaching a crucial game February 25 against the Wanderers. A loss would knock Renfrew out of contention. A win would create a three-way race with the Wanderers and Senators for first place in the NHA—and the Stanley Cup.

Lalonde was accustomed to moving from team to team. He was by nature easy-going and gregarious, and adapted quickly to new surroundings. He took a room at the O'Brien-owned hotel where most of the other players were staying for the winter, and he accompanied them north to the silver country for back-to-back games against Haileybury and Cobalt. The Millionaires won both by big margins and two nights later were back on the ice, at home, to face the Wanderers.

The Montreal seven lacked individual stars to match Lalonde, the Patricks, and Cyclone Taylor. Collectively, though, they were bigger and stronger, and they were superior. They smothered the Millionaires with their checking and kept them off balance all night with relentless hustle. The Wanderers led three–nothing at halftime and added two more after the break while holding Renfrew scoreless. A crowd of about two thousand, well above capacity, had packed Renfrew's little rink. By the end, they watched silently as their Stanley Cup hopes evaporated.

The Wanderers were hitting their peak, and on March 5 they travelled to Ottawa for the decisive game of the season. Hundreds of Montrealers made the trip as well. Some took the Grand Trunk's 3 p.m. special. Others went on regular Grand Trunk and Canadian Pacific runs. Hockey fans from small towns up and down the Ottawa Valley also converged on the capital. The Laurier Avenue Arena was full when the teams lined up for the 8:30 p.m. start, though not as packed as it had been for the Senators–Millionaires game. "It was a wildly excited throng," the Montreal *Gazette* reported, "the Ottawa supporters as usual keeping up an incessant din during the first half."

But the local fans were unable to sustain their enthusiasm. The Senators fell behind early and tired quickly. The ice was soft, thanks to mild weather, and pools of water accumulated in the corners and along the boards. None of this bothered the Wanderers. They played with their usual brisk efficiency. The forwards—Jimmy Gardner, Ernie Russell, Pud Glass and Harry Hyland—outworked the men opposite them and performed better as a unit. The defence—pointman Jack Marshall and cover point Ernie Johnson—brushed aside every Ottawa attack, ensuring that goaltender Riley Hern had an easy night. The final score was close, three–one, but not the play. Towards the end of the match, according to *The Gazette,* "a dead silence fell over the loyal Ottawa enthusiasts."

The Wanderers returned triumphant to Montreal. They had won top spot in the NHA; they had won the O'Brien Cup—a silver bowl mounted on a wooden pedestal and flanked by two silver figures of hockey players, which was donated by Ambrose O'Brien and his father to be awarded annually to the league champion. More importantly, by finishing ahead of Ottawa, the Wanderers had won their fourth Stanley Cup in five years.

As the season wound down, all the professional hockey clubs, including the Wanderers, were tallying their financial losses, incurred largely because of the extravagant player salaries. The Cobalt Silver Kings had run out of money prior to their last trip south and were about to default their remaining games until a number of wealthy backers—several of them connected with the O'Briens—contributed enough cash to pay the players and cover expenses. Ottawa wound up with a small deficit. From the outset, the O'Briens had no prospect of breaking even in Renfrew because the arena was too small to generate enough revenue to meet the payroll. There was no talk of where the Canadiens landed financially since the O'Briens were looking after them.

The Canadiens finished the season March 11 against the Shamrocks. Without Lalonde, the league scoring champion, they were incapable of generating much offence or excitement. They remained a fast-skating, hardworking team and they squeaked by the Shamrocks five–four after twelve minutes of overtime.

It was their third win of the season, but the first, against the Cobalt Silver Kings, didn't count because the game was played prior to the merger with the CHA. Their record for 1910 was two wins and ten losses. They scored fifty-nine goals, but allowed one hundred. They finished last, just behind the Shamrocks.

Given their record, their haphazard origins and their absentee, English-speaking owner, the Canadiens had failed to win the affections of French Montrealers. Some prominent members of that community refused to take the team seriously. "The Canadiens only represent the interests and the money of Mr. O'Brien and not our French Canadian nationality," Tancrède Marsil of the Montreal daily *Le Devoir* wrote in mid-February. By the end of the season, his attitude had hardened. He mocked the Canadiens as the plaything of a rich man's son. "It would have been easy to form a stronger team," Marsil wrote, "but he chose not to, and for what reason. Mr. O'Brien had assembled a hockey team of French Canadians only to create some competition to the east of him, to make money and to push Renfrew to the forefront."

Those were the final words on the Canadiens for the 1910 season. By then, the players had scattered. Some would be back as autumn turned to winter, and this time there would be an impassioned debate among French

Montrealers, a debate conducted via the columns of the French-language newspapers and centred on two questions: Who should own this team? And who should play for it if the Canadiens were truly to represent French Montreal in the world of professional hockey?

1910–1921
THE KENDALL/KENNEDY YEARS

THE TURK AND THE GERMAN, two powerful heavyweights, were struggling ferociously on the mat as the working-class crowd of men and boys at the Sohmer Park Pavilion sat silent and spellbound. Pengal, Lion of the Sultan, was on his back and writhing to avoid being pinned. Eberle, the German, had tossed the Lion quickly and easily. He was the stronger man and a better wrestler, and many of those in attendance—just over two thousand—could see that. They knew wrestling. They had been watching such bouts for five years, usually on Friday nights, sometimes on Wednesday. They lived in tightly packed two- and three-storey row houses in the east-end neighbourhoods of Ste-Marie and Hochelaga and walked or rode streetcars to Sohmer Park, at the corner of Notre Dame and Panet streets, not far from the St. Lawrence River. They had seen the biggest stars of professional wrestling, men who fought for noisy crowds and big purses in Buffalo, Chicago, New York and the famous cities of Europe.

George Kennedy, a Montrealer of Irish and Scottish descent, not long retired from the ring, had put his hometown on the North American circuit and had organized the card featuring Eberle and Pengal along with two other matches, held November 5, 1909. He promoted the evening with his customary flamboyance. He had had notices printed and posted them himself, tacking them to fences and lampposts in the side streets that ran north from Sohmer Park. He had visited the newspapers to talk up the matches, and *La Presse* had advised its readers that they would witness "UN PRO-GRAMME FORMIDABLE."

Pengal and Eberle were the main attraction. They were to fight until one had pinned the other twice. Both stood six foot one, though the German was heavier. He should have prevailed quickly, but the Turk writhed and squirmed and would not be subdued. Pengal grasped the German in a headlock and squeezed hard. Eberle gasped. He resisted violently. The Turk held fast; then he howled. The German had grabbed his toes, had squeezed and twisted and would not let go till he received a stiff blow to the chest. Eberle looked up. The referee had kicked him. The ref did it again. The German leapt to his feet and bolted from the ring. The fans jeered and the ref shouted: "Keep quiet. You know nothing."

Eberle was headed for the exit when George Kennedy accosted him. The stout, pugnacious promoter, who stood five foot three, was wielding an iron bar, his face pale as a cadaver. "If you don't wrestle," he bellowed, "I'll bust your brains out."

"George," someone yelled, "don't be crazy. You'll kill him."

Several people threw themselves on Kennedy. A young man, a member of Montreal's German community, punched Kennedy in the jaw. That brought him to his senses. He looked at Eberle and told him to get back in the ring or he wouldn't get paid.

Eberle strode back, took hold of the Lion of the Sultan, quickly pinned him and left Sohmer Park Pavilion with an escort of three police officers to prevent further trouble.

The next day, *La Presse* ran a larger-than-usual headline on its sports page—SCÈNES DISGRACIEUSES AU PARC SOHMER—and provided a blow-by-blow account of the disturbance. The accompanying story concluded with a warning: "Next Friday? Who knows. Last night's event was a colossal fiasco, which must not be repeated if the public is to be attracted to wrestling spectacles."

George Kennedy knew better. A little mayhem wouldn't hurt him. He had a solid following among the largely French-speaking working men of the east end who put in long hours in shops and factories and looked forward to their Friday evenings at Sohmer Park. He had friends in the sports departments of most of the city's daily newspapers and he was a slick promoter.

Kennedy was ambitious and self-confident, and a quick, compelling talker in French and English. He was just twenty-six and had started in the ring as a teenage lightweight who tipped the scales at about 135 pounds. He had become one of the best in the country and resolved on a career as a wrestler, but his aspirations ended on an April evening in 1903, on the floor of a Montreal armoury, when he lost a long, gruelling bout to a French-Canadian named Eugène Tremblay. Afterward, Tremblay appeared fresh and capable of continuing; Kennedy was completely exhausted. The young men soon formed an enduring and profitable partnership. Kennedy quit the ring to manage Tremblay, but his mother, a prim, church-going Irish Catholic, was aghast, and so was his Scottish Protestant father, George Hiram Kendall, the proprietor of G.H. Kendall & Co., a manufacturer of coal and gas stoves. Had he no regard for their good names? Couldn't he find a respectable profession? His siblings—three sisters and three brothers, two of whom became contractors in Montreal—questioned his judgment as well.

But George would not reconsider. He simply changed his name. George Kendall became George Kennedy, and he and Tremblay went to work for the American wrestler and promoter Martin Burns, a physical-fitness zealot who had acquired the nickname Farmer Burns in 1889 while fighting barefoot and clad in overalls in Chicago. Six years later, Burns won his first world title in catch-as-catch-can wrestling, the anything-goes American version of the sport. He had fought nearly six thousand bouts, and lost only a handful, by the time Kennedy and Tremblay joined him, and he frequently opened the show with a display of his extraordinary strength. Burns would slip a hangman's noose around his twenty-inch neck, dangle from the end of the rope and talk to the audience.

Kennedy worked as a road agent and front man for Farmer Burns. He'd been to Chicago, Des Moines and Kansas City, Omaha, Minneapolis and other booming Midwestern centres, renting venues and scheduling bouts. He visited local newspapers to talk up the matches, especially those that pitted Americans against Europeans, and challenged local strongmen to test themselves against the wrestlers.

Kennedy excelled in America, but he remained a Montrealer at heart and always returned. He began renting the Sohmer Park Pavilion. He brought in America's best wrestlers. He went to France, Germany and as far as Turkey to recruit others, and the managers of the pavilion welcomed his productions.

The park, which was privately run, thrived in the spring, the summer and the fall. Families picnicked and attended concerts at the outdoor amphitheatre in July and August. They strolled along the river during the worst of the heat and humidity. The men drank in the outdoor beer garden. Children visited the zoo, and people of all ages descended in droves when the circus came to town. In the winter, though, Montrealers turned to skating, snowshoeing and tobogganing. It was the time of year when Sohmer Park was dead—and that's when Kennedy staged his productions.

He made Montreal a wrestling centre. In 1905, his man Tremblay won the world lightweight championship in a bout held at the park. That year, Kennedy and Dr. Joseph Pierre Gadbois, his business partner and a promoter of physical fitness, formed Le Club Athlétique Canadien to train and develop amateur wrestlers. Their ambitions soon grew. They incorporated the organization in September 1908 and raised twenty-five thousand dollars through a share offering sold to French-Canadian investors. They added boxing matches to the wrestling programs at Sohmer Park, even though prizefights were prohibited under Canadian law.

Hockey caught their interest as well. In the fall of 1908, Kennedy and Gadbois tried to purchase the Wanderers, but those negotiations were not successful. They also considered starting a French-Canadian team, but were overtaken by the formation of the National Hockey Association and the creation of the Canadiens in the fall of 1909. Kennedy was vexed by this development: he and Gadbois believed they held the rights to the name "Canadiens" and that those rights were being infringed.

But what to do? Kennedy brooded over the matter throughout the winter and into the spring and slowly formed a plan. Early in October 1910, he acted. He called Frank Calder, sports editor of the Montreal *Herald,* and announced that Le Club Athlétique Canadien wanted an NHA franchise. He was prepared to purchase the Canadiens. And, if rejected, he would go to court to enforce his rights to the name.

Kennedy's timing was perfect. The annual meeting of the National Hockey Association was scheduled for November 10 at the Windsor Hotel. The last thing the owners needed, as they prepared for the 1911 season, was a lawsuit over a team none of them really cared about. Besides, they were preoccupied with more pressing issues.

The first was salaries. The previous winter, some payrolls had hit $15,000, and every club had lost money. This time, spending would be capped at $5,000 per team. The players objected vociferously. Art Ross, who had earned $2,700 with Haileybury in 1910, wrote a long letter to the *Herald* and concluded by noting, "The pros of to-day who are standing out against the salary limit aren't asking for a princely sum, but merely what they are worth as revenue producers." He and his fellow skaters threatened to form a union. They talked of a strike. They tried to start their own league. All these measures failed, and the salary cap was imposed.

Team owners also had to sort out the composition of the NHA. Ottawa, Renfrew and the Wanderers were in, but Haileybury, Cobalt and the Shamrocks had folded. The league solved the problem by awarding one of those lapsed franchises to the Quebec Hockey Club and another to the Club Athlétique Canadien, both of whom paid a fee of $7,500. It was a hefty sum, but Kennedy was flush with cash. He was refinancing the CAC through a share offering of $100,000, half of it in common shares and the balance through preferred shares. By mid-October, he had sold 2,900 shares and attracted three hundred new shareholders, including many of Montreal's political and professional elite: the mayor, a former mayor, a senator, two members of Parliament, two members of Quebec's National Assembly, six doctors and the publisher of *Le Devoir.*

Kennedy had one other big project that fall: the construction of a new CAC clubhouse at the corner of Ste-Catherine and St-André streets, a five-minute cab ride south of his home on Sherbrooke Street East. He was touting it as one of the most spacious and modern indoor athletic clubs in North America. Along with a gymnasium, it would have showers, a sauna, massage rooms, a handball court, twelve billiard tables and six bowling alleys with automated pinsetters.

Kennedy's first move as the new owner of the Canadiens was to redesign the sweater and the crest. His players would wear red sweaters with green and white stripes around the waist, neck and wrists. The crest consisted of a green maple leaf with a stylized C superimposed on it.

Next, he demanded the return of Newsy Lalonde. He had seen Lalonde's appeal to French-Canadian fans the previous summer, when big crowds watched as he won the scoring title of the National Lacrosse Union and led the Montreal Nationals to first place. But Ambrose O'Brien and the Renfrew executive had no intention of giving up Lalonde. And why would they? He was the NHA scoring champion and the most talented offensive player in the game.

They relented after Kennedy threatened to pull his team out of the league. By mid-December 1910, Kennedy had come to terms with Lalonde, who joined the veterans and hopefuls practising with the Canadiens. They trained at the Westmount Arena, their new home, till two days before the season opener on New Year's Eve against the Ottawa Senators. There was one fresh face in the opening night lineup: goaltender Georges Vézina, who was destined to have a long, distinguished career with the team.

Vézina was a quick, agile young man with a slender face and large, round eyes, and he was known as *le Chevreuil*, or "the Deer." He was twenty-three years old, homesick and too bashful to talk. Vézina was from Chicoutimi, a remote lumber and farming town 125 miles northeast of Quebec City.

Chicoutimi clung to the steep and rocky hills that lined the dark, mile-wide waters of the Saguenay River. Vézina grew up on the main street, rue Racine, in a three-storey, flat-roofed building with a sign across the front that read *Boulangerie Vézina*. His father was a prosperous baker, and Georges was the youngest of eight children. He went to school till his fourteenth birthday, and during the cold, snowbound winters, which sometimes began in early November and lasted till late April, he spent nearly every free moment playing hockey.

Vézina learned the game in streets reduced to narrow, spindly, nearly impassable lanes by the snow that fell day after day. He and his friends played with sticks hewn from the branches of trees, with a block of wood, a lump of coal or a chunk of ice serving as the puck, and with pieces of firewood, placed upright, as the goalposts. Vézina always tended one of the goals, throwing out an arm or a leg to stop whatever was hurled at him, blocking shots by the weak late-afternoon sun or the flicker of gas-fired streetlamps until the last frigid shooter was ready to go home.

He graduated from the street to the rink at age sixteen, when he joined the Chicoutimi men's team and slipped on a pair of skates for the first time. The town was too distant and isolated to be part of a league, but its hockey club travelled to Quebec City, Trois-Rivières, Shawinigan and other places along the north shore of the St. Lawrence for exhibition games.

Occasionally, out-of-town teams paid a visit. On February 17, 1910, eight hundred people packed Chicoutimi's tiny, Quonset hut–shaped arena, which had an ice surface seventy-five feet long and forty wide, to watch a game between the local side and a professional team from Montreal—the Canadiens. The home team led seven–one at the half and eleven–five at the final bell. Vézina's play so impressed the visitors that they offered him a job, but he stayed put till the next autumn, when an emissary from Kennedy came calling. Vézina joined the Canadiens on December 22, 1910. He arrived with his brother Pierre, a forward who had been given a tryout as well. Pierre didn't make it, but stuck around long enough to see Georges sign a professional contract that paid him eight hundred dollars for the season.

The Canadiens were much stronger with Vézina in net. He allowed just sixty-two goals in sixteen games, fewer than the four other goaltenders in the league, all of them veterans. Lalonde and Pitre ranked sixth and seventh, respectively, in scoring, and the team finished with eight wins and eight losses, second to the league and Stanley Cup champion Senators.

Thanks to Kennedy's astute management, there was a profit, too, of four thousand dollars, whereas the other NHA clubs lost money. Best of all, French Montrealers began to take a serious interest. Some bet on the games, and the wagering was influenced by rumours and gossip about who was injured and who was healthy. The French-speaking fans formed a noisy block at the Arena, especially for matches against the Wanderers, when crowds of six thousand were almost equally split between French and English.

The French-language sportswriters embraced the team as fervently as the fans, which was evident from the tone of their writing and their use of exclamation marks. *La Patrie*'s Raphaël Ouimet alternately referred to the Canadiens as "our boys," "our valiant athletes" or "our blue-white-red," and celebrated each victory. "They deserve all our congratulations," he declared after a win over the Wanderers. "Bravo Canadiens. Bravissimo!!! Alleluia!!!!"

Le Devoir, the nationalist daily of the political firebrand Henri Bourassa, treated the team as flag-bearers for the French-Canadian nation. After the first win of the season, the paper ran a large headline that read "UNE SUPERBE VICTOIRE," and sports editor Tancrède Marsil wrote: "Ah! What marvels can be achieved with the stuff of the country!!!!"

Kennedy made one miscue during his first season, though, and it had lasting repercussions. In mid-February, he and his general manager, Adolphe Lecours, acquired an Irish-Canadian defenceman named James (Rocket) Power from the Quebec Bulldogs. Marsil was outraged. He regarded this as a betrayal of principles. In his opinion, there was no place for English-Canadians on a team representing French Canada, and readers of *Le Devoir* agreed. The longest and angriest response came from an Ottawa subscriber named J.W. Clement. He accused Kennedy of "polluting the character of the Canadiens and of creating a deplorable and ill-advised precedent by allowing Anglo-Saxon blood to infiltrate this club which we are proud to call our own." Kennedy had slipped up, according to Clement, because he "does not understand, like us, the national pride bequeathed to us by our forefathers."

But the issue of nationality was far from cut and dried, as another reader, who identified himself as M.D., pointed out. He noted that Lalonde and a second player named Eugène Payan had French-Canadian names, yet spoke no French and were English in outlook and temperament. Power, on the other hand, had an English name, but spoke perfect French and, according to M.D., "is one of us by his language and his French-Canadian character."

Marsil ignored these complexities. He dismissed the Club Athlétique Canadien and argued that the right to represent French-Canadians "with honour everywhere and always" belonged to L'Association Athlétique d'Amateurs le National.

Kennedy commented publicly on the issue only once, late in the season, when he jokingly told the *Montreal Star*, "Anyway, if we're not all French, we're six and a half French." But those were not to be his final words on the subject.

Prior to the 1911–12 season, Ambrose O'Brien and his father pulled Renfrew out of the National Hockey Association. The NHA executive awarded two Toronto franchises, one of them to replace Renfrew, and they approved several other changes. They eliminated the position of rover, reducing a team to six players plus spares, each of whom would wear a numbered sweater. Henceforth, cross-checking, tripping, hooking, charging from behind and using foul language would be major penalties. Offenders would be fined five dollars and ejected from the contest. At the behest of Kennedy, the league agreed that only the Canadiens could sign French-Canadian players. The other clubs would be restricted to English skaters.

Kennedy's commitment to this principle was short-lived. Two games into the season, he decided the Canadiens needed help on defence. Re-signing Rocket Power was out of the question. Instead, he landed former Wanderer Pud Glass, and nobody protested—not his fellow owners and not *Le Devoir*'s Tancrède Marsil, who apparently had decided that winning was more important than keeping the Canadiens purely French.

But producing a champion proved to be more difficult than anticipated. The Quebec Bulldogs won the league and the Stanley Cup in 1911–12. The Canadiens finished last, and Kennedy concluded that the all-French approach had been a mistake. At the next annual meeting, prior to the 1912–13 season, he persuaded the league executive to allow the Canadiens two English players, while the other clubs would be permitted two French-Canadians each. He was motivated as much by financial concerns as by the desire to ice a competitive team. "What looked like a benefit at first began to assume almost the form of a curse," Kennedy said. "The French-Canadian players are convinced that I must have them and therefore they hold out for all sorts of money to which they are not entitled."

The principal culprit had been Newsy Lalonde, who deserted the Canadiens in 1911–12 for Vancouver of the new Pacific Coast Hockey Association—a rival pro league formed by Lester Patrick and his brother Frank. Lalonde returned to the Canadiens for the 1912–13 season. Prior to the opening game, he spoke to a cluster of reporters. He wore a diamond ring on the little finger of his left hand and he was full of confidence. "We are going to win the championship, boys," Lalonde predicted. "I can feel it in my bones and am so certain of it that I am going to buy cigars on the strength of it."

The Canadiens began strongly. They won seven of their first ten games, and their fans were jubilant. After one early win, a *Montreal Star* reporter wrote, "A fanfare of bugles, a roll of drums, a yell of delight, two hundred men in vari-colored suits rising and waving their toques high in the air and the Canadiens have scored again."

Things ended differently, though. After a disastrous February, the team tumbled to fifth place in the six-team league and the fans had soured. "What a boring game," declared *La Patrie* after the season finale. "That's what everyone said last night as they were leaving the Arena, where the Canadiens were beaten by Toronto by a score of six–two. A pasting."

The Canadiens redeemed themselves in 1913–14. They battled the Toronto Blueshirts for first from start to finish of the twenty-game season, and success strengthened the bond between the team and its French-speaking followers, both in Montreal and the small, outlying communities. These fans turned to their collective past to express their deepening attachment to the Canadiens. They were, for the most part, descendants of the *habitants*, the French settlers of the seventeenth and eighteenth centuries who had made dangerous ocean crossings, had taken up long, narrow plots of heavily forested land in the St. Lawrence River valley and, through years of arduous work, had turned their land into productive farms. These fans had begun calling the Canadiens "*l'équipe des habitants*" (the team of the *habitants*), then simply "*les habitants*," and by February 1914 the terms began appearing in the columns of the French-language newspapers.

In late February, the Canadiens trailed the Blueshirts by two games, with two remaining, one of them against the Wanderers. Prior to the Wanderer game, the weather turned mild. The ice was soft. A thin layer of water covered the entire surface. The lead changed hands five times, and the score was tied at five apiece after sixty minutes. Canadiens left winger Louis Berlinquette scored the winner two minutes and twenty seconds into overtime, but nobody was celebrating.

It had been a violent game. The players had butt-ended and cross-checked each other at will. Kennedy was furious and twice attacked the referee, a young French-Canadian named Léo Dandurand. Dandurand wrote a letter of protest to league president Emmett Quinn, alleging that "Mr. Kennedy seized me and threatened me with blows and at the same time speaking to me in terms unworthy of a dignified man. . . . Not content with having abused me in this manner upon my leaving the ice, the general manager of the Canadiens came back and insulted me in the worst manner in the umpires' room, calling me [as the *Montreal Star* put it] a ———."

Dandurand went further. He charged Kennedy with assault, and the two spent a day in court sorting out their differences while the Canadiens prepared for the season finale. They won that game to finish with a record of thirteen wins and seven losses, the same as the Blueshirts. For the first time, a playoff was required to determine the league champion.

A crowd estimated at 6,100 filled every seat in the Arena for the first match of the two-game, total-goal series. The ice was again a mess—a small lake, according to one witness—and the play ragged, but the Canadiens won two–nothing. The second game was in Toronto, and the Canadiens took an overnight train. "Our best wishes accompany them," Raphaël Ouimet wrote in *La Patrie*. The Blueshirts crushed them six–nothing, which ended the Canadiens' season as well as their hopes of winning the Stanley Cup for the first time.

Win one, lose two. Win two, lose one. What's wrong with this team?
Kennedy wondered. They had the talent to do better. The forwards,
Lalonde, Pitre and Laviolette, were fast and could score. The defence, Bert
Corbeau and Howard McNamara, were tough and reliable. The goaltender,
Vézina, had played every game since joining the Canadiens, and on many
nights over the years had been the team's best player. The subs—Louis
Berlinquette, Amos Arbour, Goldie Prodgers, Skene Ronan and George
Poulin—were as good as any in the league. But all of them needed a jolt, or
else this season—1915–16—would be a bust, like the last one, when the
Canadiens had won six, lost fourteen and finished last.

On the morning of January 10, 1916, prior to a team practice, Kennedy
met the players. He had a proposition for them. They would get one hundred dollars, to be shared equally, for each victory. Each loss would cost them
the same amount. Kennedy coughed up a hundred two nights later when
the Canadiens beat Quebec, but the players gave it back on January 15
after losing to Ottawa. And so it went. Money changed hands. The team
failed to advance.

By the end of January, the Canadiens were fourth in the five-team
league. Lalonde was eighth in scoring, Pitre ninth, and both were well behind
the leaders, Joe Malone and Tommy Smith of Quebec. The French-Canadian
sports writers were alarmed, and the board of Le Club Athlétique Canadien
was fed up. The directors held Lalonde, the captain and coach, responsible.
"Lalonde has received instructions from the board to produce a winning
team," *La Patrie* reported February 4. "If the team is beaten again, Lalonde
will be replaced as coach. The directors are already looking for a successor."

The ultimatum worked. The team won its next four games, lost one,
then finished the season with a seven-game winning streak. And they
needed every victory. In late February, the Canadiens, Senators and
Wanderers each had ten wins. The Canadiens pounded the Wanderers 15–4
on March 4 and knocked them out of the race. They beat the Senators twice
in four days to eliminate the reigning champs. Lalonde overtook Malone to
win the scoring race with thirty-one goals in twenty-four games, Pitre

finished fourth with twenty-three and Vézina ranked second among goal-tenders behind his perennial rival, Clint Benedict of the Senators.

The Canadiens were champions for the first time. They had earned the right to compete for the Stanley Cup and made their debut in a final series against the Rosebuds of Portland, Oregon, champions of the Pacific Coast Hockey Association. The Rosebuds arrived in Montreal the day before the best-of-five series was to begin. Local hockey fans were familiar with three Portland players: Eddie Oatman and Tommy Dunderdale, who had played for the Bulldogs, and Ernie "Moose" Johnson, a former Wanderer defence-man from Pointe-Saint-Charles, Quebec. The rest of the players were west-erners, most of them from the Winnipeg Monarchs, who had won the Allan Cup as Canadian senior champs the previous season.

The Rosebuds startled the Montrealers by winning the first game, played under eastern six-man rules. The Canadiens took the second, played western style with seven men. Game three, which the Canadiens won, was interrupted by a third-period brawl. Portland's Johnson laid out Lalonde with a stiff body check. Lalonde scrambled to his feet, and responded with his fists. Oatman jumped in, and the rest of the players joined the fracas. Then the subs came over the boards. The referee and his assistant watched helplessly until the chief of police of the Town of Westmount, where the Arena was located, came out of the crowd, onto the ice and ordered the players to behave or else charges would be laid.

Johnson was the talk of game four. He refused to dress. Money was the problem, as usual. Four seasons earlier, the big defenceman had signed with the Wanderers for two thousand dollars, but then bolted for a better offer in the west. Wanderer owner Sam Lichtenhein hadn't forgotten, and he took advantage of Johnson's return to sue for breach of contract. A judge ruled, prior to the fourth match, that Lichtenhein was entitled to Johnson's Stanley Cup prize money. Johnson was miffed and refused to dress until friends convinced him to join his teammates for the start of the second period.

Portland won that night, and Canadiens fans left sorely disappointed. Many stayed home for the fifth game, a fast, brilliant and intense contest, according to the account in *La Presse*. Ronan, a sub, scored for the Canadiens in the first. Dunderdale tied it six minutes into the third. The teams then played fierce, scoreless hockey before Prodgers, another Montreal sub, put his side ahead two-one with four minutes remaining.

Afterward, the players on both teams were exhausted, but they retired to the St. Regis Hotel for a small banquet with club executives and league officials, and the victorious Canadiens were presented with the Stanley Cup. That evening, Georges Vézina became a father for the second time. His wife, Marie, gave birth to a son at their home in Chicoutimi, and the following morning Vézina shared the news with Kennedy. "I'm going to name him Stanley," the goaltender said. "Marcel Stanley Vézina will be his name."

Later that day, the Canadiens departed by train for Chicoutimi for what had become an annual exhibition game against the local men's team, but Kennedy stayed behind to take care of business. He was in the midst of restructuring his holdings. The CAC had foundered financially. A fire on January 21, 1914, had destroyed the Ste-Catherine Street gym and clubhouse. A money-losing pro lacrosse team had compounded the problems. But the Canadiens remained profitable. So Kennedy decided to run wrestling, boxing and his other interests through the CAC, and on March 10, 1916, he incorporated the hockey team as a separate enterprise called Le Club de Hockey Canadien.

With that change came another. For the previous three seasons, the crest of the Canadiens had been an oblong C with an upper-case A tucked inside. Henceforth, the C would contain an H instead, signifying Le Club de Hockey Canadien.

By the summer of 1916, Canada had been at war for two years. Three hundred and twelve thousand men were in uniform, and half of them were serving overseas, a remarkable contribution for a small, predominantly rural country of eight million. They were an army of volunteers, fresh from towns and villages, farms and factories—and the tiny world world of professional hockey. Canada's citizen soldiers assembled in Valcartier, Quebec, for basic training, a few weeks of parade-yard marching and target shooting. They embarked at Quebec and, upon reaching England, where the real training was to begin, they marched ashore in Canadian-made boots that turned soft and rotted in the damp of the mother country. Then they were off to France to face the Hun, carrying Canadian-made Ross rifles that routinely overheated and jammed when the guns of the enemy roared and rained fire from a few hundred yards away.

The Canadians were tested early and often. They fought in Belgium in April 1915 at the Battle of Ypres, in May during a British-French counter-offensive south of Ypres, and in June near the French village of Givenchy. More than 9,400 Canadians were killed or wounded, most of them at Ypres. There, the Germans released tons of poisonous chlorine gas onto the battlefield. Wind carried greenish-yellow clouds across no-man's-land. French and Algerian troops panicked, but not the nearby Canadians. They fought even as they pulled back and their comrades gasped and vomited, or collapsed and died.

Winter in the trenches was the next test. Canada's fighting men endured rain, mud and lice, tasteless food and sporadic enemy fire, and the deaths of 546 men. Spring arrived, and they fought again at St-Eloi and Mount Sorrel, near Ypres. By then, they had chucked their unreliable Ross rifles for British-made Lee-Enfields. Still, the casualties rose, reaching thirty-two thousand at the end of June 1916, just as the bloodbath known as the Battle of the Somme was beginning.

The war had become an all-consuming national effort. It touched every corner of Canadian life, even the National Hockey Association. As the teams prepared for the 1916–17 season, nearly a sixth of the ninety-odd men who had played pro the previous winter had enlisted, and qualified replacements were scarce because most were in uniform. The world champion Canadiens lost three players: Howard McNamara, Goldie Prodgers and Amos Arbour; five members of Toronto's NHA entry, then known as the Blueshirts, had joined the army; and players from Ottawa, the Wanderers, Vancouver and Portland had also signed up.

Many had enlisted with the 228th Battalion of Toronto, also known as the Northern Fusiliers, which had filled out its ranks by recruiting athletes. The commanders realized that they had the talent for a top-notch hockey team and applied for an NHA franchise, which was granted on September 30, 1916. The Fusiliers played twelve games, winning six and losing six, before being sent overseas in mid-February 1917. Their departure caused a rift among the remaining clubs. League executives had to revise the schedule for the final three weeks of the season. Toronto owner Eddie Livingstone ended up at odds with the others, who solved the problem by voting to suspend the Blueshirt franchise for the balance of the campaign.

The Canadiens emerged from the turmoil as NHA champions and in mid-March boarded a transcontinental train for the long journey west to meet the Seattle Metropolitans of the Pacific Coast league. They won the first game, but lost the next three, and a U.S.–based team had won the Stanley Cup for the first time. The final game had been rather dull, but that made no difference to the fans, as the *Seattle Times* reported: "The largest crowd that ever saw a hockey game in the arena stood and cheered until the iron girders of the roof rattled as the Seattle team left the ice . . ."

Montreal and its mountain were ablaze with the colours of autumn. College and collegiate football teams had taken over the city's playing fields. Hockey season was a good two months off, but already the men behind the pro clubs were talking and plotting. Those who had voted to suspend Livingstone's franchise the previous winter were now determined to rid themselves of the man himself. The Toronto owner was a good promoter and a shrewd judge of talent, but as the journalist and referee Mike Roddick put it, "He had the unhappy faculty of arousing antagonism."

Livingstone ducked the first planning session of the 1917–18 season, held October 23, 1917, at the Windsor Hotel. In his place, he sent a travelling salesman, one E. Barkley, who was there only to listen. What Barkley heard was that Livingstone should relinquish his franchise and let the league find new owners. The four-hour meeting adjourned at midnight with nothing resolved. Barkley reported back to Livingstone, who responded promptly. He wasn't giving up his franchise. That meant a fight, and his fellow owners resorted to an old tactic to exclude him: they decided to form a new league, but would not award a franchise to Livingstone, an approach adopted by the Senators and their allies in the fall of 1909 to freeze out the Wanderers.

On that occasion, the move had backfired and led to the formation of the NHA and the Canadiens. This time, things worked out as planned. The demise of the NHA occurred Saturday, November 10, 1917, at the Windsor

Hotel, when representatives of the Canadiens, Wanderers, Senators and Bulldogs voted to withdraw from the association. On Monday, November 26, the same men sat at a table in the same room and created a new organization: the National Hockey *League*. Spurred on by these events, Livingstone loaned his players to the new directors of the Toronto Hockey Club, though he continued to seek redress through the courts for the next eight years.

The officers of the NHL granted a franchise to the new operators in Toronto, but the Bulldogs were suspending operations, in part because the war had left them short of players. Quebec had two stars, the forward Joe Malone and the defenceman Joe Hall, and both went to the Canadiens.

Malone, then twenty-seven, was a prolific scorer who could play centre or left wing. A native of Quebec City, he had been the Bulldogs' best player for seven seasons. He had led the team to Stanley Cup victories in 1912 and 1913, captured the 1913 scoring title with forty-three goals in twenty games, and was widely admired for his style of play, which had won him the nickname Gentleman Joe.

Malone played hard and clean for the Canadiens and scored at a prodigious rate. He had three goals in the season opener, three in the second game and two in the fourth. Ottawa's Cy Denneny challenged Malone for the scoring title till the end of January before falling behind. Gentleman Joe finished the season with forty-four goals in the twenty games he played, a record that stood until 1944–45 when Maurice Richard scored fifty.

Joe Hall filled one of the two defence postions on the Canadiens. He was lean and tough, weighing just 150 pounds, but at the age of thirty-five had played seventeen seasons of senior and professional hockey. He had started with the Wheat Kings of Brandon, Manitoba, where he lived, and went on to play for Winnipeg, Kenora, Houghton, Michigan, the Wanderers and the Shamrocks. For the previous five winters, he had played in Quebec. Hall was fun-loving and popular with teammates, but he had a volatile temper and frequently erupted.

He was known as Bad Joe Hall, and had come by his nickname honestly, which is evident from the following incidents: a fight with Frank Patrick on January 21, 1910, in which Hall tried to punch the referee, resulting in a hundred-dollar fine; an assault on a referee on January 11, 1913, which led to a fifty-dollar fine from the league, a two-week suspension and a hundred-dollar fine imposed by the Bulldogs; a cross-check on Newsy Lalonde on January 14, 1914, that sent the Canadiens star headfirst into the boards and cut him for ten stitches, an act of retribution for an earlier incident in which Lalonde had cut Hall for eight stitches; an attack on the Wanderers' Harry Hyland on January 21, 1914, which went unpunished; a post-game hit on Amos Arbour of the Canadiens on February 26, 1916, that led to a brawl involving players and spectators; and an attack on Toronto's Corbett Denneny in Quebec on February 3, 1917, with two minutes to go in the game. In the ensuing brawl, spectators threw chairs and bottles on to the ice, police escorted the Toronto players to their dressing room and the officials terminated the game.

The infant NHL nearly expired six weeks after its turbulent birth when fire destroyed the Westmount Arena, home to two of the league's four teams, the Canadiens and the Wanderers. The blaze began shortly before noon on January 2, 1918, and within twenty minutes the wooden roof had collapsed. The two-storey brick walls remained standing, but the interior was destroyed, including the ice-making equipment installed two years earlier. A late-afternoon edition of *La Patrie* described the building as "a mass of cinders and smoking ruins" and noted that heat from the inferno had shattered windows in houses across the street.

The fire brought about the demise of the Wanderers, once the best team in the country. For three straight seasons, 1906 through 1908, they were Stanley Cup champions, and they won a fourth in 1910. But they had sagged badly during the war years. Owner Sam Lichtenhein pegged his losses in two seasons at thirteen thousand dollars, and now the team had lost its home and all its equipment.

The Canadiens had lost everything as well, but Kennedy was determined to continue. They were scheduled to play a home game three nights later against Ottawa, and Kennedy booked the ice at the Jubilee Rink. Their uniforms and equipment lost in the fire, they played in gear borrowed from a Hochelaga men's team in the Montreal City League. The Jubilee was less than half the size of the Westmount Arena, but the Canadiens—and a diminished, three-team NHL survived—thanks to Kennedy's resolve.

Day after day in August 1918, Canadians reached for their newspapers to read exhilarating accounts of Allied triumphs and enemy defeats in the great war that had by then convulsed the planet. "Germans Give Ground Before French Blows," declared one headline. "British Guns Cut Retiring Foe to Pieces," said another. And on it went. "Americans Reach German Border." "To the Rhine—Cry of Canada's Gallant Sons." "World Watches for Momentous Allied Moves." "Teuton Masses Demonstrate in Favor of Peace."

As summer gave way to autumn, though, another story crept into the newspapers. On September 24, 1918, a Montreal *Gazette* headline announced, "Spanish Grippe Ravages Boston." The story reported that seventy-three people in the Massachusetts capital had died of influenza in the previous twenty-four hours. Furthermore, the U.S. War Department had disclosed that over twenty thousand cases had been diagnosed on its military bases. Three days later, 450 Canadian soldiers became ill at the barracks in St-Jean, Quebec, a town southeast of Montreal on the Richelieu River, and by the end of September twenty soldiers at the barracks in Montreal were sick.

A Canadian military official, Lieutenant Colonel F.S. Patch, told *The Gazette* that the outbreak of influenza had likely been caused by prolonged bad weather and was not considered serious. But in fact, a virulent new strain of the disease had appeared, one that killed the young and the healthy along with the old and the sick. It was named the Spanish flu, and by the spring of 1919 as many as thirty million people around the world had died of the disease.

It struck cities and towns across Canada—Toronto, Winnipeg, Vancouver, Victoria, even the remote Nipigon Indian Reserve at the northwest end of Lake Superior. Over eight hundred Quebec municipalities were affected and, in Montreal, 3,124 people died between October 1 and November 17. In its first edition after Thanksgiving, *The Gazette* observed, "All day yesterday, a constant procession of hearses winding their way over the mountain to Côte-Des-Neiges and Mount Royal cemeteries exerted a depressing influence on the holiday crowds."

Local authorities imposed emergency measures to control the spread of the disease. Schools and libraries were closed. McGill University suspended classes. Public meetings were prohibited. Theatres and moving-picture houses closed their doors. The courts did not sit. The Montreal Protestant Ministries Association cancelled services and Sunday schools. Department stores were allowed to open only till four o'clock to try to ease rush-hour crowds on the streetcars.

Still, nearly seventeen thousand Montrealers contracted the disease, and the daily death toll peaked at 201 on October 20. By mid-November, the epidemic had subsided and municipal authorities lifted the restrictions on schools, churches and places of entertainment. One month later, on December 21, the NHL opened its second season with a game between the Canadiens and the Senators at the Jubilee Rink in east-end Montreal.

The Canadiens lost that night, but proved to be the best of the three teams in the league that winter. They won the first half of the split eighteen-game season, finished behind the Senators in the second half and beat Ottawa in a best-of-five playoff to win the NHL championship. On March 10, 1919, they waved goodbye to a gathering of supporters on the platform of Windsor Station and departed for Seattle and the Stanley Cup final.

A noisy, standing-room crowd of over four thousand attended the opening game. It was played under western, seven-man rules, and the Metropolitans won seven–nothing. The Canadiens took the second game, played under eastern rules, but lost the third. The fourth ended in a score-less draw after two ten-minute overtime periods. In the fifth game, the Canadiens staged what a Seattle reporter described as "one of the greatest comebacks in hockey history."

The Metropolitans led three–nothing after two periods of play. Montreal substitute Odie Cleghorn scored early in the third, and Lalonde added two more to force overtime. Jack McDonald, another Canadiens substitute, got the winner after nearly sixteen minutes of extra play. Afterward, general manager Kennedy appeared to a reporter to be "tickled as a schoolboy" and declared: "I always claimed I had a game team and the boys certainly proved it tonight. I expect them to win the championship now."

The final game was scheduled for April 1. It was never played. Nor was the Stanley Cup awarded. A second epidemic of Spanish flu broke out in the spring of 1919. Kennedy and five of his nine players were stricken by the disease. All but one recovered.

At 3:30 on a Saturday afternoon, April 5, Bad Joe Hall died at the Columbus Sanitarium in Seattle. As with most victims, his lungs had slowly filled with mucus, he had become childlike in his final hours and drowned in his own fluids. He was thirty-eight years old. A few days later, his body was shipped to Vancouver for burial. He left behind a wife, two sons and a daughter in Brandon, Manitoba. But he had provided for them. "Hall was one of the few professional athletes who saved his money," the *Toronto World* wrote. "He worked on the railroad during the summer months and this, with his hockey earnings, allowed him to purchase property in Brandon."

Hall's fellow players had only fond memories of him. Newsy Lalonde, who had fought often with him, recalled that the two had a scrap on the same night that his wife gave birth to a baby girl. The next morning, Hall went to the hospital and apologized to Lalonde's wife for his rough play. And after Hall joined the Canadiens, he and Lalonde became roommates and close friends. Frank Patrick, who had had his own run-ins with Hall, told a newspaper reporter, "Off the ice, he was one of the jolliest, best-hearted, most popular men who ever played."

"George Kennedy Est Mort." *La Presse* announced it on October 19, 1921, *The Gazette* a day later in the same words: George Kennedy is dead. He died in his home at 1321 St-Hubert Street at 7:30 in the morning after receiving the last rites of the Catholic Church. He was thirty-nine and was survived by his wife, Myrtle, his six-year-old daughter, Doris, his mother, three brothers and three sisters.

Though his symptoms had faded quickly, Kennedy had never fully recovered from the Spanish flu. As *The Gazette* put it, "George, always of an active disposition, rose from his bed earlier than was wise and it is thought that the venom of the disease had an after effect which eventually led to his death."

The prolonged illness baffled doctors, and some of the best in Canada and the United States examined Kennedy. He collapsed on the day of a playoff game between the Canadiens and the Senators in the spring of 1921. His physician recommended prolonged rest. Kennedy spent a few weeks in the resort community of Atlantic City, New Jersey, and the summer at his farm near Ste-Agathe-des-Monts, in the Laurentians north of Montreal. He returned to the city to prepare for the upcoming hockey season, but was a mere shadow of the flamboyant promoter who had dominated the Montreal sports scene for the previous decade.

His many friends and associates were dismayed by his death. Kennedy was a man who inspired loyalty and affection. "Blessed with an affable character, a generous heart, always ready to help his friends," a *La Presse* reporter wrote, " . . . George Kennedy was adored by his hockey players, whom he always treated with the highest regard, and the wrestlers, whom he treated like brothers."

Once the obituaries had been written, the eulogy delivered, the tears shed publicly and privately and the casket lowered into the ground, all who knew him agreed that George Kennedy was gone too soon. Yet they were thankful for what he had brought them. Kennedy had entertained them. He had made them laugh. He had made them cheer. He had given them cause to celebrate. Kennedy had acquired the Canadiens when they were a novelty act and had made the team a source of civic pride. In Montreal's sprawling and ever-expanding east end, where the French lived, the Canadiens had become *l'équipe des habitants*—our team, for all intents and purposes. Wherever they played, be it Ottawa or Toronto, New York or Seattle, the Canadiens were the Flying Frenchmen, though they were not, strictly speaking, a French team. Like the city itself, they were both French and English.

Under Kennedy's prudent management, the Canadiens had survived a tumultuous decade in which the country had fought a war and many other teams had come and gone. They had remained profitable. They had won three league championships and the Stanley Cup. The Canadiens were a valuable property. Within days of Kennedy's death, prospective buyers approached his widow, and not long after that a bidding war for the team had begun.

1921–1931
LES CANADIENS SONT LÀ

THE STATION WAS GRAND, it was crowded, it was noisy—almost as noisy as the stadiums Léo Dandurand had visited to watch Chicago's professional baseball teams, the Cubs and the White Sox. People stood in clusters, sat on luggage, lined up at ticket windows. There was laughter. Tears. Hurried, whispered conversations between people about to part company. But Dandurand was oblivious to it all. He stood with his mother, Aurélie— a tall, gangly, awkward boy clutching a heavy, overstuffed suitcase, his beloved baseball glove tucked under one arm, the ticket to Montreal stowed securely in the breast pocket of his jacket. He had packed under his mother's watchful eye (he was only seventeen and had never been away from home) and had insisted on bringing his glove, though he now wondered: did they even play baseball in Canada?

He knew almost nothing about this strange country except that there had been Dandurands there since 1690 and that his great-grandfather, Marcel Dandurand, had left in 1810—loaded his wagon, gathered up his family, joined a caravan of wagons and emigrated to the United States, where he acquired land and took up farming in Bourbonnais, Illinois, a French-Canadian community fifty miles south of Chicago. And now, in early September of 1906, Léo was going back, very reluctantly. French was his mother tongue, but he was American. He dreamt of becoming a wealthy businessman and was eager to get started.

A priest was responsible for changing the direction of the young man's life—a Montreal Jesuit named Father Louis Lalande, who had come to Bourbonnais in May 1906 (the month of Mary, the Blessed Virgin) to lead the faithful in prayer and strengthen the bonds of faith and race. Father Lalande had visited the Dandurand farm, dined with the family and invited Mrs. Dandurand, a widow, to send the fifth of her nine children, young Léo, to one of Montreal's Jesuit-run classical colleges. She had accepted and the matter was settled.

Father Lalande had chosen a school—Collège Ste-Marie on Bleury Street—and sent a ticket. Dandurand said goodbye to boyhood friends, his siblings and his mother and boarded the train with five dollars in his pocket and a box of sandwiches, fruit and sweets for the journey.

Dandurand gradually became accustomed to his new surroundings. He became a busy student athlete and he graduated in June 1909. He was well educated, ambitious and now dreamed of becoming a sports promoter, though he began his working life as a three-dollar-a-week messenger and office boy for a Montreal real estate company. Soon, he was selling homes. On a really good week, he could earn a hundred dollars in commissions. He drove a fancy Chandler automobile worth three thousand dollars and, come winter, wore a luxurious fur coat.

Dandurand devoted almost all his spare time to sports. In 1910, he managed the intermediate lacrosse team of the Association Athlétique d'Amateurs le National, and his boys won the eastern Canadian championship. He helped organize the City Baseball League of Montreal and played second base for one of its eight teams. He participated in the creation of the Montreal City Hockey League, where the top amateurs played, and he served as league manager, publicist and secretary-treasurer. In 1912, he promoted a strongman competition at Sohmer Park and a baseball game between two all-star teams assembled as a supporting cast for Ty Cobb, the Detroit Tigers star who was travelling from city to city to participate in such exhibitions.

Along the way, Dandurand befriended Joseph Cattarinich, a high-profile Montreal sports figure who was known as Mr. Joe at the track, as Silent Joe among those who gathered at bars and taverns to discuss sports and as Catta among the city's sportswriters. They had written about him for twelve seasons when he was a star defenceman with the Nationals, French Canada's premier lacrosse team. They had watched him play goal briefly for the Canadiens, and they often reminded readers that Catta had discovered Georges Vézina.

Dandurand and Cattarinich formed a business partnership in 1913, and it endured until December 7, 1938, when, at age fifty-seven, Cattarinich died while undergoing cataract surgery in New Orleans. Léo was a talker and a backslapper, Catta was reserved and soft-spoken. Despite their disparate personalities, the two men were an ideal match. During World War I, they ran a real estate company and a tobacco wholesaler on Ste-Catherine Street East. But their real interest was horse racing, and the best opportunities lay south of the border.

In 1919, Dandurand and Cattarinich brought in a third partner named Louis Létourneau, a merchant who sold fish from a stall in the Bonsecours Market on Montreal's waterfront and ran a bar a few blocks north on St-Laurent Boulevard. He was known as Little Louie, and he commanded attention wherever he went. At the market, he used his booming voice to announce his products and prices and to greet customers, and he entertained the regulars at his tavern with stories about earlier exploits promoting boxing and wrestling and running a stable of thoroughbreds.

The three Montrealers took over the management of a track at Chagrin Falls, Ohio, twenty-two miles south of Cleveland, and ran it for two seasons until local opponents had it closed. Undaunted, they moved to Cleveland and built a one-mile course called Maple Heights at a cost of four hundred thousand dollars. It opened in the spring of 1921 and became the cornerstone of a sporting empire that would come to include some of the finest race facilities in North America. Eventually, they owned or managed Fair Grounds Park and Jefferson Park in New Orleans, Washington Park and Arlington Park in Chicago, Hamilton County Park near Cincinnati, Lagoon Park in Salt Lake City, Utah, and the Delorimier,

Dorval and Blue Bonnets tracks in Montreal. In 1921, though, they were novice operators who had enjoyed a profitable season and had most of their money tied up in Maple Heights.

One day, late in October 1921, Dandurand was alone in the Cleveland hotel suite he shared with Cattarinish and Létourneau when he received a long-distance phone call from Montreal. The caller was Cecil Hart, an insurance broker and old friend who had helped organize the city's amateur hockey and baseball leagues, and who had played in both and coached as well. Their conversation was brief and to the point. George Kennedy is dead, Hart said. The Canadiens are for sale. Are you interested? Of course, Dandurand responded, without hesitation and without consulting his partners. He authorized Hart to act as agent for them and issued clear, simple instructions: "Make sure you outbid the other people and get that club."

Two competing parties were interested: the owners of the Mount Royal Arena Company, who had appointed managing director Tom Duggan to act for them, and an unnamed Ottawa businessman who had asked NHL president Frank Calder to represent him. On November 3, everyone gathered at the offices of Mathieu Papineau, Mrs. Kennedy's lawyer.

Duggan bid first. He pulled from his pocket ten bills, lay them on the table and declared, "I have ten thousand dollars in cash to pay for the club." Calder matched him. Hart asked for time to call Dandurand, and he reached him in Cleveland. "Listen closely, Cecil," Dandurand said. "Just make sure you outbid the others. I'm giving you a free hand."

Hart duly offered eleven thousand. Duggan collected his cash and snapped, "If you're playing me against Léo and his partners, I'm through." Calder was finished as well. A few minutes later, Hart broke the news to Dandurand, who was jubilant and raced down to the lobby to share the news with Cattarinich and Létourneau. "Well, partners," he said, "we've just bought a hockey club for eleven thousand dollars. I'm leaving within an hour for Montreal to complete the deal and sign the papers."

The new owners had acquired an aging but competitive team. The Canadiens could hold their own against two NHL rivals, the Toronto St. Pats and the

Hamilton Tigers, but they had been eclipsed by the powerful Ottawa Senators, winners of the Stanley Cup in 1920 and 1921.

Dandurand's first move was to trade for the defenceman Sprague Cleghorn, whose younger brother Odie had been a substitute forward with the Canadiens for the previous three seasons. The Cleghorns were born a year apart, Sprague in 1890, Odie (given name Ogilvie) in 1891, and they had grown up in the Montreal suburb of Westmount. They began as amateurs there, graduated to Montreal junior and intermediate clubs, and in 1910 earned fifty dollars playing in the five-team New York Hockey League. The following winter, they joined the Renfrew Creamery Kings. In 1912, the Cleghorns moved on to the Montreal Wanderers and stayed until the Wanderers folded after the Westmount Arena fire of January 1918. From there, Odie went to the Canadiens, Sprague to the Senators.

Odie was a slick stickhandler and a skilled offensive player who scored 230 goals in seventeen professional seasons, good enough for eighth place among the scorers of the era. Sprague, who stood six foot one and weighed 185 pounds, was a high-scoring rushing defenceman and one of the roughest players the game had ever seen. "To get by him," Charles L. Coleman wrote in *The Trail of the Stanley Cup,* "opponents had to face up to body checks, charging, cross-checks, elbows, butt ends and fists."

Cleghorn paid a high price for his style of play. He once told an interviewer, "You'd need a battery of adding machines to tabulate all the minor cuts, bruises, torn ligaments and pulled tendons my quarter century of hockey gave me." And when one writer asked him how many fights he'd had, Cleghorn replied, "Do you mean stretcher-case fights?" The reporter nodded. "I guess I've been in fifty of those kind."

There were no stretcher-case brawls in the 1921–22 season, but Cleghorn was guilty of some vicious stickwork, mostly when playing the Senators, a team he hated for having traded him the previous year. In a January 9 game in Montreal, Cleghorn attacked three Senators. According to a report in the *Ottawa Citizen:* "He jabbed goaltender Clint Benedict in the face with the butt end of his stick and it is miraculous that the victim was not maimed for life. Cleghorn openly slashed George Boucher across the face, causing a deep gash on that player's nose and he also disabled Frank [Nighbor's] left arm with a wicked slash which landed above the elbow."

In a game in Ottawa on February 1, Cleghorn whacked Nighbor across the arm and nearly broke it; later in the contest he cut Eddie Gerard below the eye with a high stick. Afterward, two Ottawa police officers visited the Canadiens' dressing room and threatened to arrest Cleghorn. Outside the arena, five or six hundred angry fans waited for him. On the advice of proprietor Ted Dey, the Canadiens left through a back entrance.

Cleghorn's menacing presence was not enough to make the Canadiens winners. Newsy Lalonde, who had been the heart of the team's offence for years, found that his scoring touch deserted him that winter. After an early loss, Dandurand accused Lalonde of lack of effort. Stung by the criticism, the proud veteran quit. NHL president Calder intervened, and Lalonde returned after four games. But he was not the player he had once been. On February 15, Montreal fans booed him during a thrilling game against Ottawa. A record crowd of nearly seven thousand packed the Mount Royal Arena. Lalonde started at centre, but Dandurand pulled him early in the second. Odie Cleghorn went in, and Lalonde watched as his teammates fought back from a six–one deficit. Early in the third, rookie Billy Boucher tied the score. "The crowd went almost frantic," *The Gazette* reported. "Hats were thrown in the air while men and women pounded one another with delight."

Dandurand put Lalonde back out, but the crowd disapproved and a chant arose from the bleachers at one end of the rink: "Send out Cleghorn. Send out Cleghorn." Lalonde watched the rest of the game, including a twenty-minute overtime period. He was a substitute forward three nights later when Canadiens played Toronto, and he never started again. He had scored 280 goals in eleven seasons with the Canadiens, and his feats included four five-goal games, three six-goal games and one nine-goal game. At the end of the 1921–22 season, Dandurand traded Lalonde to the Saskatoon Sheiks of the Western Canada Hockey League for a pint-sized dynamo named Aurel Joliat, the son of an Ottawa police officer. He stood five feet, seven inches tall and weighed 136 pounds. He wore a black cap when he played, and would fight like an enraged bulldog if anyone had the nerve to knock it off his head.

———

In the fall of 1922, the Canadiens held their training camp in Grimsby, Ontario, a small town at the western end of Lake Ontario in the Niagara fruit-growing district. They were invited by Leslie Farrell, the manager of the local arena. The Canadiens' home at the time, the Mount Royal Arena, did not have ice-making equipment, but Grimsby's rink did—it was used to produce the playing surface as well as the ice required to preserve fruit while it was being shipped across the country. Farrell promised a smooth, fast sheet of ice, a modern building and comfortable accommodations at the Village Inn across the street.

Dandurand accepted, and on December 3, two weeks before the season opener against the St. Pats in Toronto, he left Montreal with the team trainer and seven players: Vézina, the Cleghorns, Boucher, Louis Berlinquette, William Bell and the newcomer Joliat. The facilities were as good as promised, and the townsfolk were delighted to have the French-Canadian hockey players in their midst. They hosted a civic ball for the team, and a good crowd turned out daily to watch the workouts.

The Canadiens' new manager was an advocate of fitness and conditioning. The players began their days with a brisk run—sometimes up and down the Niagara escarpment. They practised late in the morning and were back on the ice in mid-afternoon. Dandurand directed the drills himself, and he gave the players Sunday off so they could attend Mass and have lunch in Niagara Falls.

Joliat was the most closely watched player in camp, and he made a big impression. "He is an extremely fast skater, handles the stick with rare skill and is very dangerous when he has the puck near the net," *La Presse* reported. Joliat was tested early, encountering Lalonde in a pre-season exhibition game. He was wearing number four on his sweater, Lalonde's old number, and behaving brashly. Joliat carried the puck up the ice, straight at the former Canadiens star, who was playing defence. "He was the big rooster at everything he played in those day," Joliat later recalled. "He was waiting for me. One second I was on left wing, the next I was on right wing. He crushed me. Split my lip in two."

Apart from the addition of Joliat, the Canadiens did not make any major player moves. They finished the twenty-four-game schedule in second place and met the league champion Senators in a two-game, total-goal series.

Hundreds of Montrealers lined up outside the Arena the morning of the first game to purchase tickets. Others ordered by phone and kept two box office employees busy. Between 10 a.m. and 2:30 p.m., all 3,800 reserved seats were sold. The three thousand bleacher seats went on sale at 7 p.m., and they, too, were quickly snapped up, and every bit of standing room as well.

The teams played a dull, scoreless first. The mood of the capacity crowd soured after referee Lou Marsh called three penalties against Joliat. Twice the crowd objected by hurling projectiles, including bottles, onto the ice, and the contest was stopped to clear the debris. The game took an ugly turn in the second when Ottawa's Cy Denneny scored from a bad angle. "Billy Couture followed in behind," *The Gazette* reported, "and with his stick struck Denneny over the head, sending him rolling over and over on the ice to finally come to a stop some twenty feet away."

Denneny was bleeding and unconscious. Teammates carried him to the dressing room, and Marsh ejected Couture. Late in the game, the Canadiens trailed two–nothing. Ottawa rookie Lionel Hitchman, a big man who had quit the Ontario Provincial Police to play pro hockey, carried the puck into the Montreal end. Sprague Cleghorn cross-checked him on the side of the head. Woozy and bleeding, Hitchman struggled to the Ottawa bench and collapsed.

At the final gong, the Arena band began playing the national anthem and Marsh left the ice. A small mob of furious fans descended on him. One man punched the referee in the face before police formed a phalanx and escorted Marsh to the dressing room.

Many Montrealers were appalled. A *La Presse* editorial described the incidents as disgraceful and concluded, "We cannot denounce them with too much vigour." Dandurand pre-empted NHL president Calder and suspended Cleghorn and Couture for the second game. The Canadiens prevailed by a score of two–one, but lost the series by a single goal. Vézina stopped sixty-four shots, but in the eyes of many the night belonged to

Didier Pitre, the last of the original Canadiens. By now, Pitre was thirty-nine. He had played eighteen seasons of professional hockey and scored 240 goals. Under Dandurand, he was a substitute, seldom used and frequently berated for being overweight. But on this occasion, he played one of his finest games. "Didier Pitre was sensational on defence," *La Presse* reported. "One expected him to be exhausted after a few minutes, but he was like a wall against the Ottawa attack." Afterward, he announced his retirement.

Ernest Sauvé was the first to see him play, and immediately afterward he drove from the Mount Royal Arena to the Windsor Hotel to tell Dandurand what he had witnessed. Sauvé was a former player in the Montreal City Hockey League. That day, a Saturday in December 1922, he had refereed a game between two Canadian National Railway teams, one from Pointe-St-Charles, the other from Stratford, Ontario.

"Léo," he said, "today I have discovered a player who I believe to be the fastest I have ever seen. He is faster than Jack Laviolette, Didier Pitre or Cyclone Taylor."

He continued: "On the visiting team, a player named Howie Morenz, a young man of eighteen or nineteen, scored nine goals and could have had ten more if the coach had not taken him off the ice. You should take a look at this young man."

Dandurand watched Morenz at Stratford in January 1923. The youthful centre, who was actually twenty, had played five seasons with the Stratford Midgets, a junior team in the Ontario Hockey Association, and led the Midgets to the Memorial Cup final in 1921. They lost eleven–nine to the Winnipeg Falcons in a two-game, total-goal series. Later, Falcon defence-man Harry Roth said: "It was Morenz, Morenz, Morenz as the fastest junior I ever saw scored goal after goal. Howie had speed to burn. He would come right up to you and when you tried to check him he wasn't there."

Dandurand was immediately captivated by his speed, checking and strength, and in April he met with Morenz and his father William. He brought along Riley Hern, a Stratford native and former Wanderer who ran a men's clothing store in Montreal. The elder Morenz did most of the talking because, legally, Howie was still a minor. "I don't want my son leaving Stratford," he told his visitors. "He still has two years to go before finishing his apprenticeship at the CN factory. It would be regrettable if he abandoned his trade."

In July, Dandurand bumped into *Toronto Star* sports editor Lou Marsh at Delorimier Park, a Montreal racetrack he operated with Cattarinich and Létourneau. Marsh informed him that Morenz and his father had been to Toronto several times to meet with Paul Ciceri and Charlie Querrie of the Toronto St. Pats. Dandurand promptly phoned his friend Cecil Hart and asked him to take a train to Stratford that day. He gave Hart three signed cheques, each for a different amount, and a standard player's contract. "It is absolutely necessary to call on young Morenz," he said. "Don't come back to Montreal without having the bird in the cage."

Hart reached Stratford at noon the following day. At 9 p.m., he phoned Dandurand. Morenz and his father had both signed the contract in the presence of a lawyer. It was for three years at $3,500 per season. Dandurand told Hart to stay overnight and deposit the cheque for $1,000 as a signing bonus. It was July 7, 1923, Dandurand's thirty-fourth birthday, and the Canadiens' manager decided that his new recruit would wear sweater number seven.

Over the next several weeks, the senior Stratford Indians and many local residents pressured Morenz to reconsider. Eventually, he relented. On August 10, he wrote to Dandurand, sending the letter by registered mail. It arrived August 23 and read:

> Dear Sir:
>
> I am enclosing Check and contract to play pro Hockey with your club owing to Several reasons of which family and work are the most to consider. I find it impossible to leave Stratford. I am sorry if I have caused you expense and inconvenience and trust you will accept the returned contract in a Sportsmanlike way.
>
> Yours truly
> Howard Morenz

Dandurand phoned Morenz. "I want you to take the train to Montreal this evening and to be at my office tomorrow morning," he said, adding that the manager of the Stratford train station would have a ticket waiting for him.

Morenz arrived as instructed. He began to explain his reasons for reneging on the contract, but broke down and cried. Dandurand was adamant. "If you refuse to play for the Canadiens," he said, "you can say goodbye to your career. Young man, you will never play professional hockey."

Morenz spent the day in Montreal. He met the Cleghorn brothers and tossed a football around with them at a park, had dinner at Dandurand's home, and boarded the 11 p.m. train, having promised to report to the Canadiens' training camp in Grimsby in the fall.

Morenz kept his word. On December 3, 1923, he left for camp. He had a trunk full of clothing and a battered pair of skates that Dandurand called wheelbarrows and replaced with new ones. Morenz quickly impressed his new teammates and opened the season at centre, with Aurel Joliat on his left and Billy Boucher on the right.

Why would anyone call at this hour, Dandurand wondered as he pulled himself from a deep, dream-filled sleep. It was 4 a.m. The house was dark, the floor cold, and the phone rang a good number of times before he made his way downstairs, lifted the receiver and said "Hello."

"Mr. Dandurand," said the caller. It was Morenz's middle-aged landlady. She spoke with a thick Scottish accent. "Howie's not here."

She explained that something had awoken her, she had walked quietly down the hall and been surprised to find Howie's door open. She had listened attentively before turning on the light. The bed was made and the room just as he'd left it nearly twelve hours earlier when he left for the game. Dandurand told her not to worry. The players were to be at the rink at 10:30 a.m. Morenz would be there.

Sure enough, he showed up, ahead of his teammates. "Yes, I have been out part of the night," he told Dandurand. "First I walked to Bonaventure Station to stretch my legs. Then I took a taxi out to the CNR motive power plant in Pointe-St-Charles to visit an old Stratford friend who is on night shift there. I'm sorry to have caused you worry, but, gosh, what's a fellow to do when he can't sleep a wink?"

Dandurand had seen his kind before. Morenz was like those thoroughbreds known as stall walkers. They had fiery, competitive spirits and could not relax after a race. That was Morenz—restless, unable to sleep, replaying the match in his mind, blaming himself for mistakes and missed opportunities where others saw only brilliance.

He impressed the sportswriters from the start, none more so than Elmer Ferguson of the Montreal *Herald*. Three games into the season, Ferguson wrote: "Here's the best-looking youngster who has broken into the NHL in quite some time. If he isn't a star of the first magnitude before the season's over it'll be because he's lost a leg."

Besides his speed, Morenz could handle the puck, he possessed extraordinary stamina and he was tough. The Senators tested him in their first meeting. Jack Darragh ran at him, but Morenz flattened him with his shoulder and sent him to the bench. He also laid out George Boucher, Billy's older brother, with a stiff check. And he outplayed Harry Broadbent, a rough player, who hit him all night and cut his nose with a butt end.

Morenz, Joliat and Boucher formed the youngest forward line in the league, and they led the Canadiens to the top of the NHL standings in 1924, giving the team its first title in five years. The Canadiens met the Senators in a two-game, total-goal playoff. At noon on the day of the opening game, fans began lining up for rush seats, and they stood in wind and sleet till the box office opened at 7 p.m. By game time, the Mount Royal Arena was packed. Young men were perched in the girders forty feet above the ice. Montreal radio station CKAC had an announcer in the building to broadcast the contest. And, prior to the opening faceoff, Cecil Hart presented NHL president Frank Calder with a trophy donated by his father, Dr. David Hart, to be awarded annually to the league's most useful player.

The game began on a good, fast sheet of natural ice that deteriorated as the evening progressed, becoming what Ferguson described as a surface disfigured by "holes, bumps, ridges and pools of water." Morenz scored the only goal, early in the second period.

The Canadian Pacific Railway put on a special train of twelve cars for the second game. Close to a thousand fans travelled to Ottawa, the largest contingent ever, and the same number were turned away. In all, twelve thousand spectators witnessed the game. Morenz scored twelve minutes in, and the youthful Canadiens used speed and energy to overpower the veteran Senators and skate to a four–two victory. On the way back to the train station, Montreal fans walked through the quiet streets shouting, *"Halte là! Halte là! Halte là! Les Canadiens sont là!"*

The Canadiens next faced two western champions, the Vancouver Millionaires of the Pacific Coast Hockey Association and the Calgary Tigers of the Western Canada Hockey League. They beat the Millionaires in two close, hard-fought games and began the second series by trouncing Calgary six–one. In the third period, Dandurand replaced Sprague Cleghorn with the rookie Sylvio Mantha—the first time in seventy-one games, going back three seasons, that Cleghorn had taken a break.

The Canadiens defeated Calgary again two nights later, this time in Ottawa because the Mount Royal ice was unuseable. They were forced to play the second and third periods without Morenz and Boucher. Unable to cope with Morenz's speed and tenacity, Calgary's Cully Wilson clubbed him over the head with his stick, while another Calgary player took out Boucher with a blow to his knee.

On April 1, the team held a banquet in the Rose Room of the Windsor Hotel to celebrate its second Stanley Cup. Over four hundred people connected with Montreal's French- and English-language sporting communities attended. The Windsor Orchestra provided musical accompaniment, and there were free cigars and cigarettes at every table. The players received gold watches and, after all the speeches, head-table guests joined Dandurand in drinking to the health of the champions from the bowl of hockey's most hallowed prize.

For several seasons, the Canadiens had been the team of both French and English Montreal. That was about to change. In October 1924, the National Hockey League awarded two new franchises. One went to Charles Adams of Boston, who hired Montrealer Art Ross as his coach and general manager. The other went to the Montreal Professional Hockey Club, an organization formed to represent the English community.

Three men were originally behind the new club: William Northey, a longtime hockey organizer and past president of the Montreal AAA; Donat Raymond, a French-Canadian businessman who operated in both linguistic communities, was majority owner of the Windsor Hotel and was a Liberal Party organizer; and Edward Beatty, president of the Canadian Pacific Railway. They formed the Canadian Arena Company to build a new rink, and they purchased land at the corner of Ste-Catherine Street and Atwater Avenue, one block east of the old Westmount Arena. The property had been the site of a grand roller skating rink called the Forum and, before that, a vacant lot on which local boys such as Art Ross, Russell Bowie, and Lester and Frank Patrick had learned to play hockey.

English Montrealers with deep pockets and long memories rallied to support the venture. Two Molsons, Herbert and his cousin William, were early investors. The architect John Smith Archibald put in money and designed the building. Sir Herbert Holt, president of the Royal Bank, and Sir Charles Gordon, president of the Bank of Montreal, both bought shares, as did a number of stockbrokers and company presidents. Some of these men had played hockey as youths, and they knew that over the past half-century their community—English Montreal—had transformed hockey from a crude game into a polished sport, had created the rules and set the dimensions of the playing surface. Their teams, the Montreal AAA, Victorias, Shamrocks and Wanderers, had combined to win the Stanley Cup more often than any other city or town in the country. Yet they had been not been represented at hockey's highest level since January 1918, when fire destroyed the Westmount Arena and Sam Lichtenhein folded the Wanderers.

A Canadian Arena Company prospectus issued on June 19, 1924, announced that investors had purchased $750,000 worth of stock and that the company had borrowed another $500,000. Construction began June 23, and 159 days later, on November 29, the Montreal Forum opened. In a twist of fate, it was the Canadiens who inaugurated the new building, beating the Toronto St. Patricks in a game moved from the Mount Royal

Arena because the latter structure's newly installed ice-making plant wasn't functioning properly. Nine thousand people turned out, at that time the largest crowd ever to watch a hockey game in eastern Canada.

By all accounts, the new building was well designed, the seating spacious, and every fan enjoyed a perfect view of the ice surface, unobstructed by columns. Montreal finally had an arena befitting its place as Canada's metropolis, according to *La Presse,* which went on to say, "The Forum is the biggest, the most beautiful and the most comfortable rink on the continent."

A month later, on December 27, the Canadiens visited the Forum to meet the new Montreal club, whom fans had nicknamed the Maroons because of the colour of their uniforms. That night, eleven thousand people packed the building, setting yet another attendance record. The teams played intense, hard-hitting hockey, and the Maroons held on to a one–nothing lead till late in the third. "The closeness of the score kept the crowd continually jumping to its feet," according to *The Gazette,* "and bedlam reigned for the greater portion of the game."

With two minutes remaining, Aurel Joliat tied it, and Canadiens supporters cheered for three solid minutes. "It was a delirious demonstration . . . a thunderous clamour . . . that will remain unforgettable to all who witnessed it," *La Presse* reported. The teams played two ten-minute overtime periods. Neither scored, but that night a new rivalry was born, one that would soon become the most heated in hockey.

On the final day of February 1925, the Canadiens travelled to Ottawa for a crucial late-season game against the Senators. Both teams were fighting for third place and a playoff berth. Eight thousand fans attended, including several hundred from Montreal. Also present were Governor General and Lady Byng, who watched from a box. Between periods, the smartly attired British aristocrat visited the Canadiens' dressing room and shook hands with the flushed and sweaty players. Afterward, Lord Byng had a brief conversation with Léo Dandurand. His wife, he said, was so taken with the speed and beauty of hockey that she wanted to create a trophy that would be awarded annually to the player who best combined athletic skill with gentlemanly qualities.

"Would that be in order?" the governor general asked.

"Certainly," Dandurand replied, "and would you please pass on to Her Excellency my most sincere thanks, as well as those of all my colleagues in the National Hockey League."

There were no candidates on the Canadiens for the new trophy, and not much interest, either. The team's sole objective was to repeat as Stanley Cup champions. They finished third, and defeated second-place Toronto in two straight playoff games.

Next, they should have played the Hamilton Tigers, who had finished first in the regular season, but the Hamilton players demanded two hundred dollars each to continue. Red Green, their spokesman, pointed out that he and some of his teammates had signed contracts the previous season for a twenty-four-game schedule. The league had extended the 1924–25 campaign to thirty games without compensating the players. NHL president Frank Calder was unsympathetic, and, when the Tigers refused to play, he awarded the league title to the Canadiens.

On the evening of March 15, a Sunday, the players boarded a transcontinental train to play the Stanley Cup final against the champion of the Western Canada Hockey League, which that season had absorbed the remnants of the Patrick brothers' PCHA. The Canadiens travelled in a private car around Lake Superior and across the Prairies. They played cards, listened to jazz records on a phonograph and wondered about the identity of their opponent. The Calgary Tigers and Victoria Cougars were still playing for the WCHL title when the Canadiens reached Alberta. Shortly before midnight on March 19, during a stop at Brooks, Alberta, a CPR inspector delivered a telegram stating that the Cougars had prevailed.

The best-of-five series lasted four games and changed forever the way hockey was played. The Cougars were a veteran team, but fast, and they skated the Canadiens to exhaustion. Lester Patrick, their coach, switched his forwards at every opportunity, whereas Dandurand used Morenz, Joliat and Boucher for the full sixty minutes. The previous season, in fact, the Canadiens forwards had set an endurance record by playing six playoff games—two each against Ottawa, Vancouver and Calgary—without being relieved other than when they were injured. This proved to be a losing strategy against the Cougars, who won the first two games decisively. Facing elimination, Dandurand roused his players for the third game. "He waved a raft of telegrams in front of their eyes, told them what the East was expecting of them, and if they didn't win there would be no joy around the breakfast tables in Montreal in the morning," the *Victoria Daily Times* reported. Morenz scored three times and the Canadiens won four–two, but the Cougars demolished the Montrealers in game four to win the Stanley Cup.

This series signalled the end for the sixty-minute men, and twenty-five years later, in an interview with *Maclean's,* Patrick recalled his strategy. "The Canadiens came west and those easterners who came with them in their hard derby hats bet their last dollar that an upstart team in Victoria couldn't stop them," he said. "Who could stop Morenz, Joliat and Boucher? Who could score on the great Vézina? But I knew we'd win because our second line would just tire them out, and it did. From then on, with three, then four interchangeable lines spelling each other, the game speeded up and is immeasurably faster now."

Georges Vézina had two nicknames, one English, the other French. He was both the "Chicoutimi Cucumber," a player who remained cool and unflustered no matter how hot the action around him, and *"l'Habitant silencieux,"* a veteran who was quiet even with teammates. He had his own corner of the dressing room, where trainer Eddie Dufour placed Vézina's skates, pads and other equipment, and where he would sit prior to practices, smoking a pipe and reading the newspapers in which he was rarely quoted. When he was, someone else had usually spoken for him—George Kennedy when his son, Marcel Stanley, arrived the same evening that the Canadiens won their first Cup, and Léo Dandurand when the team met the press in the lobby of the Empress Hotel in Victoria prior to the 1925 final.

"He is a real French Canadian," Dandurand told the reporters, pointing to the tall, thin man with the crewcut. "He speaks no English and has twenty-two children, including three sets of triplets and they were all born in the space of nine years." It was an outlandish and oft-repeated story, but not true. Apart from Marcel Stanley, Vézina had one other boy, Jean-Jules, born in 1912.

He played the 1925 Stanley Cup final with thumbs "swollen like balloons," according to one reporter, but said nothing about his injuries. He felt awful in November 1925, when he arrived in Montreal for training camp, his sixteenth. Again, he kept this to himself. He practised daily, took shots, played in the scrimmages and attended a dinner held at the Windsor to honour the Cleghorns—Sprague, who had been sold to Boston for five thousand dollars, and Odie, who was leaving to coach the Pittsburgh Pirates, one of the NHL's new U.S. expansion teams. And he was in net for the season opener on November 28 at the Mount Royal Arena against Cleghorn's Pirates.

Vézina was gaunt and pale. He had lost thirty-five pounds during training camp. He was running a fever of a hundred and two. He finished the first period, took off his pads and remained in his corner. Another player, Alphonse Lacroix of Boston, a U.S. Olympic goalie, finished the game for Montreal—one of the rare occasions in Vézina's sixteen seasons that he had not completed a night's work.

He went home and the next day saw his doctor, J.-E. Dubé, who diagnosed tuberculosis. The physician told Vézina that he was gravely ill and recommended he go home to Chicoutimi. The goaltender visited the Canadiens' dressing room for the final time on the morning of December 3. Afterward, his close friend Dandurand spoke to the reporters: "Vézina reported at his usual hour. I glanced at him as he sat there and saw tears rolling down his cheeks. He was looking at his old pads and skates that Eddie Dufour had arranged in George's corner. Then he asked one little favour—the sweater he had worn in the last world series."

Vézina left Montreal that evening aboard a Canadian National overnight train—bundled and bedridden and cared for by his wife, Marie. Lacroix lasted five games before Dandurand signed Herb Rhéaume, an Ottawa amateur. Rhéaume made his debut on December 15, in a contest against the New York Americans at Madison Square Garden. The Americans were the second U.S. team admitted to the NHL that season, and they had drawn most of their talent from the Hamilton Tigers, who had folded, leaving the league with seven franchises.

The game between the Canadiens and Americans represented the debut of professional hockey in New York. It was also the "official, royal and gala opening" of the latest iteration of Madison Square Garden. Seventeen thousand fans attended, in part because the game was a benefit for the Neurological Institute Society, and the lower-level boxes were filled with men in suits and women in furs and jewels. So many high-society New Yorkers turned out that the next day's *New York Times* filled a column and a half naming them box by box.

The building was draped with multicoloured bunting as well as American and British flags. Two bands provided musical entertainment. The Governor General's Foot Guard—performing outside Canada for the first time—welcomed the Canadiens with a rousing number and played the national anthem. The West Point Cadet Band greeted the Americans, who were clad in their extravagant red, white and blue uniforms emblazoned with stars and stripes.

The Canadiens prevailed by a margin of three–one and afterward received the newly created Prince of Wales Trophy, which was theirs to keep until the end of the season, when it would be presented to the team that finished first. Both sides showered, then headed for the Hotel Biltmore, where, along with several hundred upper-crust guests, they enjoyed dinner and music provided by the Paul Whiteman Orchestra.

The New York game was one of the few highlights of an otherwise dismal season for the Canadiens in which they lost five of six games against the Maroons, completed the thirty-six-game schedule with twelve straight losses, finished last and watched the Maroons beat Pittsburgh, Ottawa and Victoria to win the Stanley Cup. And before going separate ways for the summer, they mourned the loss of a teammate.

Georges Vézina died in the pre-dawn hours of Saturday, March 27, 1926, at l'Hôtel-Dieu, the small, three-storey stone hospital in Chicoutimi that stood on the summit of a hill overlooking the ice-bound Saguenay River and the streets where he had learned to play hockey. He was thirty-nine. He had earned eight hundred dollars as a rookie, six thousand in his final season, and the Canadiens had paid him in full in 1925–26 though he started only once.

Vézina played 367 games between December 31, 1910, and November 28, 1926, and never missed a start. On six occasions, including his last two full seasons, he posted a better goals-against average than any of his rivals, and he had the second-best average five times.

Vézina was well liked in Montreal and revered in his hometown. His widow, Marie, received hundreds of telegrams and letters of condolence. Over eight hundred Catholic masses were devoted to his memory. Close to 1,500 people packed the cathedral in Chicoutimi for his funeral. Newspapers across the province paid tribute to the man, the athlete and the Christian. "He died a fervent Catholic," a local journalist wrote, "confident in divine mercy and knowing that his soul would enjoy eternal happiness."

For three decades starting in the mid-1890s, hockey operated on an east-west axis—just as the country was supposed to work, according to the Fathers of Confederation. One year, the eastern champions, be they from Montreal or Ottawa, Quebec or Toronto, rode a train across the continent to play the winner of the west for the Stanley Cup. The following year, the Stanley Cup final was played in the east, and the western champions travelled.

The last of these transcontinental showdowns occurred in the spring of 1926, when Lester Patrick's Victoria Cougars came east to play the Montreal Maroons. That fall, professional hockey succumbed to the forces of continentalism. The game's axis shifted, and it became a north-south enterprise. The Western Canada Hockey League folded, and the NHL awarded franchises to the New York Rangers, Detroit Cougars and Chicago Black Hawks, becoming a ten-team league. The Patrick brothers, who held the rights to many of the western players, sold their contracts to NHL teams for an estimated three hundred thousand dollars.

The Chicago franchise purchased the Portland Rosebuds roster, while Detroit acquired the Victoria Cougars. The other NHL clubs grabbed the best individuals available to fill holes in their lineups. The Canadiens desperately needed someone to replace Georges Vézina, and Dandurand signed George Hainsworth of the Saskatoon Crescents. A stocky, moon-faced, thirty-one-year-old, Hainsworth stood five foot six and weighed

150 pounds. When he leaned into his goaltender's crouch, a really sharp shooter might, on a good night, put the puck over his shoulder and under the crossbar. Hainsworth had begun his career prior to World War I as a child mascot for the Berlin Seniors of the Ontario Professional Hockey League, had ridden trolley cars to games in Galt, Guelph, Brantford and Toronto, and learned goaltending from one of the early greats, Berlin's Hugh Lehman. He played junior and intermediate with the Berlin Union Jacks and senior for ten seasons with the Kitchener Greenshirts.

In his first season with the Canadiens, he played all forty-four games and shut out the opposition fourteen times. He became the first recipient of the Georges Vézina Trophy, which the Canadiens had created to honour their departed goaltender, and he made the job look easy, according to the *Herald*'s Elmer Ferguson. "He is never excited, no matter how tough the going," Ferguson wrote. "He stands in net with a bored, detached air and seems to yawn with indifference as he tosses aside the wickedest drives. He seems unconcerned when he plunges into a maelstrom of flying skates and sticks to retrieve a puck."

Hainsworth and Morenz were the cornerstones of the Canadiens' second great team. In 1927–28, his second season in Montreal, the squat little goaltender allowed just forty-eight goals and earned thirteen shutouts and another Vézina trophy, while Morenz captured the scoring title and the Hart Trophy. The Canadiens finished first overall, but lost to the Maroons in the playoffs. Despite that disappointment, Dandurand organized a sumptuous banquet and told the assembly of several hundred admiring fans, "There is not enough money in the coffers of Wall Street to buy the players of the Canadiens."

The team was just as good in 1928–29. The Canadiens lost only one of their final twenty-five games. They won the league championship and played the Bruins in the first playoff round. The team left for Boston on a Monday evening, March 19, accompanied by Louis Létourneau and two hundred ardent supporters. The players were healthy and their coach, Cecil Hart, confident. "Certainly, we are going to beat Boston," he told *La Presse*. "I have no worries. Pittsburgh, which nearly finished last, gave us as much trouble as Boston."

Four days later, the Canadiens returned to Montreal having lost twice before wild, noisy, overflow crowds at Boston Garden. Thirteen thousand Montrealers packed the Forum for the third game. The Canadiens scored twice in the first period, while the Bruins replied with three in the second. The Canadiens mounted a ferocious assault on Boston in the third but could not score. Afterward, Dandurand, Hart and Létourneau behaved like true sportsmen, according to *La Presse*. They walked down the long, narrow corridor under the Forum stands to the visitors' dressing room and congratulated Art Ross and his jubilant Bruins.

The Bruins won their first Stanley Cup that spring and were nearly unbeatable the following winter. They lost only five games and set new NHL records for most goals (179), wins (38) and points (71). Cooney Weiland won the scoring title with an unprecedented 73 points, while linemate Dit Clapper finished third and goaltender Tiny Thompson took the Vézina Trophy. The Bruins beat the Maroons in a preliminary round to reach the best-of-three final against the Canadiens, and they were certain that a second Stanley Cup was as good as theirs.

They had beaten Montreal seven straight times during the season and finished twenty-six points ahead of them. But the Canadiens had speed and momentum on their side and skated to a startling three–nothing victory in the series opener. "Light and fast, the Montrealers swept around the champions like a Texas cyclone," *The Gazette*'s L.S.B. Shapiro wrote. "A stunned, silent crowd of seventeen thousand sat in the Garden and watched the favored Boston team rendered almost helpless by the amazing vitality of the Flying Frenchmen."

The second game, played at the Forum, was tense and exciting. The working-class fans known as the Millionaires, who were packed into the bleachers behind the goal at the north end of the rink, showered the Canadiens with confetti as they skated onto the ice and roared with delight as their team ran up a three–nothing lead by the middle of the second period. Boston's bruising defenceman Eddie Shore scored late in the second, but Morenz got that one back and the Canadiens led four–one at the break.

The powerful Boston offence produced two goals early in the third, and the Bruins played with a fury and desperation that kept the crowd quiet as the minutes ticked away. At the sound of the gong, anxiety turned to joy. "The spectators threw their hats on the ice," wrote *Le Devoir*'s X.-E. Narbonne. "They waved handkerchiefs and scarves, danced and sang and created an infernal ruckus."

The Canadiens had won their third Stanley Cup, though this triumphant moment passed quietly. The players appeared at a number of private events, but made only one public appearance. On the evening of April 15, the management of the Palace Theatre, a Ste-Catherine Street movie house, introduced the players individually on stage between showings of a western called *Under a Texas Moon*.

"The Stanley Cup, an undistinguished-looking silver mug, scrawled inside and out with names that make up the history of hockey, stands in a corner of the Canadien Hockey Club rooms at the Windsor Hotel," the Montreal *Gazette* reported on March 24, 1931. It had been there almost a year, and that day the Canadiens began their defence of the trophy. They had finished first in their division in 1930–31. Morenz won the scoring championship and the Hart Trophy and Hainsworth had the second-best goals-against average. Under the league's playoff system, divisional winners met in the opening round, which meant the Canadiens played the Bruins. It was the third straight post-season showdown between the teams, and fans in both cities got value for their money.

Four of the five games were decided by a goal, three of them in overtime. The teams were so close, and interest so high, that Montrealers peppered newspaper offices with calls seeking the scores while the contests were in progress. The *Gazette* operators couldn't keep up, prompting the paper to run a daily notice pleading with fans to phone "only after the time at which matches may be expected to be concluded and to limit their enquiries to final scores."

The series was decided at the Forum after eighteen minutes of overtime in the fifth game, a match described by one observer as "thrilling and hardbitten." Both sides were banged up and physically spent, but played with speed and ferocity. The partisan crowd cheered nonstop, led by the Millionaires and their war cry: "*Halte-là! Halte-là! Halte-là! Les Canadiens sont là!*"

The game ended when defenceman Marty Burke broke up a Boston attack and carried the puck down the ice. Centre Pit Lepine was on his left; winger Wildor Larochelle was open on the right. Burke passed to Larochelle at a bad angle. The crowd rose to its feet. Larochelle faked a shot to the far side. Tiny Thompson shifted that way. Larochelle pulled the puck back, snapped his wrists and picked the opening.

"The entire Canadien team jumped to the ice and almost smothered Larochelle," L.S.B. Shapiro wrote. "After a few seconds of wild struggling he was lifted to the shoulders of his exhausted teammates and carried to the dressing room. . . . It was a stirring finish and took place to the roar of a capacity crowd."

The Canadiens left for Chicago at 3 p.m. the following day, a Thursday. Several hundred fans cheered from the platform at Bonaventure Station as the players boarded their train. The trip took eighteen hours. They arrived at 9 a.m. Friday and had to face the Black Hawks that night with a lineup weakened by injuries.

Left winger Armand Mondou received a nasty cross-check in the final Boston game and landed in hospital with damage to his shoulder and ribs. Albert Leduc, a bruising defenceman known as Battleship, was concussed and occupied a nearby bed. Both were expected to be back in uniform when the team returned home for game three. *The Gazette* added that "Marty Burke, Aurel Joliat, Georges Mantha, Pit Lepine and Howie Morenz all are wearing a certain amount of adhesive tape and have mercurochrome covering cuts, bruises and scrapes . . . but will not permit such minor ailments to affect their play."

The Black Hawks, playing in their first final, were healthy—or, as Shapiro put it, "Sixteen men and not a scratch to mar them." They had tier upon tier of roaring fans cheering them on—16,500 in the first game, 17,500 in the second—and a sharp mind behind the bench in Dick Irvin.

This was Irvin's first season as a coach. He had begun his pro career with the 1916–17 Portland Rosebuds and played until the spring of 1929, when he retired after three years with the Hawks. In 1930–31, he led his team to second place in the NHL's American Division and past the Maple Leafs and Rangers in preliminary playoff rounds. The Canadiens, according to one observer, possessed "more genuine hockey ability and infinitely more championship experience," but Irvin's coaching evened things up. He used three forward lines equally, rolling them over the boards in short shifts of two to three minutes. His players were fresh from start to finish, which produced a final as tight as the Boston series, though not as emotional.

The teams split the games in Chicago. In the third, the Canadiens led two–nothing with less than five minutes remaining, but they allowed the Hawks to tie it and then lost in the fifty-third minute of overtime. The Hawks jumped to a quick two–nothing lead in the fourth game, which silenced the Forum's capacity crowd, but surrendered a goal in the second and three in the third.

"When the final gong sounded," a *Gazette* reporter wrote, "that sure sign of a triumph for the Flying Frenchmen—Les Canadiens Sont Là— pealed forth from lusty lungs among the famous Millionaires at the north end of the rink." The players were as excited as the fans, and so was coach Cecil Hart. In the team's crowded dressing room, he told a writer: "It's the most wonderful team imaginable. And we'll take 'em Tuesday night."

The fifth game was played Tuesday, April 14. The temperature in Montreal rose to sixty degrees Fahrenheit that day. Major league baseball opened in half a dozen American cities, making this the first time the two seasons had overlapped. But Montrealers were preoccupied with hockey. Fans began gathering at the doors of the Forum early in the morning, and by late afternoon several thousand stood in line. The box office and the doors opened at 6 p.m. Hundreds of eager fans—buddies and brothers, fathers and sons, most of them working-class residents of the French-speaking east end—snapped up every available rush ticket and dashed two-hundred-odd feet for the seats at the north end of the rink, where—for the fifty-cent price of admission—they got to be Millionaires for the biggest game of the season. Their less fortunate brethren, those left behind in line, waited till almost 8:30 and the opening faceoff for the few hundred standing-room tickets.

Most of the city huddled around radios to catch the action. Foster Hewitt, described by a reporter as "one of the leading sports broadcasters of the continent," came from Toronto to call the play-by-play, and CPR transmission lines carried his voice to Winnipeg, Regina, Saskatoon, Edmonton, Calgary and the west coast.

The teams played fast, hard, end-to-end hockey. The goaltenders, Hainsworth and Chicago's Chuck Gardiner, were sensational. Montreal opened the scoring midway through the second. Johnny Gagnon, the speedy rookie on Morenz's right wing, who stood five foot five and weighed 140 pounds, took a pass from Joliat. Gagnon burst around a defender, cut to the front of the net and lifted the puck over a sprawling Gardiner.

That was all the scoring till 15:27 of the third, by which time a good portion the thirteen thousand Forum fans were on their feet. Some watched the clock, some prayed and some held their breath, but they cheered as one when Morenz picked up a loose puck near the Canadiens' blue line, sped down the right boards, beat a defenceman, faked a shot to the far side and drilled the puck shoulder-high past Gardiner. He turned—arms raised in triumph, face lit by a radiant smile—and skated into thunderous applause and the embrace of jubilant teammates. His goal assured their victory and ended Morenz's own miserable nine-game scoring slump, brought on by injured shoulders and zealous checking.

Thanks to the radio broadcast, Montrealers celebrated that night in their homes, at private gatherings and in the nightclubs. At the Forum, most of the crowd stayed put for forty-five minutes, talking and laughing, shaking hands and embracing, and some continued to vent their joy on the streetcars afterward. None were noisier than the cars that travelled down Ste-Catherine to the east end, each one packed with Millionaires who chanted and cheered all the way home.

The following evening, nearly five hundred members of the city's sporting and corporate elites packed the grand ballroom of the Windsor Hotel for a celebratory banquet. They came in suits and tuxedos and sipped pre-dinner drinks to the jazzy melodies of Jimmy Rice and the Frolics, a five-member nightclub band, which performed on the stage at one end of the room. The head table sat eighteen men, their backs to the room's enormous windows. Mr. Justice Joseph Archambault, the first after-dinner speaker, called the Canadiens "the most valiant hockey team that ever existed" and declared that he was proud to pay tribute to them.

Dandurand spoke briefly and from the heart. He addressed the businessmen and sportsmen first. "You can be certain, gentlemen, that if the Canadiens won to keep the Stanley Cup in Canada, if they fought for the honour of French Canadians, if they battled to give Montreal a coveted championship, it was also with thoughts of you in their hearts, for you their great friends always."

And how to thank the players? It was not easy. "To cite names, to recognize the most brilliant of you, would seem to me an injustice," he said. "You have all given to the best of your abilities . . . to the benefit of professional hockey. I cannot emphasize too much the admirable spirit of harmony which you have brought to your work. I recognize among you men of splendid courage, of strength, of determination, of generous hearts, accomplished athletes of whom I am, this evening, enormously proud."

When the speeches were over, there was prolonged applause. Jimmy Rice and the Frolics began to play. Men lined up to buy drinks or to congratulate the players, and some headed for home in cars or streetcars, all certain on this warm April night that, with Hainsworth in goal, Burke and Mantha on defence, Morenz, Joliat and Gagnon up front and top-notch reserves behind them, the Canadiens would win again and the Stanley Cup would be theirs to behold and to admire.

1931–1946
INTO A BIND AND OUT

THE CITIES AND TOWNS OF THE ST. LAWRENCE slipped past one by one—Lachine, Pointe-Claire and Beaconsfield on the west island, Cornwall, Brockville and Gananoque further west in Ontario—and he scarcely noticed. Likewise, the communities of Lake Ontario—Kingston, Belleville, Cobourg and a host of smaller places.

Howie Morenz had made this trip many times over the previous eleven years, boarding a westbound train destined for Toronto or Detroit or Chicago when the Canadiens were on the road. He had always been surrounded by teammates, his closest friends after all the years in Montreal. They had joked and laughed and played cards while Léo and Cecil, as close to him as a father and a brother, talked quietly in the background. But this trip was like none of those. On this mid-October day in 1934, he was alone in his compartment. He was hurt, he was angry and his mind was filled with doubt and anxiety. He was haunted by memories of his beloved *bleu, blanc, rouge*. How had it all come apart, he wondered? Why did it have to end like this?

He and the Canadiens had enjoyed one more splendid season after their triumphant spring of 1931. The team finished atop the Canadian Division in

1931–32 for the fourth time in five years. Morenz, who had placed third in scoring, won his second straight Hart Trophy and the third of his career. But he and his mates lost to the Rangers in the opening round of the playoffs. And that summer, things began to change.

Louis Létourneau sold his interest in the Canadiens to Dandurand and Cattarinich, and some of the fun went with him. Little Louie had been a familiar face at home games and a welcome presence in the dressing room, a short, rotund, avuncular man bundled up in a fur coat and hat, always a smile on his face, generous in his praise and encouragement and frequently slipping someone twenty or twenty-five dollars for an extraordinary performance.

Cecil Hart was next to leave. Coaching had always been a part-time proposition for him. He did it because he loved hockey and the rink and the players, especially these young men. How many times had he said it: they were the greatest. His bonds with them were as deep and strong as those between father and son. If he only had to keep his players happy, he could have stayed for years. But the fans had to be kept content, and those who followed the Canadiens could be as harsh and fickle as winter weather. The more cantankerous of them had been complaining about him for years. A few had even written to X.-E. Narbonne, sports editor of *Le Devoir*. They questioned his coaching decisions, and that wasn't all. Surely, some said, French Canada's team should be coached by a French-Canadian, not an English-speaking Jew.

Léo Dandurand heard the hateful sniping and listened to some of it. He had expressed some of the same doubts as the fans, and Hart was resentful. Their friendship—formed twenty years earlier when they organized hockey and baseball leagues for the city's best amateurs—had suffered.

Hockey had also interfered with Hart's business. He was a broker who sold, as his advertising put it: "Insurance of all kind. Fire, Life, Accident, Sickness, Burglary, Liability, Automobile, Plate Glass, Etc., Etc., Etc." He had been able to juggle hockey and business when he took on the Canadiens' coaching job in 1925–26, the winter of George Vézina's demise. NHL teams played thirty-six games and the season lasted about four and a half months. Within seven years, the number of matches had grown by one-third, to forty-eight. Training camp started a month earlier, in mid-October, and the playoffs lasted into April. There were long road trips to Detroit and Chicago. Coaching was becoming a full-time occupation. Hart had had enough and resigned late in August 1932.

A few weeks later, Dandurand announced that Newsy Lalonde would take over. The players were untroubled by the changes. On October 14, they showed up for physicals, weigh-ins and fitness tests at a downtown Montreal armoury, but golf seemed uppermost in everyone's mind, according to *The Gazette*'s L.S.B. Shapiro. "The Flying Frenchmen gathered for the first physical training drill and immediately fell into a deep and scholarly discussion on slices and mashie shots," he reported. "They rolled around on their stomachs on the gym floor still arguing about how to correct a hook. Back in the locker room, the discussion of scores was waged with considerable fervor. When they were ready to go, foursomes were arranged and all paths led to the fairways."

This lighthearted bunch played its home opener on November 12 against the Boston Bruins. Mayor Fernand Rinfret dropped the puck in a ceremonial opening faceoff and then presented the Canadiens with an immense, horseshoe-shaped floral arrangement, a gift from the fans known as the Millionaires, who packed the benches at the north end of the Forum as usual. Elsewhere, though, there were some three thousand empty seats, and the Canadiens did not sell out the Forum till December 1, when they met the Maroons. By then, they were accustomed to less-than-capacity crowds.

Attendance was down across the league because unemployment was up almost everywhere and nearly every sort of business activity was declining. The Great Depression had taken hold. By the spring of 1932, the volume of shares traded on the Montreal Stock Exchange—Canada's largest—was one-quarter of the peak in 1929. The value of stocks listed on the exchange had fallen by over a billion dollars. Thirty-four thousand unemployed Montrealers had registered with the city, hoping for temporary work on relief projects. Forty thousand families and over a hundred and fifty thousand individuals were receiving social assistance. A municipal refuge on Vitré Street was serving fifteen thousand meals daily and providing beds for 1,800 homeless. Helping the unemployed and the down-and-out was costing the city seven hundred thousand dollars a month, and idleness was fuelling discontent.

The Canadiens fared no better in 1932–33 than the city itself. They posted a losing record—eighteen wins, twenty-five losses and five ties—for the first time since the departure of their great goaltender Vézina. The fortunes of the once-fabulous Morenz declined with those of the disenfranchised tradesmen and factory workers who had worshipped him in his prime. His point production slipped—he finished behind Aurel Joliat in team scoring—and Lalonde moved him to the second line.

His slide continued the following season. His scoring touch deserted him, and on January 2, 1934, he suffered the first serious injury of his career when he twisted his right ankle in a game in New York. Doctors determined that he had bruised a bone and torn ligaments. He missed a month and, upon returning, displayed only occasional flashes of his former brilliance. After a game in mid-February, *The Gazette* reported, "He staged his headlong rushes, bounced off defenceman like a rubber ball, almost bowled over goalkeepers with the intensity of his shot and brought inspiration to the rest of the team." Morenz had other good nights in the last two months of the season, but not enough of them. On at least one occasion, the Forum crowd booed him. Trade rumours surfaced in *La Presse* as the Canadiens were about to open a two-game, total-goal playoff against Chicago, and Dandurand confirmed that the Bruins, Rangers, Red Wings and Black Hawks had expressed interest. Morenz played with his customary speed and recklessness in the first game of the series, but was knocked out of the second with a broken thumb.

The Hawks beat the Canadiens, and afterward Morenz told an Associated Press reporter: "You can say that I am good for five more years—make it four, just to be safe. Right now, only one thing can make me quit. When the Canadiens don't want me then I'm all done. When I can't play for them, I'll never put on a skate again."

Morenz had never worried about the future, but that spring and that summer he was troubled by recurring doubts. He stayed active. He golfed. He played tennis. His injured ankle healed completely. By the time summer turned to fall, he was ready to go.

But the talk in hockey circles and in the newspapers was all about trades. Several teams would be involved, numerous players would be moved, and his name was always mentioned. He waited, and wondered. Why hadn't he heard from Léo or Joe? He hoped he would wake one morning and it would all be gone, like a bad dream. Instead, he picked up his morning paper on October 3, and there it was: Howie Morenz was going to Chicago.

He told the sportswriters otherwise. He'd quit before he'd join the Black Hawks, even though they were a good team and had won the Stanley Cup the previous spring. Dandurand knew better. "When we get together," he said, "Howie will find he is not being tossed around as he claims. His interests are not being neglected. I am sure that if he had any intention of retiring he would have come to us first."

Morenz couldn't quit. He loved Montreal, but he loved hockey even more. The team honoured him with a banquet on the evening before his departure. It was held at the Café Martin, one of the two popular downtown nightspots that Dandurand owned. Two hundred people attended, including Fernand Rinfret, now the ex-mayor, and Camillien Houde, his successor. Morenz sat between Dandurand and NHL president Frank Calder. He looked grim, according to Al Parsley of the *Herald*, who wrote: "He bit his lips and a jagged white scar stood out dead-white in the half-light. Morenz sat so still you could almost count the criss-crosses of the surgeon's stitches."

There were toasts and speeches. Dandurand announced that no one would ever wear Howie's number seven again. Joliat spoke for the players. "We all like Howie Morenz," he said. "He played every day, practised every day with us. We knew him as pals. The owners and league officials only knew him as the big gate attraction. They didn't know the Howie I know. Our lockers were in the same corner for eleven years. Always together. This season it's going to be different. All I can say is: good bye, Howie. You won't be here. There'll be a stranger in our corner."

The next morning, Morenz cleaned out his locker. Elmer Ferguson stood with him, notebook open, pen poised. He saw tears in Howie's eyes. "It's all in the game," said Morenz bravely. "I'll give the best I have to Chicago and I sincerely think I have plenty of good hockey left in the old frame. I never felt better." He continued talking and Ferguson kept taking notes, and when his bag was packed he left. He hailed a taxi, boarded the train and began the long journey west to Chicago.

There were strange faces sprinkled throughout the Canadiens' dressing room that winter. There was the goaltender, Wilf Cude, taking the place of Lorne Chabot, who had been sent to Chicago as part of the Morenz deal. Defenceman Roger Jenkins had been secured from Chicago in the same transaction. Centreman Jack Riley came from the Red Wings organization. Right winger Joe Lamb arrived from Boston in exchange for Johnny Gagnon. Then there were the McGill graduates, Nelson Crutchfield and Jack McGill, who had led the Redmen to the Quebec senior title the previous year.

The Canadiens began the season with seven players between the ages of twenty-one and twenty-four. Dandurand hoped new leaders would emerge to form the nucleus of another great team, as Morenz and Joliat had done a decade earlier. But his reconstructed Canadiens faltered from the start, losing their season opener at Maple Leaf Gardens.

They opened at home against Detroit. During the pre-game ceremonies, Les Canadiens of the Montreal and District Ladies Hockey League presented a blue, white and red floral horseshoe to Aurel Joliat and Sylvio Mantha. The Millionaires gave a horseshoe of bright yellow chysanthemums to coach Lalonde. Mayor Houde dropped the puck between the sticks of the opposing centres. But late in the third, with the Canadiens trailing three–nothing, the Millionaires booed Lalonde and called for the return of Morenz and Gagnon.

The Canadiens briefly fell to the bottom of their division, and the Millionaires began jeering and banging the boards. Attendance was down, though the papers seldom published actual figures, and senior games played mid-week and Sunday afternoons were drawing bigger crowds. By New Year's Day, the Canadiens were battling the New York Americans for third, but had little chance of catching the front-running Leafs. Lalonde was under so much duress that his health suffered, and he turned over coaching duties to Dandurand. The Canadiens held on to third and made the playoffs, but lost to the Rangers in a two-game, total-goal series.

That spring, Dandurand and Cattarinich tallied their losses. Forty thousand this season, twenty thousand the previous winter. They were ready to quit pro hockey. "We like to be loyal," Cattarinich said, "but we can't go on losing at that rate."

They held discussions with a Cleveland businessman, A.C. Sutphin, who was interested in buying the team and moving it to the Ohio city, but talks broke off when a group of local buyers emerged. By mid-September 1935, the sale of the Canadiens was complete. Colonel Maurice Forget and Ernest Savard, president of the Montreal Exhibition and a shareholder in the Montreal Royals baseball club of the International League, led a syndicate that paid $165,000 for the team.

Savard promised an overhaul for the upcoming campaign, but he and his partners barely had time to take stock of their assets when they lost one of their most promising young players. Crutchfield was a passenger in a car that collided with another and flipped over near Shawinigan Falls. He was thrown from the vehicle and suffered a compound basal fracture of the skull.

The new owners also had to appoint a coach quickly and decided on Sylvio Mantha, the team's veteran defenceman. Mantha, now thirty-three years old, was the first Montreal-born member of the Canadiens. He grew up reading about the original Canadiens—Newsy Lalonde, Jack Laviolette and Didier Pitre—but never saw them play, nor did he dream of a professional career. Hockey was just a game and the ticket to a decent factory job. In his late teens, Mantha had applied at Imperial Tobacco, told them he was a good hockey player and promptly landed a position with the company, not to mention its team in the Manufacturers' League.

The following season, he led Les Nationales to the championship of the Montreal City Hockey League. One night, a stranger approached him between periods in the Nationales' dressing room. They talked. The visitor looked at his skates and equipment, chuckled and asked how he played with such gear. "Who was that guy who had the nerve to laugh at my outfit?" Mantha later asked his manager. It was Léo Dandurand. The Canadiens' managing director watched him several times that winter and offered him a tryout the following autumn.

Mantha had spent eleven seasons on the Canadiens blue line, winning three Stanley Cups along the way. But he proved unable to manage the dual role of player and coach. The Canadiens, with eight new faces on the roster, finished last. Worse still, gate receipts were down sixty-five per cent from 1930–31, the last Cup-winning season.

The team needed yet another shakeup, and it happened during the off-season. The new owners searched for a qualified coach and concluded that Cecil Hart was the best available. Hart was fifty-three. He had never married. He had devoted his life to sport and business. Since leaving the Canadiens, he had been coaching the senior Verdun Maple Leafs, and his team often played big games before roaring crowds of ten thousand or more at the Forum. Hart was prepared to return to the Canadiens, but on one condition.

He wanted Morenz back.

Howie Morenz could hardly believe his good fortune. After a season and a half with Chicago, and a second trade, this one to the Rangers, he was back where he belonged: back on the ice at the Montreal Forum, wearing the blue, white and red of the Canadiens, centring a line with Aurel Joliat and Johnny Gagnon, who had also been reacquired. And the fans. Where else would you get a crowd like this on the opening night of training camp? There must have been five thousand people in the seats, and most were there just to see him.

"The old spirit is back," he told the sportswriters who clustered around his locker afterward. "The old gang is together again. It's like when we won the Stanley Cup back in 1930 and '31. Just watch us go this year. We can't miss."

The Canadiens made one other smart off-season move. They acquired Babe Siebert from the Boston Bruins, a left winger who stood five foot ten, weighed 180 and played a "crushing offensive and rugged defensive game," according to Elmer Ferguson. With Siebert on the wing, Morenz at centre and Hart behind the bench, the Canadiens were a different team.

From the start, they battled the Maroons for first place in the division. Their old rivalry heated up again, and the fans began to return. They beat the last-place New York Americans twice over New Year's, once before a noisy home crowd of nine thousand, and started 1937 atop the NHL standings. Afterward, the mood in the dressing room was celebratory. "Players were buzzing around joyously," Ferguson wrote. "The team spirit never ran higher. You wouldn't know there are any racial divisions on the team, that its units are French-Canadian, a Welshman, two German-Canadians, a Belgian-Canadian, Irish-Canadians and Scotch-Canadians. They're a harmonious whole, a great organization, one for all and all for one."

In mid-January, the Canadiens and Maroons played before twelve thousand fans, their biggest crowd since 1932, and Canadiens won five–nothing. Later that month, they went undefeated for five games and pulled ten points ahead of their intra-city rival. Gagnon was third in league scoring with twenty-six points, while Joliat was fifth with twenty-four. Morenz lagged behind with twenty, well below the pace of his peak years, but he was happy.

"You know, there was something missing inside when I was away the last two seasons," he told Ferguson at one point. "I got it back when I came back with the Canadiens. I'm going to the limit right now. I'm giving the fans everything I've got. The end may be in sight, but the heart is still sound."

On January 28, a Thursday, the Canadiens played the Black Hawks at home. They were expecting an easy game because the Hawks were in last place in the American Division. Early in the first period, Morenz raced into the Chicago end, two steps ahead of Earl Seibert, the big Hawk defenceman. Both were going at full speed. Morenz lost his footing and slid into the end boards. The blade of his left skate penetrated a crack between two planks. Seibert couldn't stop and piled into him.

The momentum of the crash carried the two players one way, but Morenz's leg didn't move. Instead, it snapped. Seibert scrambled to his feet while Morenz writhed. The referee blew the play dead. Fans stood and stared. Gagnon, Joliat and the defence helped Morenz to the bench, where ushers waited with a stretcher.

Hart sent Paul Haynes out to take the faceoff, and play resumed. The Canadiens built a four–one lead before the first period was out. The Hawks rallied and made it close, but Hart's men won six–five. Georges Mantha, the second-string right winger, had the best night of his career, with four goals and an assist, but he was subdued afterward, and so were his teammates. Joliat sat with his chin cupped in his hands, staring at the floor. The chair beside him was empty, and Morenz's sweater was draped over it.

A sportswriter congratulated Mantha. "Thanks," Mantha said. "But what are we going to do without Howie?"

Hart leaned against a wall and spoke to the writers. "The greatest player of all time," he said. "What a fighter, the way he came back this year. Then to be suddenly snuffed out like this . . ."

His voice broke. He paused for a moment.

"Perhaps Howie will play again, but I doubt it," he said. "As he lay on the rubbing table waiting for the ambulance, tears were pouring down his face and he kept sobbing 'I'm all through. This is the finish.' It was my saddest experience, by far, in hockey."

Morenz was taken by ambulance to Hôpital St-Luc. X-rays showed that his leg was fractured in four places between the ankle and the knee. Doctors administered a full anaesthetic and inserted a steel pin to stabilize the bone.

The *Herald* sent a reporter to his room early the next morning, and Morenz appeared in good spirits. A traction device held his injured leg aloft to stretch it and to ensure that the bones meshed together properly. There was a phone next to his bed, and he handled one call after another from well-wishers. Between calls, he told the *Herald*'s representative: "It's just one of the misfortunes and it is a tough blow. I wanted to finish out this season and make it a good one."

Later that day, Hart paid a visit. So did Maroons coach Tommy Gorman and a delegation of his players, all of whom liked Howie despite hating the Canadiens. Letters and get-well cards arrived daily, bags full of them, such a deluge that he couldn't possibly respond to each one. Instead, he had cards printed with a thank-you note inside.

Visitors showed up unannounced at all hours. Everyone signed his cast, which extended from the ball of his foot to the middle of his thigh. By mid-February, there were over a hundred signatures on it. Newspapermen dropped in periodically, and one day a reporter from Stratford, Tom Duggan, paid a surprise visit. Players from other NHL teams came to the hospital when they were in Montreal to play the Canadiens or the Maroons. Most brought drinks. One veteran later noted, "The whisky was on the dresser and the beer was under the bed."

Howie talked bravely on such occasions. The leg would heal. He'd soon be out of here. He'd be back next year. The visitors would nod and concur, and he would feel better until they were gone. Morenz was a gregarious man, accustomed to being around teammates, fans and sportswriters. But during those weeks in the hospital, he often lay alone, flat on his back, for whole mornings and afternoons with nothing to do and no one to talk to. He read the papers, but that only distressed him.

The race had tightened. The Maroons had gained on the Canadiens. First place was no longer a sure thing. His team needed him. And he needed the team. He needed to play. Soon, he was consumed by an idea: he would never play again; he was finished. What would he do? He had no skills. He had very little money. He was frightened. He slept poorly and ate far less than normal. He became irritable and depressed.

In late February, the team physician, Dr. J.A. Hector Forgues, made another diagnosis: Morenz had suffered a nervous breakdown. No more visitors, Dr. Forgues said, except for family and team officials. Mary Morenz came by after school most days with Howie Jr., the oldest of their three children. William Morenz, Howie's father, came down from Stratford in the first week of March and stayed until the fifth, a Friday.

Howie passed the weekend quietly and on Monday, March 8 was the same. He ate a light dinner and afterward he slept. Later, he awoke with chest pains. A doctor determined that he was suffering a heart attack. The hospital called Mrs. Morenz and Cecil Hart. Around 11:30 p.m., Howie got out of bed. He tried to hobble to the washroom, but collapsed and died on the floor just before his wife and coach arrived.

The newspapers were notified, and the next day's editions informed Montrealers that Howie Morenz, hockey's greatest star, was dead. He was thirty-four. He had played fourteen seasons. He had scored 270 goals and assisted on 197.

Canadiens president Ernest Savard echoed the response of most Montrealers when they heard the news: "It is unbelievable. I thought Howie was on the road to recovery."

"We were close," Hart said. "Real pals. I don't know what to say, what to do or how we can carry hope to carry on tonight."

The Canadiens were scheduled to play the Maroons on the evening of March 9. Club officials offered to cancel, but Mary Morenz said no, Howie would have insisted that the game be played. The players on both sides wore black arm bands. Prior to the opening faceoff, they stood along their blue lines. The crowd stood also and everyone observed two minutes' silence. Afterward, buglers played the Reveille.

The game, which the Canadiens lost four–one, was fast and hard-hitting, though, according to Elmer Ferguson, it lacked the fireworks that often accompanied these contests—"fist fights, spectator battles, missile-hurling, referee-baiting and all the other factors that make up this thing we call hockey."

Howie's funeral was held March 10 at the Forum. That morning, Montrealers lined up three and four abreast all the way around the building. The doors opened at eleven o'clock and the faithful filed past the bier and casket, which had been placed above the centre-ice dot where Morenz had lined up to start so many games. Boards covered the playing surface, and a rotating honour guard of four teammates stood by their fallen friend. Wreaths, flower baskets and floral tributes—a hundred and fifty of them, by one count—nearly engulfed the casket. Most people noticed the big number 7 in lilies and roses with the card that read, "To Howie from Aurel." Far fewer saw the spray of roses that Mary Morenz had slipped under her husband's hands and the note, "To Our Daddy."

The service began at 2:30. Thousands stood in the streets around the Forum. Inside, every seat was occupied, including five rows of chairs across the ice surface. Mrs. Morenz and her children, Howie Jr., four-year-old Donald and the baby, two-year-old Marlene, sat in the first row.

Radio station CFCF broadcast the service, which was brief and simple: a hymn, a prayer and the eulogy, delivered by Reverend Malcolm Campbell, a Presbyterian minister. "He was a hero in the true sense of the word,"

Reverend Campbell said. "He never knew what it was to quit. . . . Howie Morenz was not only the idol of thousands upon thousands of fans who went to see him weekly play hockey, but he was above all the hero of his teammates. It was his spirit that appealed to every player to do his best.

"He chose hockey as a profession and he made an unqualified success of it. He was the fastest skater, I am told, in the business, a star, a superstar, a star on the ice and a star off the ice. He came into the dressing room whistling and singing, the cheering spirit of all his teammates. Everyone loved him . . . opponents as well as supporters. It is commonplace to say that no single player ever won such publicity as did Howie Morenz and yet it left him the same gentle, unassuming, plain man."

At the conclusion of the service, eight teammates lifted the casket from the bier and carried it to the hearse. They took their places in the automobiles that made up the funeral cortège and followed the hearse north, into the sea of faces that lined Atwater Avenue, and proceeded toward Côte-des-Neiges Cemetery on the north slope of the mountain.

The sudden, unexpected departure of this powerful, young man was incomprehensible to family, friends, fans and most of his teammates. Aurel Joliat offered the best explanation while speaking to a reporter: "When he realized that he would never play again, he couldn't live with it. I think Howie died of a broken heart."

Joliat played his last game one year later, on March 12, 1938. The Canadiens tied the Leafs that night, three–three in Toronto. Joliat left early with an injured shoulder and missed the balance of the regular season and the playoffs. Two days after the Canadiens were eliminated, he gathered his teammates at the grave of Howie Morenz, where they laid a wreath and bowed their heads in prayer. The next day, Joliat informed team officials he was retiring. He had played sixteen seasons and 708 games, more than any player up to that time—a remarkable achievement considering his stature. He scored 270 goals, the same number as Morenz, and 467 points.

Most people wondered how such a small man had lasted for so long in such a tough business. There was no obvious answer, according to Elmer

Ferguson. "The source from which he gets his strength, the virility to play robust games, to out-drive sturdier opponents at golf, to outwit them at hockey, to carry on the testing, wracking game over a span of years far beyond average—that's a mystery," he wrote. "Try and solve it. I gave up long ago."

Joliat was quick and clever and a superb stickhandler. He was so hard to hit that a Toronto right winger named Babe Dye once skated up to the Canadiens bench and shouted to Léo Dandurand, "I'm tired of chasing that shadow of yours, that Frenchman, Joliat."

The Mighty Mite, as he was called, had a ferocious temper, and from early in his career there was a sure way to provoke him. "To knock off his black cap was to start a battle," Ferguson wrote. "It drove Joliat into a hysterical frenzy, from which he lashed out blindly with fists or stick, and he didn't pick his opponents."

Aurel Joliat outlasted every player who was in the league when he started out, *and* he survived longer in the NHL than the Montreal Professional Hockey Club.

The Maroons competed for fourteen seasons. They began playing in the fall of 1924. They won the Stanley Cup in 1926 and again in 1935. A professional hockey franchise had become more expensive to run over the Maroons' lifespan. There were more games, longer road trips, higher salaries and bigger rosters. And the Great Depression had eroded support for both the Canadiens and the Maroons. The city could not support two pro teams. The great rivalry, in which the teams served as proxies for the English and French communities ("Only the dead and the dying were neutral," Milt Dunnell once wrote), was no more.

A Montreal industrialist with six hundred workers captured the spirit of the rivalry when he told Dunnell: "Half of my employees bet on the Maroons. On Monday, they're busy selling pools for games on Tuesday nights. On Wednesday, they fight over the results. Thursdays, there's another pool. Friday we have more fights. Saturdays the plant is closed. There isn't any more room for me and hockey. One of us has to go."

After the final game of 1937–38, in which the Maroons finished last, club officials told the players to leave their equipment, but handed out paper bags so they could take their sweaters home as souvenirs. The club's demise was made official on August 25, 1938, when the governors of the NHL met in New York and voted to suspend the franchise for a year. It was never reinstated.

The Canadiens picked up six players from the Maroons, but had only three vacancies, created by the departure of Joliat and two other retiring players, Marty Burke and Pit Lepine. Cecil Hart put together a team that appeared to be fast and tough, and he expected the Canadiens to contend for the Stanley Cup. In a pre-season assessment, *The Gazette*'s Marc T. MacNeil wrote: "Strengths: Speed to burn; Balanced offensively and defensively. Weaknesses: Hard to discern."

But the Canadiens of 1938–39 were a disappointment. They lost their first seven games, were in last place on December 1 and stayed there. By late January, they had won six, lost eighteen and tied six, and Montreal's sporting public was unforgiving. The Canadiens fired Hart, even though he had guided the team to the playoffs in each of his eight seasons and had twice won the Stanley Cup.

On the afternoon of September 3, 1939, a Sunday, Prime Minister William Lyon Mackenzie King addressed the nation, and people from coast to coast huddled around radios to hear his words. "For months, indeed for years, the shadow of impending conflict in Europe has been ever present," King began. "Through these troubled years, no stone has been left unturned, no road unexplored in the patient search for peace.

"Unhappily for the world, Herr Hitler and the Nazi regime in Germany have persisted in their attempt to extend their control over other peoples and countries and to pursue their aggressive designs in wanton disregard of all treaty obligations and peaceful methods of adjusting international disputes. They have had resort increasingly to agencies of deception, terrorism and vengeance. It is this reliance upon force, this lust for conquest, this determination to dominate throughout the world, which is the real cause of the war that today threatens the freedom of mankind . . ."

Two days earlier, Germany had invaded Poland. England and France declared war, Australia and New Zealand entered the conflict and Canada would join the Allies as soon as Parliament approved. Canadians immediately rallied to support the war effort.

The Royal Canadian Artillery placed advertisements in the Montreal newspapers. "RECRUITS WANTED," the ads said in big, bold letters. Candidates had to be eighteen or older and at least five feet, four inches tall, with chests measuring thirty-four inches or more. The Department of National Defence took over the Canadian Pacific Railway's chateau-style Viger Place Hotel, which had been closed for some time, and set up a medical examination centre. In Sunday sermons, clergymen tried to come to terms with the evil loosed upon the world, and the faithful prayed for divine assistance.

In many realms, life continued as usual in the autumn of 1939. Children started a new school year. Farmers harvested their crops. Merchants ran their businesses. The sports pages were full of news about high school and university football, the World Series and the opening of NHL training camps.

The Canadiens were in disarray. They had hired Babe Siebert as coach. He was thirty-five and retired after a fourteen-year career, but he drowned on August 25 while swimming in Lake Huron. Ernest Savard and his partners turned to Pit Lepine, a tall, smooth centre who had played thirteen seasons, mostly in the shadow of Howie Morenz.

Lepine's Canadiens started the season with four wins and two ties and briefly held first place. Then they went nineteen games without a win. They spent much of the season in last place. Montrealers retaliated by turning their backs on the team. The Canadiens could not fill more than a third of the Forum's nine thousand–odd seats and were a poor attraction on the road.

"It's not like your agent to cry havoc and ruin," Al Parsley of the *Herald* wrote in early March 1940, "but I have heard rumblings and rumours by those very close to the higher ups among the American clubs in the National Hockey League that they could just as well get by with a six-team league next year and leave the Canadiens entirely out of the picture."

By the end of that awful season, the team was hemorrhaging financially and Savard and his partners were looking for a way out. They talked of suspending operations for a year, or even for the duration of the war.

Instead, the Canadian Arena Company—owner of the Forum—stepped in and purchased the team. Senator Donat Raymond became president. The deal closed on April 6, 1940, and less than two weeks later the new president called a press conference.

"Senator Donat Raymond . . . exploded a bombshell in hockey circles this afternoon," Elmer Ferguson wrote, "when he announced that Dick Irvin has been appointed manager and coach of the local National Hockey League club. The announcement came as a startling surprise since Irvin, coach of the Toronto Maple Leafs, was not even considered for the position with the Canadiens."

Ferguson interviewed Irvin the following evening. They talked till one o'clock in the morning. Afterward, the *Herald* sports editor returned to his office and began to write. "He is quiet, soft-spoken, doesn't drink or smoke, has a way with young talent and undoubtedly is a real capture for the Canadiens. Now, all they need is to get some hockey players to be coached, some material to be molded and everything will be alright."

Dick Irvin was forty-seven. He was a thin man with an angular face and snowy white hair. He was born near Hamilton, Ontario, but grew up in Winnipeg. Irvin learned the game outdoors. He played indoors for the first time in 1907, at age fifteen, when his father, James Irvin, a butcher, loaded him and his playmates into a horse-drawn sled and drove them fourteen miles east in sub-zero weather for a game in Dauphin, Manitoba.

"I remember the rush we made to get into that rink," he would recall later. "The goalposts were poplar poles, extending from the ice to the roof and there were no nets. A lantern hung on each goalpost above the goalies' heads. There were no boards around the playing surface. Oil lamps provided dim light and splattered big shadows across the ice. The ice was fast, and smoother than on the outdoor rinks in backyards and on ponds and streams. There was no wind to almost blow a kid off his skates. It was just a sort of fairyland to me, that's all."

Irvin played hockey in the west as a young man. He was a member of the 1915 Winnipeg Monarchs, who won the Allan Cup. He turned pro with the Portland Rosebuds of the Pacific Coast Hockey Association, and when they folded he joined the Regina Capitals of the Western Canada Hockey League. Irvin signed with the Chicago Black Hawks after the western league ceased operations in the summer of 1926. He played three seasons in the NHL, finished second in scoring in the first, fractured his skull in the second and retired after the third.

Irvin returned to Regina, where he maintained his home, and worked as a travelling salesman for Burns Meats of Calgary until the Chicago owner, Major Frederic McLaughlin, offered him a coaching position. Irvin led the Hawks to the 1931 Stanley Cup final. They lost to the Canadiens in part because some of his players got drunk the night before the fifth game in Montreal. Afterward, the erratic and unforgiving owner fired the coach. Conn Smythe hired him in November 1931 to run the Leafs, and he guided the team to a Stanley Cup championship the following spring. The Leafs made the final in six of the next eight seasons, but lost each time, and Smythe decided to make a change in the spring of 1940.

"I'm no miracle man," Irvin told Ferguson. "I hope no one expects me to win the Stanley Cup first crack out of the box."

In each of the next two seasons, the Canadiens finished sixth in the seven-team league and lost in the first round of the playoffs, which may have made Irvin's words seem prophetic. But he was building a team. The cornerstone was left winger Toe Blake, the only player who possessed leadership qualities and championship potential.

Blake's given name was Hector. He became Toe as a boy in Coniston, Ontario, because a younger brother pronounced his name Hec-Toe. Soon he was Toe to his friends, classmates and teammates. Blake was a member of the Sudbury Cub Wolves, who won the Memorial Cup in 1932, and he left home the following season to play senior with the Hamilton Tigers.

He began his pro career with the Montreal Maroons in 1934, but played only eight games with them before being traded to the Canadiens prior to the 1935–36 season. Blake became the team's top left winger after Aurel Joliat retired, and he quickly earned the respect of his peers. "The hallmark of Blake's success is his doggedness," Marc T. MacNeil of *The Gazette* wrote. "He never ceases trying. He doesn't know what it means to quit." MacNeil was watching the Canadiens one night with Blake's injured teammate Bob Gracie. "There goes the best left winger in the National Hockey League," Gracie said as Blake dashed down the ice. "What a worker that guy is."

In February 1939, with the team in sixth place, Blake was leading the league in scoring when he injured his knee in a Saturday night game against Toronto. "Trainer Jimmy McKenna treated the bruised, puffed and swollen joint until three o'clock Sunday morning coming home on the train," *The Gazette* reported. "And on arrival Blake went straight to the hospital." Two nights later, he was back in uniform against the Bruins. Blake played all forty-eight games that season. He won the scoring championship with forty-seven points and captured the Hart Trophy.

Blake spent the summer of 1940 in an army reserve unit and was not in shape when he reported for his first training camp under Irvin. The new coach checked each player's weight before they stepped on the ice, and Blake was carrying a few extra pounds.

"You can play for this team this year, Mr. Blake," Irvin snapped. "But if you look the same this time next year don't bother showing up."

Irvin held his first camp in St-Hyacinthe, a town on the south shore, thirty miles east of Montreal, and he signed four rookies from western Canada: defenceman Ken Reardon and forwards Jack Adams, Joe Benoit and Elmer Lach, all of whom had been recruited by Canadiens centre Paul Haynes during a scouting trip the previous spring.

Lach, a twenty-two-year-old centre, proved to be the best of the three forwards. He was a fast, smooth skater, tenacious in the corners, had good vision and deft hands and could fire a puck through a churning thicket of legs and skates and place it on the blade of a teammate's stick. Lach grew up in Nokomis, Saskatchewan, about seventy miles north of Regina, and learned to skate on blades borrowed from a neighbour. The village doctor saw him play school hockey as a sixteen-year-old and recommended him to the Regina Abbotts, a junior team.

"I took the train into Regina and there was a fellow waiting for me at the station," Lach recalled years later. "He said, 'Where's your baggage?' I said, 'It's in my back pocket.' I'd left home with a tooth brush and a handkerchief."

Lach played a season with the Abbotts, two with the senior Weyburn Beavers and another with the Moose Jaw Millers. Haynes saw him with the Millers in the 1940 Allan Cup final and tried to recruit him, but Lach had to be persuaded to leave Moose Jaw. "Fall came along and the Canadiens sent me a letter asking if I'd like to come to camp. I had a job in Moose Jaw as a meter reader with National Heat, Light and Power. I was happy where I was. I talked to my boss, a guy named Cliff Henderson, who ran the hockey club. He said, 'You might as well go. You've already been skating. You'll be that much ahead of the other guys.' In Moose Jaw the weather had turned cold and we were skating on the river."

Lach had a solid rookie season, scoring seven goals and adding twenty-one assists. He played only one game as a sophomore in 1941–42. On opening night against Detroit, he raced past a Red Wing defenceman who reached out with his stick and tripped him. Lach slid toward the boards with his left arm extended. The impact broke his wrist, shattered his elbow and dislocated his shoulder. It was the first of a series of injuries that earned him the nickname Lach the Unlucky. In fourteen seasons, he fractured his skull, leg, thumb, jaw (twice in one season), cheekbone (twice) and nose (on seven occasions). His left arm did not heal properly, and in July 1942 doctors had to operate on his elbow, rebreak his wrist and set it again. Yet, Lach was in uniform to start the season.

Irvin built his defence around Reardon and a big Montrealer named Émile Bouchard. Reardon grew up in Winnipeg, where he had a hard childhood. His mother died when he was thirteen, his father a year later. He and his three siblings went to live with an uncle, and Reardon took a job as a railway messenger boy, delivering telegrams on his bicycle. He showed great promise as a defenceman, but his job was so exhausting that he barely played for two seasons. And he didn't play at all in 1937–38, when his uncle moved to Blue River, British Columbia. The following year, Reardon wrote to the Edmonton Athletic Club and asked for a tryout. He played two seasons for the ACs, as they were known. They advanced to the Memorial Cup final in his first year, though Reardon hardly saw the ice. The following season, they met Kenora in the western final. Reardon was a regular and that's when the Canadiens' Paul Haynes spotted him.

"One look was enough," Haynes later recalled. "Even at seventeen he was a hell-bent-for-rubber kid who electrified the stands. I slapped him on the Canadiens' [protected] list pronto."

Reardon was a choppy skater who seemed to run on the ice, but he was fast, fearless and reckless, and he became one of the most colourful performers in the NHL. At various times, sportswriters called him hockey's toughest hombre, the Hammering Hab, Mayhem Inc., the burly bumping terror of hockey's big time, and Reardon the Irrepressible. But no one ever questioned his integrity or his courage. He once hurt his shoulder and should have missed three weeks; he was back after ten days and hitting as hard as ever. He ran at an opponent, missed and slammed his damaged shoulder into the boards. Afterward, his arm was throbbing and he visited the team physician. "It's your head I should be examining, not your shoulder," the doctor said.

Reardon played most of his seven NHL seasons partnered with Bouchard, a Montrealer who made the team in the fall of 1941 at age twenty-one. They were an intimidating presence on the Canadiens blue line. At six foot two and 185 pounds, Bouchard was one of biggest players in the league and a punishing checker.

Bouchard grew up in Le Plateau, a working-class Montreal neighbourhood east of the mountain and overlooking downtown. He was the youngest of four children of a house painter who provided his family with the essentials, which did not include hockey equipment. Bouchard loved the game, so he borrowed skates or rented them from other kids for five cents a night and played at neighbourhood parks. And, when he had no skates, he tended goal in his winter boots.

At age sixteen, he borrowed thirty-five dollars from an older brother and bought a set of equipment—gloves, pants, pads for his shins, shoulders and elbows and his first pair of skates—to play high school hockey. He played well, and the teacher who ran the team arranged a meeting at the Forum with Arthur Therrien, coach of the Verdun Maple Leafs, the Canadiens' junior affiliate. "I had never been to the Forum," he would recall years later. "I didn't even know where the place was. We didn't have a radio at home so I didn't know anything about the Canadiens."

Bouchard played three seasons under Therrien and twice competed in the eastern Canadian final, losing both times to the team that went on to win the Memorial Cup. Following another season split between junior and the minor pros, Bouchard was ready to try out for the Canadiens. He lived then in Longueuil, on the south shore opposite downtown Montreal, and rode his bicycle thirty miles to St-Hyacinthe for the opening of training camp.

He spoke almost no English and considered himself a poor skater compared to some of the men whizzing around him, but he was smart. He had a feel for the flow of the game. He knew when to join the attack and when to retreat and was adept at forcing forwards to the outside, toward the boards, where he administered jarring checks that invariably forced them to surrender the puck. Irvin liked Bouchard's robust approach and put him on the team. Bouchard was thrilled, but had the presence of mind to negotiate before signing.

"I went to see Armand Mondou, who had played with Morenz and Joliat," Bouchard says. "Elmer was getting thirty-five hundred. Kenny Reardon was getting the same. I said, 'If I ask for four thousand, what do you think?' Mondou said, 'Good luck.' And I did. It took ten days before they signed me, but I got five hundred more than Lach and Reardon."

Maurice Richard lay crumpled and helpless. He was consumed by pain that took his breath away. He was oblivious, momentarily, to the teammates at his side, the trainer kneeling over him, the Bruins standing near their net and the fans who filled the Forum. Then he heard voices: "You're going to be okay." "You'll be all right, Maurice." "Don't worry. We'll get you up." He felt hands under his shoulders, lifting him. He was up on his left leg, arms draped over two teammates in red sweaters. He wanted to weep. This time, he had fractured his right leg, and a dreadful thought filled his mind: he was finished. Three days after Christmas 1942. After sixteen NHL games, five goals and six assists. And he had never been happier. He was a newly signed rookie *and* a newlywed. His bride was Lucille Norchet, the sister of his boyhood friend and former teammate Georges Norchet. Lucille was seventeen, Maurice twenty-one. They had met four years earlier, at the Norchet family home. Georges had often invited Maurice and the other players back after games to drink pop and listen to music. Maurice was dark-eyed and handsome, but shy and quiet. Lucille was the opposite, and it was she who pursued him. They danced. They dated and soon were inseparable.

On September 12, 1942, they were married, and one month later the Canadiens' training camp opened. Richard signed on October 29, the second-to-last day of camp. He scored his first goal November 8 against Steve Buzinski of the New York Rangers. The Canadiens tallied ten times that night, the Rangers four, and the next day's edition of *Montreal-Matin* said, "The most spectacular goal of the evening, which brought back memories of the famous Howie Morenz, was scored by Maurice Richard, the popular left winger of the Canadiens."

Imagine that, he thought. He had been compared to Howie Morenz, one of his boyhood heroes. Aurel Joliat was another. And Toe Blake, now his teammate. He knew these players through radio broadcasts. As a boy, he would stay in on winter nights when the Canadiens played and he would listen to the games. Otherwise, he didn't like being inside. The family home was small and crowded, like all the other houses on Avenue de Bois-de-Boulogne in the Bordeaux district on the northern edge of the island of Montreal. He was one of eight children. There was always a baby, always noise. Better to be outside, on a rink or the river, where he was free—and faster than the boys his age and most of the older ones too.

His parents, Onésime and Alice Richard, had bought him his first pair of skates when he was four. His father built a backyard rink, but as an older boy Maurice spent the long, hard Montreal winters playing hockey at neighbourhood parks or on the Rivière des Prairies. He joined his first team at age fourteen while attending l'École St-François-de-Laval. He played fiercely. He could score goals, and he was noticed quickly. A team that represented Bordeaux recruited him, and his teammate Georges Norchet introduced him to Paul-Émile Paquette, who owned a parcel delivery service and sponsored a team in the Ligue des Parcs de Montreal.

"Our team was the best in the juvenile division," Paquette recalled later. "I went to see Richard with Bordeaux . . . and immediately asked him to play for us. In his first game he scored six goals. With Richard on our team we won the juvenile championship three consecutive years."

In 1938–39, his last season in juvenile, the team won forty-three games, tied two and lost one. Richard scored all but eleven of Paquette's team's 144 goals. Paquette and his coach, Paul Stuart, believed that this young man could play junior, maybe even professionally, but he would have to be tough. Stuart introduced Richard to Harry Hurst, a promising young light-weight fighter who gave him boxing lessons. Stuart also took him to see Arthur Therrien, who offered a tryout with the Verdun Maple Leafs.

A hundred and twenty-six players attended the Leaf camp in the fall of 1939, including Richard in a frayed yellow and green sweater with a Marvelube crest stitched on the back. He was the last player picked. He was eighteen and had very bad teeth. Therrien said something had to be done about that and took Richard to a dentist, who pulled most of them. Richard played very little that season until the playoffs. Verdun beat the Montreal Royals to win the Quebec championship, but lost to the Oshawa Generals in the eastern Canadian final. Richard appeared in seven playoff games. He scored seven goals and assisted on nine, which earned him a tryout with the Montreal Canadiens of the Quebec Senior Hockey League.

He made the team, but played only one game, early in November 1940. "Canadiens have probably lost the services of one of their ace forwards for the balance of the season," the Montreal *Gazette* reported. "The casualty was Maurice Richard, the speedy youngster who figured in the first goal of the game and who was one of the best men on the ice.

"The former Verdun junior was pulled down by Quebec's Stu Smith on a breakaway in the third period and crashed into the boards at the south end of the rink feet first. He was helped off the ice with a broken bone in his left leg and was taken to the Western Division of Montreal General Hospital."

The following season, Richard returned to the Senior Canadiens. This time he played thirty games before breaking his left wrist in the third week of January. He had eight goals and nine assists and was about thirtieth in league scoring. He went home to heal, and the hockey world forgot about him.

His days had been full. Now they were empty. Idleness bred boredom, anger and doubt. When he looked to the future, he saw work, not hockey.

His father was a carpenter with the CPR, and at sixteen Maurice had become an apprentice machinist with the railway. He had worked days and played hockey at nights and on weekends. Sitting at home now, with his arm in a cast, he fretted.

Fortunately, he had Lucille. She had watched him more often and more closely than anyone when he had played for Paquette, for Verdun and for the Senior Canadiens. She knew how good he was and how much desire he had. It was only his wrist, she reassured him. It would heal. He would be back.

And she was right. By late February, the cast was off. He resumed practising with the team and played the final game of the regular season as well as all six games of a closely contested playoff against the Ottawa Senators. He scored two goals, including the winner in the series opener.

Early in the playoff, the NHL Canadiens disclosed that Richard and his teammate, Marcel Bessette, would be offered tryouts in the fall of 1942. The parent club had a problem: it had become too English. The coach and the general manager, Dick Irvin and Tommy Gorman, were both English-Canadian, the former from the west, the latter from Ottawa. The best recruits—Elmer Lach, Joe Benoit, Kenny Reardon and his older brother Terry—were westerners or, like Buddy O'Connor, were from Montreal's Irish community. There were just three French-Canadians: goaltender Paul Bibeault and defencemen Émile Bouchard and Clifford "Red" Goupille.

Richard was the best French-Canadian prospect in years. He was a goal scorer with an explosive style who reminded some observers of the great Morenz. And as he played his first NHL season, he fulfilled expectations. He was scoring at a good pace and was considered a candidate for rookie of the year—until the evening of December 28, 1942, when he raced into the Boston zone, absorbed a ferocious check from Bruins defenceman Johnny Crawford and went down with a fractured leg.

In the summer of 1943, Maurice Richard decided to put his career on hold and join the Canadian Army, as many others were doing. Nine of the Detroit Red Wings and six Toronto Maple Leafs had enlisted during the off-season. The Rangers, who had won the Cup in 1940 and made the playoffs in fifteen of their first sixteen seasons, lost ten players over a two-year span and fell to the bottom of the standings. By the start of the 1942–43 season, Richard's rookie year, about eighty NHL players or prospects had gone to war and the league's governors considered suspending operations.

The army took a look at Richard's medical history—a fractured arm and two broken legs—and declared him unfit to serve. In the fall of 1943, he was back with the Canadiens. They had lost only one key player, Ken Reardon, to the military, and they continued to build. The team was weak in goal, but had a good prospect in Bill Durnan of the Montreal Royals.

Durnan was a native of Toronto. He was twenty-seven and, in the words of general manager Tommy Gorman, was "big as a horse and nimble as a cat." He played goal like no one before or since. Durnan was ambidextrous. He could catch and wield his stick with either hand, and he wore specially adapted gloves that allowed him to do so. If a shot came from the right side, he would hold the stick with his right hand and catch with the left. He would switch when the shooter approached from the left. Durnan had acquired this skill as a boy in Toronto and perfected it during his long amateur apprenticeship.

Durnan played a few games of junior hockey with the Sudbury Wolves in 1932–33 and spent most of the next three seasons bouncing around Toronto's industrial leagues. He tore ligaments in a knee one summer, which affected his play, and he quit hockey in 1935–36. He continued to play fastball, though. Durnan was a pitcher, and a good one. He once struck out twenty-four batters in a nine-inning game. He hurled fourteen no-hitters, and fans flocked to parks in Toronto to watch him.

Durnan's fastball feats kept his name alive in sporting circles, and in the fall of 1936 the Kirkland Lake Blue Devils, a senior hockey team, recruited him. He spent four seasons with the Devils and won the Allan Cup in 1940, their only trip to the finals. The Montreal Royals signed him next and he played three seasons with them before the Canadiens decided in the fall of 1943 that Durnan was ready for the NHL.

But Durnan was content where he was. The Royals were paying him, and he had a job in a CIL munitions plant. The Canadiens could not persuade him to sign, so they applied some subtle leverage. A director of the

Canadiens, Len Peto, was also a senior executive with CIL. He issued an ultimatum: If you don't play, you don't have a job. According to Gorman, the goaltender signed ten minutes before game time on opening night. "Bill hadn't even put down the pen when I informed him he was going in the nets that night and I pointed to the clock," Gorman later recalled. "He raced down the corridors and yanked his equipment out of the Royals dressing room. He dressed in near-record time, went into goal and was spectacular."

With Durnan behind them, the Canadiens led the league from the start. Their record stood at thirteen wins, two losses and three ties when Dick Irvin boarded a train for Regina on December 21 to spend Christmas with his family. Buddy O'Connor was the team's top scorer with twenty-nine points. Lach was next with twenty-six. Richard had four points and was tied with Émile Bouchard.

Irvin had tried Richard at right wing on a line with Blake and Lach to start the season, the first time the left-shooting Richard had played that side. But he injured his shoulder and skated with various forward combinations until Christmas. Blake, the team captain, ran the practices while Irvin was away. He, Lach and Richard practised together, and Irvin kept the line intact when he returned on December 30 for the twentieth game of the season.

That night, a star was born. The Canadiens beat Detroit eight–three, and the next day's *La Presse* reported, "Maurice Richard was the principal architect of the victory with three goals and two assists."

Richard scored thirty goals and assisted on twenty others in the final thirty games of the season. Teammates who had to keep pace with him in practice or check him during drills began to call him the Rocket, and journalists picked up on the nickname. Richard, Blake and Lach formed the NHL's most potent forward combination, which came to be known as the Punch Line. Blake finished 1943–44 with fifty-nine points and Lach with seventy-two, ten back of Boston's Herbie Cain, who won the scoring title.

They led an unusually powerful offence. Two other forwards, O'Connor and Ray Getliffe, both earned over fifty points, and three others—Murph Chamberlain, Phil Watson and Gerry Heffernan—tallied close to fifty.

Durnan won the Vézina Trophy and earned the respect of his teammates, though the Forum fans regularly chanted the name of his predecessor,

Paul Bibeault, if he let in a soft goal or had a bad game. "We knew as long as we got back for the rebound, Bill would stop the first shot," recalled Glen Harmon, a member of the defence corps. "It was almost guaranteed."

The Canadiens lost only five of fifty games in 1943–44. They finished with a record eighty-three points, twenty-five ahead of Detroit, and were equally dominant in the playoffs. They lost the opening game of the semifinal to Toronto and then won eight straight to win the Stanley Cup. The Punch Line accumulated an unprecedented forty-eight points in the playoffs. Blake's eighteen points and Richard's twelve goals were both new NHL records.

In the first round, Richard scored every Montreal goal in a five–one win over Toronto, and he lifted the Forum fans out of their seats in the fourth game of the Stanley Cup final against Chicago, a game the Black Hawks led four–one midway through the third period. Lach cut the Hawks' lead to two goals with five minutes remaining. Up in the press box, Calgary broadcaster Doug Smith called the game—working alone, without a colour commentator. The stands were packed. The air was thick with tobacco smoke. The play went back and forth, end to end and Smith described each attack in crisp, clipped phrases:

> . . . the pass to Mosienko. He relays it ahead to Bentley. It was too far. Bentley goes into the corner, works out in front of Durnan and is blocked by Toe Blake. Blake now for the Canadiens, with Lach and Richard against the three-man defence. The pass to Richard. He cuts in from the side. He stops. He shoots. He scores.
>
> Richard the Rocket has scored. The house is in an uproar. It was one of the most sensational goals scored in a Stanley Cup series. This boy, Richard the Rocket, beats you all the time. Just when you think he's scored a goal that defies all description he comes across with another one . . .

The score was now four–three, with four minutes left in the period. Irvin left his big line out. The Canadiens attacked, but the Hawks gained possession. Doug Bentley drove toward the Montreal net, where Bouchard stripped him of the puck.

> Now Bouchard returns for the Canadiens. Up over the blue line. Holds the puck inside. A flip shot to Blake. Blake passes it out front. They score. Richard scores. Richard . . .

Smith said nothing for twenty seconds and let the roar of the crowd fill his microphone.

> That time Richard took a pass from back of the Chicago goal and put it into the net with terrific force. Maurice Richard, twenty-two years old and the idol of Montreal, banged it in. His second goal in less than a minute to tie the game four–four. The ice has been littered with debris . . .

The game went into overtime. Nine minutes in, Bouchard passed to Blake at the side of the net. Blake cut to the front and scored.

> Toe Blake. Toe Blake. The game is over. . . . The Stanley Cup is won by the Montreal Canadiens for the first time in thirteen years. . . . They're raising him up on the shoulders of Elmer Lach and Bill Durnan. Toe Blake is up on the shoulders of his teammates. Flash bulbs are popping down there on the ice. The Stanley Cup stands on a table. A presentation will be made . . .

The next day, April 14, the team honoured the players with a small private lunch at Senator Raymond's Queen's Hotel. From there, it was off to work in wartime industries. Lach, Watson, Getliffe and several others had jobs in an airplane factory. Blake had a position in a shipyard, Richard and three others in a munitions plant.

They all assembled once more to celebrate their victory. Paul Stuart, Richard's mentor, organized a tribute to French Montreal's new hero on April 29. Twelve hundred people attended, including Aurel Joliat, Léo Dandurand and Onésime and Alice Richard. Dignitaries spoke glowingly of the young star, and many gave gifts. Richard went home that night with, among other things, a new wallet, a cigarette lighter, a walnut coffee table, a set of luggage and a four-by-five-foot action photo of himself.

The Canadiens held their training camp at the Forum in the fall of 1944 and admitted the public for the opening session—a spirited scrimmage on October 13. Over six thousand fans attended and, according to Elmer Ferguson, "They raised the roof when their favourites scored." Autograph hunters besieged the players. Gangs of youngsters ignored the ushers who tried to control them. Dick Irvin couldn't maintain the attention of his players, and that was the last the public saw of the Canadiens, apart from exhibition games, till the home opener November 7 against Toronto.

The game revived what Ferguson called "the ancient bitterness" between the teams and turned into "a tale of slug and sock and whose teeth are these?" There was only one fight, but the referee called sixteen penalties, eleven of them against Montreal. The imbalance so enraged the fans that they hurled bottles and chairs onto the ice. The Canadiens lost four-one, and in the dressing room afterward, Ray Getliffe seethed: "We hate those Toronto guys so much we want to kill them."

In the corridor outside, NHL president and former player Mervyn "Red" Dutton bellowed to reporters: "What a game. There's nothing wrong with hockey when teams go out and play like that. It reminded me of some of the battles between Maroons and Canadiens. Those are the games that fill the rinks."

The Canadiens lost only eight times in 1944–45. Again, they led the league most of the season, but sportswriters and some club officials in other NHL cities began to denigrate the team as a wartime powerhouse and nothing more. The critics said the same about Blake, Lach and Richard, who were the top three scorers most of the season. The race remained close until mid-January, when Blake began to fall behind. Lach and Richard were never more than a point or two apart, and they duelled for the lead till late in the season. Lach piled up the assists, while Richard scored goals.

On January 19, 1945, *La Patrie* reported that Richard had a chance to break all NHL scoring records. Three days later, Elmer Ferguson wrote, "It was game No. 30 for Canadiens and goals No. 30, 31 and 32 for Richard, a feat of outstanding note." Ferguson also addressed the pundits who had begun to snipe at Richard. "We all know about goals being cheaper this wartime season and the quality of hockey having deteriorated," he wrote. "But this is still the major league of hockey and 32 goals in 30 games is a remarkable feat."

On February 10, he scored his forty-third goal, equalling what was regarded as the modern record, set in 1929 by Boston's Ralph Weiland. The Canadiens were playing their thirty-eighth game, at home, and the Forum crowd saluted Richard with two minutes of uninterrupted applause.

One week later, in Toronto, he scored the winner with five minutes remaining. He had tied Joe Malone's all-time record of forty-four, which Malone scored in twenty games in 1917–18 while playing for the Canadiens. Some of the fans recognized the significance of the goal and spontaneously applauded, but the Maple Leaf Gardens announcer did not acknowledge the record, nor did referee King Clancy retrieve the puck as a keepsake.

The Globe and Mail's Jim Coleman chided the Leafs for the oversight, but concluded by taking a swipe at Richard: "In our book, he isn't as good a hockey player as his centre man Elmer Lach. As for comparing him to Howie Morenz—well, it's improbable that he'll ever have Howie's gift for lifting the customers out of their seats."

Richard was out to set a new record the following Saturday night, February 25, when the Canadiens and Leafs met again, this time at the Forum. At game time, an estimated five thousand people were unable to buy tickets and were left standing in the streets around the building, causing traffic jams for blocks in all directions. Inside, just under fourteen thousand fans packed the seats and every bit of standing room.

The Leafs used left wingers Nick Metz and Bob Davidson, two of the game's best defensive forwards, to cover Richard. By then, Richard was accustomed to such attention. Every team in the league had tried to stop him. Earlier that season, the Rangers had employed a tough guy named Bob Dill to provoke and intimidate him. Dill had marginal skills, but had trained as a fighter with two uncles who were pro boxers. Dill and Richard fought twice on the same night at Madison Square Garden, once on the ice and again in the penalty box. Both times, Richard knocked Dill out. The Canadiens' general manager, Tommy Gorman, thought the abuse so excessive that he sent a letter to Dutton demanding action. "It is evident," he wrote, "that some players are being sent on to the ice . . . to stop Richard by any means. Richard can defend himself against individual opponents, but not when teams become a Wreck Richard Club. Richard must be protected and we ask that the referees give him this protection."

Metz and Davidson took turns shadowing Richard as he pursued his forty-fifth goal. They skated with him stride for stride. They hammered him into the boards at every opportunity. They hooked and held him to prevent him from getting loose. The Leafs were so focused on Richard that others got a free ride. Blake, Lach, O'Connor and Bouchard all scored in what proved to be a wild game. Clancy called eighteen penalties, and there were six fights, some of them involving fans. The third altercation unleashed a bench-clearing brawl.

With three minutes remaining, the Canadiens led four–two. Irvin had played Richard far more than usual that night, hoping he'd score, and he kept his star player out as time wound down. The play was in the Toronto end.

"Richard was so exhausted that . . . when checked into the boards, he leaned there wearily as though completely through," according to Ferguson. "But at the face-off he gathered himself together gamely and swung out in front. . . . Blake gave him a pass. Richard, coasting twenty feet out, whistled a waist-high blast between [Leaf goalie] Frank McCool and the left post. A perfect shot, a perfect goal."

Richard's teammates mobbed him, after which he staggered to the bench and collapsed. The fans threw hats, pennies, fruit, bottles, programs and toe rubbers onto the ice. They cheered for ten minutes. Clancy retrieved the puck and turned it over to Joe Malone, who presented it to Richard. The crowd cheered for another two minutes.

"This Richard is a great hockey player," Malone told reporters after the game. "He's fast, game and powerful. Really strong. Look at the way he fights off checks, tears loose from them, fights for the puck. Richard, I tell you, would be a great hockey player in any day, age or league."

Having surpassed Malone's record, Richard began pursuing another milestone: fifty goals. Prior to the season, he had signed a new contract that included a bonus if he scored thirty and an even heftier one if he hit fifty, a clause that was added almost in jest because few thought such a thing possible. Richard got the milestone goal in the final game of the season, in Boston, with a minute and forty-two seconds remaining in the third period.

He finished with seventy-three points, seven back of Lach, the scoring leader. Blake was third, with sixty-seven. Durnan won his second Vézina Trophy. The Canadiens finished first with eighty points, but lost in the opening round of the playoffs to the Leafs, who had earned only fifty-two points.

Richard's friends Paul Paquette and Paul Stuart organized another tribute, held April 29, 1945. This time, fans and admirers gave Richard seven hundred dollars in cash and five hundred gifts. But the adulation could not erase the pain of the playoff loss to the Leafs. "As my wife will attest," he later told an interviewer, "I spent many sleepless nights during the summer thinking of nothing but that."

Ken Reardon served three years in the Canadian Army. He saw action in France, Holland and Germany. His superiors cited him for bravery after he led a team that erected a bridge while under enemy fire, and Field Marshal Bernard Montgomery awarded him the Certificate for Gallantry. Reardon returned to Montreal on October 24, 1945, aboard a train carrying hundreds of discharged veterans. They pulled into the station at nine o'clock in the morning and the platform was packed with parents, siblings and sweethearts waiting to greet them. Reardon had no family in Montreal, but when he stepped off the train he saw Tommy Gorman and Dick Irvin wading through the crowd.

"Welcome home, kid," Irvin said. "And by the way, be at the Forum at eleven. We're practising."

"How many defencemen are there on the club?" Reardon asked.

Eight, Irvin replied.

"Wait till I get a hold of them," he snapped.

Reardon skated that afternoon and worked out with the team in the evening. He finished training camp with the Canadiens, but played five games with the Montreal Royals of the Quebec Senior Hockey League, mainly for conditioning, before he rejoined the Canadiens November 10 against Boston. He started slowly, but by the end of the season he had made a good team better.

"The life of the party these days in the Canadiens' camp is none other than Kenny Reardon," *The Gazette*'s Dink Carroll wrote in late February 1946. "He's the guy who put the buckle back in swashbuckle. . . . When he hits 'em, they buckle."

He and his partner, Émile "Butch" Bouchard, were nearly unbeatable at the blue line. At season's end, Bouchard was named to the league's first All-Star team, while Reardon made the second team. Durnan won his third straight Vézina Trophy and Toe Blake, who received one penalty all season, became the first Canadien to win the Lady Byng Trophy. Montreal finished atop the standings for the third year in a row, though the Punch Line was overshadowed by Chicago's Pony Line, made up of Bill Mosienko and the Bentley brothers, Doug and Max.

In the opening round of the playoffs, the Canadiens swept the Hawks four straight. They outscored Chicago twenty-six–seven, and the Punch Line shone while the Pony Line wilted. Montreal advanced to the finals against the Bruins, who put up a much better fight. Boston had a strong goaltender in Frank Brimsek, who was known as Mr. Zero. Boston also had one of the league's best forward combinations. Milt Schmidt, Bobby Bauer and Woody Dumart, all of German descent and hailing from Kitchener, Ontario, were called the Kraut Line and were together again after fighting in the war.

The first two games were played in Montreal. Both were fast and wide open and were decided in overtime. In the opener, Richard scored the winner nine minutes in and, as *The Gazette*'s Carroll reported, "Delirious fans poured over the boards and hoisted him high in as spontaneous a victory salute as you'll ever see."

Montreal rookie Jimmy Peters was the hero in game two. He slipped a backhand past Brimsek after nearly seventeen minutes of extra play. "For a moment, the big crowd was too stunned to realize what had happened," Carroll wrote. "Then the Forum rocked with the triumphant roar of the Habitants' followers."

The teams split two games in Boston and returned to Montreal for the fifth. Thirty minutes before the opening faceoff, at least four thousand people stood in line outside the building, as several thousand more spilled into the streets and blocked traffic. After ticket sales ended, hundreds forced their way into the lobby, tore doors off hinges and broke windows.

The building was packed so tightly that young men sat in the rafters. The teams scored five goals in the first period, the Canadiens leading three–two. Boston's Milt Schmidt tied the game seven minutes into the second, and it remained even until midway through the third. Blake, playing with a back injury, scored the winner and the Canadiens added two more to make the final score six–three.

Afterward, dozens of fans tried to push their way into the dressing room, but ushers blocked the entrance. Radio stations had set up microphones and the players spoke directly to fans across the province in French and English. One of the last to speak was Dick Irvin. After congratulating each player individually, he declared: "You see, I was right. The Canadiens are the best team of all time."

1946-1955
SELKE BUILDS AN EMPIRE

IT WAS A WARM EVENING, a Monday in early July 1946, and most sports-minded Montrealers were outdoors enjoying the fine weather. They watched men's fastball at neighbourhood parks. They cheered Jackie Robinson and the Montreal Royals. Or they wagered on the horses at Blue Bonnets racetrack. Still another crowd gathered for the wrestling matches at the Forum, though it was hot in the building and the air muggy and blue with tobacco smoke. Wrestlers stretched and loosened their muscles in the ring that stood over the faceoff circle where opposing forwards lined up at the start of hockey games. There were rows of seats on the floor around the ring, and most were occupied. The fans smoked, mopped their brows with hankies and talked—not about that night's bouts, as one would expect, but about Tommy Gorman, general manager of the Canadiens, and the news that he had resigned.

A radio station broke the story over the dinner hour, and the city's sportswriters had to play catch-up. Where was Gorman, they wondered? No one had seen him, so they tracked down Senator Donat Raymond, director of the syndicate that controlled the Forum and the Canadiens. The senator, a reserved and dignified man, rarely spoke to the press and was reluctant to discuss the matter. But the writers persisted and Raymond finally acknowledged that, yes, Gorman was departing after running the Forum for a decade and turning the nearly bankrupt Canadiens into money-making champions. And that was all he would say.

Gorman was popular with both English- and French-speaking fans. He was T.P., short for Thomas Patrick, to the English, and Tay Pay to the French. He was many things to the sportswriters: a buoyant and jovial personality; a stranger to tranquility; a man who seemed happiest when hemmed in by trouble; a notoriously bad loser; a practical joker who once nominated a Montreal goal judge as league MVP; a promotional genius and a prodigious worker.

Gorman, an Ottawa native, had been involved in pro hockey for thirty years. He had represented the Senators at the founding meeting of the NHL in November 1917, and two years later he and a partner bought the team. His Senators were Stanley Cup champions in 1920, 1922 and 1923. He created the New York Americans. He coached the Chicago Black Hawks to their first Stanley Cup in 1934 and the following season guided the Montreal Maroons to their second and last championship. He had taken over the Canadiens when they were on the brink of going under and, along with Dick Irvin, had brought the team back to life.

During his final season in Montreal, he had invested in a new arena in Ottawa and then bought the building. He was also managing a track called Connaught Park Raceway. The directors of the Canadian Arena Company thought he had taken on too much and told him in the spring of 1946 to decide whose business he wanted to run: theirs or his.

When the news of his departure leaked out, Gorman was working at the track in Ottawa. The Montreal sportswriters reached him there by phone. He said the same thing to one and all: that the people of Montreal had treated him wonderfully and that he was "leaving the Forum itself in splendid financial condition and Canadiens with one of the greatest hockey teams the game has ever produced."

One week later, Gorman's successor, Frank Selke, spent a morning at his new office in the Forum. He fielded calls from friends and acquaintances and spoke with a Montreal *Gazette* reporter who happened to drop by. Selke, who was fifty-three, had resigned that spring as assistant general manager of the Toronto Maple Leafs. He was very different from the affable and flamboyant Gorman. He was five feet, two and a half inches tall. He wore rimless glasses, his close-cropped hair was greying and he spoke softly.

"Senator Raymond asked if I wished to sign a contract—for a year, two, three, five," Selke told the *Gazette* writer. "I told him no contract is necessary, that his word is good with me. I will never leave him in a hole and if at any time he finds he has no use for me then I will step aside."

The Canadiens may have been champions, but they played in a run-down building that badly needed refurbishing. There were about nine thousand bench-style seats, most without backs, all painted a drab brown. Nearly half were set aside for the Millionaires and were sold on game day for sixty cents apiece. Fencing that resembled chicken wire ran from the boards to the promenade on both sides to keep the Millionaires in place. Reporters worked in cramped cubicles scattered throughout the building and filed their stories from a dingy telegraph room beneath the stands at the south end of the rink.

By opening night, October 16, Selke had put his stamp on things. He had spent $115,000 to upgrade the plumbing. He had ordered construction of a new press box that seated fifty reporters. The seats had been repainted. There were now blue, white and red sections and a new pricing regime put in place. The Millionaires' section was gone. Selke had also replaced the wire mesh behind the nets with glass, and for the first few games fans ducked when ever they saw a puck coming at them.

The Canadiens began the 1946–47 campaign against the Rangers, and Selke organized a pre-game ceremony to celebrate the team's past and its most recent accomplishments. Four ex-players—Jack Laviolette, Newsy Lalonde, Joe Malone and Eugène Payan—were introduced at centre ice. NHL president Clarence Campbell presented Toe Blake with the Stanley Cup, and together they raised banners commemorating Montreal's first-place finish and Cup victory.

The Canadiens won that night, and the capacity crowd went home happy, but not the new general manager. Selke was concerned about the team's underlying strength. He had seen weaknesses, not apparent to others, from day one of training camp.

———

The NHL schedule was extended to sixty games for the 1946–47 season, and the Canadiens began training earlier than ever before—on September 19, a humid day when the temperature in Montreal hit eighty-one degrees Fahrenheit. After watching fifty-eight veterans and prospects skate, Selke called a meeting of the directors and said: "You have problems. Canadiens only have six players who are better than any other team. Durnan, Reardon, Bouchard and the Punch Line of Blake, Richard and Lach. And you have nothing in reserve. Your minor-league Royals are older than the Canadiens."

Senator Raymond asked Selke how he proposed to solve the problem.

"I'd like to inaugurate a farm system," Selke said, "with a team in every province to build up young reserves, as in Toronto. The players there will be haunting me for years."

"We owe the people of Montreal a good hockey team," the senator replied. "Go ahead and build an empire."

Selke was just the man to do it. He had been running hockey teams since he was a boy in Berlin (later Kitchener), Ontario. Hockey was big in pre-war Berlin, and Selke, the son of Polish immigrants, loved the game, but was too small to play. He began organizing teams in 1906, the year he quit school. He was thirteen and he formed the Iroquois, a seven-member squad of friends and neighbourhood acquaintances.

At age twenty-one, he put together his first junior team, the Berlin Union Jacks, who won the OHA title for western Ontario, but lost in a provincial playoff to a Toronto team whose captain was a young man named Conn Smythe. Selke joined the Canadian Army and organized a soldiers' team that played in an OHA intermediate league in 1916–17. After the war, while working as an electrician at the University of Toronto and raising his growing family, Selke coached and managed bantam and midget teams at the churches he attended. But he had grander ambitions, and in 1924 he lined up financial support to form his second junior team— the Toronto Marlboros.

Among his many duties, Selke scouted, often standing around outdoor rinks in frigid winter weather, and he proved adept at spotting talent. His

Marlies won the Memorial Cup in 1929, and four players from that team moved on to the Leafs: defencemen Reginald "Red" Horner and Alex Levinsky and wingers Harvey "Busher" Jackson and Charlie Conacher. In the fall of 1929, Selke quit his electrician's job and went to work as assistant manager of the Leafs for his old friend and occasional opponent Conn Smythe.

He was responsible for scouting, publicity and producing the Leaf program, though he did much more. Selke helped raise money for the construction of Maple Leaf Gardens and saved the project in the spring of 1931. The Great Depression had begun. Smythe's financial backers were nervous and wanted to hold off for a year or two. Selke, honorary business manager of his local branch of the International Brotherhood of Electrical Workers, went to the Allied Building Trades Council of Toronto with an ingenious idea. He convinced the council to allow its members, many of them unemployed, to take twenty per cent of their wages in Gardens stock.

Smythe presented the idea to Sir John Aird, a key financial backer and president of the Canadian Imperial Bank of Commerce. A startled Aird replied: "This to my knowledge is the first time that labor has indicated a willingness to co-operate with capital. If the workers are willing to subscribe twenty per cent of their wages, I'll recommend that the bank do its share too. We will invest $25,000."

The Gardens opened in November 1931, and a few games into that season Smythe fired his coach, Art Duncan, and hired Dick Irvin. Selke and Irvin quickly became close friends. They were both in their late thirties. They disliked smoking, drinking and gambling, and were keen chicken fanciers who raised and exhibited exotic breeds.

Early on, Selke gave Irvin some advice about working for Smythe. "I told Dick that, above everything else, Smythe was the Boss, with a capital B."

Selke worked comfortably in the shadow of the Boss for a decade. When World War II started, Smythe, then in his late forties, enlisted, formed his own battalion and went overseas. By default, Selke ran the Leafs, made the trades and recruited young talent, though Smythe kept up with everything and occasionally sent Selke orders even as he fought the Germans and recovered from serious wounds suffered in France.

Selke defied Smythe once, by trading a young defenceman, Frank Eddolls, for a Canadiens prospect named Ted Kennedy. Smythe never forgave Selke and made him miserable upon his return for the 1945–46 season. He accused his reliable and trustworthy assistant of trying to usurp him. He blamed him for the Leafs' poor performance that winter. One day, he sent a memo that read, "Anytime I am in the building you are not to leave for lunch or any other purpose without my permission in case I need you."

"Lincoln freed the slaves eighty years ago," Selke replied. "I'm done. Goodbye."

In Montreal, Selke found the ideal boss. Senator Raymond gave him a mandate—to build an empire—and provided the resources and operating latitude necessary to get the job done. Selke used the approach he had developed with the Leafs. Toronto had begun sponsoring junior teams, offering them financial support in return for access to their best players. During the war, Selke had adopted another practice that put the Leafs ahead of their competitors. NHL rules allowed teams to sign players as young as sixteen, but most clubs waited until their prospects turned eighteen. When eighteen-year-olds began enlisting, Selke recruited sixteen-year-olds, brought them to Toronto, enrolled them in schools and put them on the rosters of Leaf affiliates. "Before the other NHL clubs caught on," he wrote in his autobiography, "we had signed most of the good lads in Canada."

Selke built a network of Montreal-sponsored teams that far exceeded those of his rivals. The Canadiens had affiliates in Halifax, Quebec City, Trois-Rivières, Victoriaville, Montreal, Peterborough, Fort William, Winnipeg, Regina and Edmonton. By 1950, the Canadiens were spending $150,000 a year on player development, a figure that would eventually reach $250,000 per season. "We just haven't got that kind of money," Red Wings coach Jimmy Skinner would observe in the mid-1950s.

But for a few seasons, until the farm system began producing talent, the Canadiens went with the powerful but aging team that Gorman and Irvin had built. In 1946–47, they won the league championship for the fourth consecutive year and met their Toronto rivals in the Stanley Cup final for the first time.

Irvin tried to motivate his players with the battle cry, "Let's win for Elmer." Early in the season, Lach had suffered a fractured cheekbone in a game against Chicago. He returned to the lineup in late January. On February 6, the Leafs' Don Metz charged the width of the ice and hit Lach with such force that he landed on the back of his head and fractured his skull. Prior to the start of the playoffs, Lach bid his teammates farewell, boarded a train and went home to Saskatchewan to recover. Many were sure they'd seen the last of him.

Montreal won the first game six–nothing and in the dressing room afterward, Bill Durnan told reporters: "The boys got that one for me. I had a good seat." However, one Toronto paper quoted him as wondering, "How did those fellows ever get into the playoffs?"

That lit a fire under the Leafs for game two. They skated to a three–nothing, first-period lead and pounded the Canadiens until Rocket Richard snapped. After a mid-ice collision, Richard swung his stick and hit Vic Lynn over the left eye. Lynn left with blood flowing from the wound, and Richard received a five-minute major. Early in the second, Richard clashed with Bill Ezinicki, a stocky, pugnacious checker who could hit with devastating force. The sticks came up. An official stepped between them. Richard reached around him and cracked his tormentor over the head. Ezinicki skated to the bench with his scalp bloodied, while the Rocket left with a match penalty and game misconduct. The Canadiens played shorthanded for twenty minutes and, afterward, league president Clarence Campbell suspended Richard for game three.

French Montrealers were incensed. It was excessive and unfair, they said. Some even saw the power of English Canada at work. Paul Parizeau, sports columnist for the Montreal daily *Le Canada*, reminded his readers that Don Metz had ended Lach's season and received a two-minute minor. "Here's indisputable proof of the influence of Smythe on the National Hockey League," Parizeau wrote, adding later, "Campbell is president of the league in name only, but in fact is the advocate of Conny Smythe."

The Richard incident proved to be the turning point in the series. The Canadiens lost the third game four–two in Maple Leaf Gardens, but the

Rocket couldn't bear to watch. In his hotel room, he listened to the play-by-play broadcast over the radio. He was so disgusted when Ezinicki was named one of the game's three stars that he hurled the radio to the sidewalk outside his room.

The Canadiens lost game four with Richard back in the lineup and returned home facing elimination. Selke anticipated trouble if things went badly and decided to clamp down on the fans' habit of hurling objects onto the ice. He announced prior to the opening faceoff that plainclothes spotters were scattered throughout the crowd. Anyone—even season ticket holders—caught throwing things would be arrested and prosecuted.

Richard redeemed himself with a two-goal performance that led to a Montreal victory, but forty-eight hours later the Canadiens lost by a single goal "before a howling mob of 14,546 at Maple Leaf Gardens," as *The Gazette*'s Dink Carroll put it.

Toronto took possession of the Stanley Cup and Carroll concluded, as Selke had at the start of the season, that it was time for an overhaul. "It's apparent to one and all," he wrote, "that the Canadiens will have to do some rebuilding if they hope to regain the Cup."

That fall, Conn Smythe predicted that the Canadiens would be the team to beat in 1947–48. New York Rangers coach Frank Boucher thought otherwise. He believed that Montreal had slipped while their rivals had improved, and he was proven correct.

Injuries were a problem from the start, and an off-season trade haunted the Canadiens all winter. Selke sent Buddy O'Connor to New York, but received little in return. O'Connor, a Montreal native, was a small, slick centre. The Forum fans liked him and gave him a three-minute ovation when he appeared in a Ranger uniform for the season opener. On his second visit, in late November, they applauded again when he scored the winning goal.

With O'Connor gone, the Canadiens did not have a good second-line centre and relied excessively on the Punch Line for offensive output. Lach had recovered from the injuries of the previous season and, as one observer noted, "still has all his old speed, skates opponents into the ice and is setting up plays with his usual skill." But on January 10, 1948, in a game against the Rangers, he and the Rocket lost their longtime left winger, Toe Blake.

Late in the third period, the Canadiens were on the attack. Defenceman Bill Juzda delivered a stiff body check that sent Blake into the boards. "Toe seemed to catch his left skate in the ice," Carroll reported. "He tried to get up but fell back again and players and officials crowded around him. As he was carried off the ice on a stretcher, the crowd of 11,211 seemed stunned into silence."

X-rays revealed a complete break of the fibula and a tear fracture of the tibia—two bones in the lower part of the leg. Blake was finished. He was thirty-five. He had played fourteen seasons. He was second on the NHL's list of all-time top scorers, just five points behind retired Bruin Bill Cowley, the leader. Blake had won a scoring title, the Hart Trophy, the Lady Byng, and held the league record for playoff points with sixty-two. What most impressed the fans was his fiery temperament. "If ever there was a player in the league with more spirit, we haven't seen him," Carroll wrote.

The Canadiens missed the playoffs that year, but they had one reason to smile. Elmer Lach won the scoring championship. He went into the final weekend trailing O'Connor by four points. O'Connor failed to score in the last two games. Lach picked up three assists in one game and scored twice in the last contest to finish on top by a single point, a remarkable accomplishment considering the severity of the injuries he'd suffered the previous year.

Dick Irvin boarded a plane and flew home to Regina at the end of the season. For the first time in his seventeen-year NHL coaching career, his team had missed the playoffs. Frank Selke headed for Regina, too, but he took the train. Selke was going west to sign a sponsorship agreement with the Regina Pats of the Saskatchewan Junior Hockey League, and before leaving he told a reporter: "We are more anxious than ever before to take junior clubs and their minor-league affiliates under our wing. We frankly do so with the idea of building up an endless reservoir of future talent for our pro teams . . ."

Selke was planning for the long term, but in the short run the Canadiens sorely needed some capable young prospects. They had been eclipsed by the

Leafs, who finished first and won the Stanley Cup in 1948 and repeated as Cup champions in 1949, to become the first NHL team to win it three years in a row. Then the Red Wings became a powerhouse. They finished first for seven straight seasons beginning in 1948–49. Twice they accumulated one hundred points or more and they won the Stanley Cup three times.

These were trying times for the Canadiens and their supporters. By the late 1940s, the Canadiens were more than just Montreal's team. They had fans in nearly every town and village in Quebec. Radio broadcasts had made it possible for French-Canadians across the province to listen to the games. La Société Radio-Canada, the CBC's French-language arm, began providing play-by-play accounts in 1937, and two years later the network had transmission technology in place that allowed it to reach ninety per cent of Quebec households.

Initially, though, most French-Canadians could not tune in. They had to wait until the electrical grid was extended from cities to towns to villages and beyond to the countryside. Rural electrification occurred in phases throughout the 1940s and gathered speed after the war. By the end of the decade, ninety-four per cent of Quebec homes had electricity, well above the national average of eighty-three per cent.

With the advent of this new form of energy, French-Canadians could buy electrical stoves, refrigerators, clocks, lamps and many other goods, including radios. They could set their dials to receive the Radio-Canada signal—the only one available in many places—and on Saturday nights, at the end of a hard week, they could gather around this magical device and listen to Michel Normandin call the play-by-play from a booth above the ice at the Forum. They could hear the buzz of the crowd rise and fall with the ebb and flow of the game, and periodically an eruption of applause, followed by a stirring announcement over the Forum public address system: "*Le but des Canadiens. Montreal goal. Maur-r-rice R-r-rocket R-R-Richard.*"

French-Canadians of every age revered the team and its great star. Richard gave them strength and confidence, as Roch Carrier wrote in his 2001 memoir *Our Life with the Rocket*. Carrier grew up in Ste-Justine, a village of one street and some two thousand inhabitants on the Quebec–Maine border, southeast of the provincial capital. Carrier first listened to the games in his grandparents' home in the days prior to rural electrification. They used a windmill to pump water from the ground and to generate electricity. The whirling arms of the mill would illuminate a single bulb above the kitchen table and power the radio until the wind began to wane. Then the light would falter and Normandin's voice would vanish like a wisp of smoke.

Once the electrical grid reached villages like Ste-Justine, the lights would stay on and the radios would play all evening. Every member of the family, every family in the village, every village in the province could sit transfixed and listen to the entire broadcast, which in those days began at the end of the first period, and in listening they were transformed. On Sundays, when they congregated at church, they talked about the games. On Monday mornings, in shops, factories and walking to school, it was the same.

"We're five schoolboys," Carrier wrote, "wearing aviators' helmets with the fur-lined flaps pulled down, parkas with fur-lined hoods and felt boots. . . . We're seven, eight, nine years old. . . . We schoolboys are happy. Last Saturday the Canadiens won their game against Toronto. . . . We climb the hill. Nothing is impossible. Maurice Richard has won. The Canadiens have won. We have won. Under the blue sky we're taller now, stronger, more important."

The Rocket had the same uplifting effect on their elders. "With his muscles strained as taut as bowstrings, Maurice Richard lays claim to the territory of hockey. He occupies it with authority. And through this ritual, French-Canadians are regaining confidence in themselves, in their future. Each of them feels a little less defeated, a little less humiliated, a little more strong."

A Stanley Cup victory was nothing less than a vindication of the race. "In this Canada that their ancestors discovered, the French-Canadians are the servants, the hewers of wood and drawers of water. The language of their ancestors, their language, is looked down on. Winning the Stanley Cup is a proud revenge."

But the Canadiens could not win every year, even with Maurice Richard leading them. There were painful defeats, and these only deepened the bond between the team and its followers. In 1948–49, the Canadiens finished third, ten points behind the league champion Red Wings. Richard scored his two hundredth goal that season, but otherwise had a poor year. His output fell to twenty goals. He slipped to seventeenth in the scoring race and was ineffective in the playoffs against Detroit, in part because Elmer Lach got knocked out early by an elbow to the jaw, which he had fractured during the regular season. Lach left with two black eyes—and a cut over one of them—teeth missing and his jaw so sore he could hardly eat. Irvin tried to prod Richard by telling a reporter between games, "I may play Floyd Curry in place of Joe Carveth or Maurice Richard."

The ploy didn't work. Richard scored just twice in seven games while twenty-one-year-old Gordie Howe connected six times and led Detroit to the final. The fans grumbled, and some questioned Richard's value. "You would be surprised," *The Gazette*'s Dink Carroll wrote, "at how many of the team's followers believe The Rocket has outlived his usefulness and should be traded now when the Canadiens could expect to get some good players in return."

Richard proved them wrong in 1949–50. He scored forty-three goals, and the team had a better season, too. The Canadiens moved up to second, but still trailed Detroit by eleven points. They met the Rangers in the Stanley Cup semifinal, and Richard again had a poor playoff. New York's Pentti Lund checked the Rocket and held him pointless through the first three games, which the Canadiens lost, while picking up seven points of his own to lead the playoff scoring race.

Prior to game four, Bill Durnan told Selke he was through. The big goaler had just won his sixth Vézina Trophy. He was the quintessential team player. He never blamed his teammates for a weak goal or poor performance. But his nerves were shot. He had been hit in the face by too many pucks, sticks and errant skate blades. He had been jeered too often by Montreal's unforgiving fans. He couldn't sleep before or after games.

The Canadiens turned to Gerry McNeil, a Quebec City native who had played senior for the Royals and for the minor-league Cincinnati Mohawks. Irvin asked Durnan to give the newcomer a private pep talk as he dressed for the game, and the two goaltenders retired to a back room.

"A few minutes later I stepped into the room myself," Irvin said after the game, "and what do you think I saw? The two of them were in there crying. Yes, crying. And Bill, his voice shaky and his hands trembling uncontrollably, was saying, 'Now, Gerry, don't be nervous. Don't be nervous. Everything will be all right.'"

McNeil and the Canadiens won that night, but were eliminated in game five, and Selke began the task of rebuilding in earnest.

The Canadiens were confident they could start the 1950–51 season with McNeil in net, but they had a big hole to fill on defence. Butch Bouchard was still there patrolling the blue line like a surly gatekeeper, but his partner, the irrepressible Ken Reardon, had retired over the summer, his shoulders nearly ruined by too many high-velocity collisions with the dasher boards, goalposts and opposing forwards.

Reardon's departure created opportunities for two young players. The first was Doug Harvey. He was twenty-six, a veteran of three seasons and a superb athlete. Harvey had excelled at every sport he played as a youth growing up in Notre-Dame-de-Grâce, an English-speaking Montreal suburb of working- and middle-class families. He was one of the best high school football players in the city—"an unstoppable ball carrier, a ferocious tackler and a thunderous punter," according to biographer William Brown. He played minor-pro baseball with the Class C Ottawa Nationals, and in his second season hit .357, won the batting title and was drafted by the major-league Boston Braves. He spent two winters with the Montreal Royals of the Quebec Senior Hockey League, and in the spring of 1947 was named that league's "Best Pro Prospect." Harvey could skate with anyone. He could handle the puck or make a pass like no one else, *and* he could rattle opponents at the blue line or in the corners.

But Harvey's unorthodox approach often left the fans gasping and his coaches fuming. He held on to the puck too long in his own end. He carried it in front of the net. He appeared to be skating at half-speed much of the time. People sat on the edge of their seats. "Pass it!" they shouted. "Get rid of it." "Why doesn't he play with more intensity?" they asked each other. On more than one occasion, Selke came close to trading him.

With Reardon gone, Harvey became a steady and reliable performer. In mid-March 1951, Len Bramson of *The Hockey News* reported: "The once loud chorus of boos from the rafters of the Montreal Forum have now changed to cheers. Harvey's showings in the last five games have been the greatest of his career."

Reardon's spot on the Canadiens roster was filled by Tom Johnson, a twenty-two-year-old rookie who wore bow ties, smoked cigars and showed up at training camp driving a convertible. Johnson was from Baldur, Manitoba, a farming hamlet about a hundred miles southwest of Winnipeg, and did not play indoors until he joined the Winnipeg Monarchs of the Manitoba Junior Hockey League in the fall of 1946. Toronto sponsored the Monarchs, but Leaf management thought Johnson had too many rough edges and left him off their protected list. During a western scouting trip, Frank Selke watched Johnson score twice in one game on end-to-end rushes and that was enough. He acquired Johnson's rights for five hundred dollars.

The Canadiens brought him to Montreal at the start of the 1947–48 season, and he played for the senior Royals. The fans were perplexed. "They took one look at him and they laughed," Bransom wrote. "They said, 'He can't skate.' Every time he was on the ice the fans gave him a good razzberry. They even took to throwing insults at Selke for they knew Johnson was a protege of the little general manager. It got so bad that one night a fan actually had to run from Selke, who was going after him with his fists cocked. Irvin had to restrain him."

Johnson honed his skills with the Royals and the Buffalo Bisons of the American Hockey League before graduating to the Canadiens. Initially, he struggled against the faster, tougher competition. He also received a memorable tongue-lashing from Dick Irvin between periods one night. "Johnson, you remind me of that convertible you drive," Irvin said. "When the sun is out, your top is down. When the rains come, up goes the top. You run for cover as soon as things go bad."

By the latter half of the season, Johnson had made a believer of Irvin. He was a stronger, faster skater than he appeared to be. He was tough and fearless. He moved the puck well and was one of the best at stealing it from attacking forwards. "Tom Johnson is the steadiest defenceman in the league today," Irvin told a hockey writer in February 1951. "He's one of the main reasons why we're still in the battle. And, what's more, he's a future all-star."

Irvin was correct. Johnson was twice named to NHL All-Star teams (the second team in 1956 and the first in 1959) and won the James Norris Trophy once. He might have earned more individual honours, except he played on the same team as Harvey, who was an all-star for ten consecutive seasons (1952–62) and won the Norris Trophy seven times in eight seasons beginning in 1955.

With Harvey, Johnson and the veteran Bouchard on the blue line, the Canadiens had built the foundation of a great defence. They still needed help up front, though. The team played poorly in the fall of 1950, and by mid-December Frank Selke was exasperated. He was in his fifth season. The Canadiens had not won the Stanley Cup, nor were they a contender. "I'll trade anyone for someone I think will strengthen the club," he told *The Hockey News*. "Right now, I'm looking for a French-Canadian right winger."

A few days later, he *traded* a French-Canadian right winger, Léo Gravelle, to Detroit in exchange for Bert Olmstead. Gravelle was known as the Gazelle because of his speed, but he was short and slight. Olmstead was a tough left winger from Sceptre, Saskatchewan. He stood six foot two. He weighed 183 pounds and filled the hole on the Lach–Richard line that had been created by the departure of Toe Blake.

Olmstead would spend eight years with the Canadiens, always on a top line even though he never scored more than eighteen goals per season. He was one of the best at fighting for possession of the puck in the corners and could make perfect passes to teammates waiting in the faceoff circle or in front of the net. The writer Scott Young once described Olmstead as "implacable, immovable, unforgiving of friend or foe alike." He was like a blunt-force instrument on the ice, and he spoke bluntly, too. After a win over the Bruins one night, Olmstead told a youthful Frank Orr, "The big reason we won is that we knocked a lot of those bastards on their asses."

Selke found his French-Canadian right winger on one of the many junior teams the Canadiens sponsored. His name was Bernie Geoffrion and he played for the Montreal Nationales of the six-team Quebec Junior Hockey League. Geoffrion had size—he was almost six feet tall and weighed 185 pounds—and he could score, thanks to a shot that was both spectacular and intimidating.

Geoffrion is usually credited with inventing the slap shot. But NHL players had already begun lifting their sticks to slap the puck by the time he joined the Canadiens, and sportswriters were using the term slap shot in their copy. Geoffrion did, however, take it further than other players. In his autobiography, he recounts how he developed a golf-style swing as a teenager playing for a parish team.

One day, he was alone on the ice before a practice, shooting pucks at the net. After missing several times with a wrist shot, he raised his stick high over his head and slapped the puck in frustration. "I couldn't believe it," Geoffrion wrote. " . . . the puck . . . went through the back of the net. When I saw the puck come out the other side I said to myself, 'This is something that goalies are going to be afraid of for a long, long time.'"

Geoffrion had perfected his technique by the time he joined the Nationales at age sixteen. His shot attracted a lot of attention from fans and sportswriters—one of whom nicknamed him "Boom Boom" for the sound of his stick smacking the puck and the reverberation of the puck crashing against the boards. Geoffrion scored from the start of his junior career, and in 1949–50, his fourth season, he won the league scoring title with eighty-six points, six better than the runner-up, Jean Béliveau of the Quebec Citadelles.

Geoffrion played three games as a call-up from junior before joining the Canadiens permanently on February 14, 1951—that season's trading deadline. "The date is forever etched in my mind," he wrote in his autobiography. "I got the call from The Boss [Selke] and went to his office where he laid out the three-year offer. Quite frankly, I would have played for nothing. That's how desperate I was to play in the National Hockey League. Who cared about money?"

In his first six games, Geoffrion scored four times and added an assist—much-needed offence for a team that had spent most of that season in fourth or fifth place. The Canadiens finished third, which meant a playoff series against the league champion Red Wings. Montreal had earned sixty-five points, Detroit a record 101. Yet the Canadiens prevailed in six games, an upset that ranked as one of the biggest in Stanley Cup history.

The final contest was played at the Forum, and afterward players and team officials were "crazy with joy," according to one French-language newspaper account. "This is the greatest sensation in my young life," said Gerry McNeil, who sat in his corner puffing on a cigarette. Frank Selke and team president Donat Raymond went around the room, congratulating each player individually. A dozen newspaper photographers snapped photos, and reporters surrounded Dick Irvin, who shouted, "And everybody thought I was crazy when I said I would rather play Detroit than any other club."

Four nights later, the final began at Maple Leaf Gardens. The Leafs won the first game after five minutes and fifty-one seconds of extra play, and the Canadiens took the second when Maurice Richard scored his third overtime goal of the playoffs. "Doug Harvey's long pass put the Rocket a half step ahead of Gus Mortson, the Leaf defenceman," Dink Carroll of *The Gazette* wrote. "He shifted into high gear, pulled away from Mortson, raced in on Turk Broda, faked him into a pretzel and flipped the puck into the empty net." Afterward, an admiring Conn Smythe told reporters: "There's no comparison between the Rocket and Gordie Howe. Richard is the best in the game today."

The series shifted to Montreal, and the entire city was swept up in the excitement. "We thought we had detected an acute case of hockey fever in Toronto," Rhéaume Brisebois wrote in *Le Canada* on the day of the third game. "But it was nothing compared to the malady which has struck here. Fans started lining up yesterday at noon in the hope of obtaining tickets. Forum officials are not exaggerating when they say that if there were forty thousand seats they would all be occupied."

Fans that night watched another overtime thriller—a two–one Toronto victory—and the Leafs took the fourth match with a sudden-death goal by Harry Watson. Back in Toronto for game five, the Canadiens fought valiantly till the end. They led two–one with under a minute to go. Leaf coach Joe Primeau pulled his goalie, and Toronto forward Tod Sloan tied it.

The delirious home crowd let loose a deluge of hats and programs that nearly covered the ice, and they roared like thunder as the final thirty-two seconds were played.

The overtime session lasted just short of three minutes. Leaf forward Howie Meeker passed from the corner to Bill Barilko at the blue line. Barilko skated in, fired blindly toward the net and took a hit that sent him flying, but the puck sailed past McNeil into the top corner.

The 1951 series is the only one in Stanley Cup history in which every game was decided in overtime. Leaf fans would wait eleven years for another championship. The Canadiens were improving, and their junior affiliates were about to produce a bumper crop of prospects who would put them on the road to greatness.

December 1951, and the Canadiens were in another slump. They had earned only one point in their previous four games. They hadn't won on the road in two months and were, as one writer put it, "a breath away from last place."

Frank Selke again turned to the farm system for help. He announced that Dickie Moore of the Senior Royals would join the Canadiens for a three-game trial. The twenty-one-year-old left winger was the Royals' leading scorer and had had a great junior career.

A native Montrealer, Moore grew up in a north-end neighbourhood called Park Extension, in a family of nine boys and one girl, all of them talented athletes. The Moore brothers boxed, played softball, soccer and hockey, and one was an accomplished figure skater. Their sister, Dolly, had the opportunity to play pro softball in Chicago and would have run the 100- and 200-metre sprints for Canada at the 1940 Olympics had the games not been cancelled due to the war.

Dickie, the youngest, was a scrappy, cocksure player who had led the Junior Royals to a Memorial Cup championship in 1949 and the Junior Canadiens to the national title the following year. "Crowds streamed to the rinks to either support or hoot the brash kid who was forever in a feud with the league's top stars," Ian MacDonald of *The Hockey News* wrote. "Quebec

Citadels' Jean Beliveau was a prime target . . . Dickie is reported to have blackened Big Jean's eyes on one of the few occasions when Beliveau resorted to fighting."

Moore signed a two-year contract on Christmas Day, scored a hat trick on February 16, 1952 and another a week later. In his first twenty-seven games, he collected twenty-nine points and was being touted as a candidate for rookie of the year. His most serious rival for that honour was Bernie Geoffrion, who was still eligible because he had played only eighteen games the previous season. Geoffrion was on his way to a thirty-goal season, and Dick Irvin said of him: "That kid is better than Rocket was in his first season. He can do more things with the puck, he can stickhandle, skate both ways and take care of himself. He can score with the best."

Others agreed, and Geoffrion was named rookie of the year. He was elated and said: "If I am proud, it's above all because I am the first French-Canadian player to win the Calder Trophy. We are ambassadors for French Canada . . . and that's why, today, I feel a great senses of pride at having a French-Canadian name."

Elmer Lach also enjoyed a landmark season. The Elegant One, as the papers liked to call him, became the NHL's all-time scoring leader. He surpassed retired Bruin Bill Cowley's record of 594 points, and Montrealers paid tribute before a Saturday night game in early March. They gave Lach cash and gifts worth an estimated eleven thousand dollars. He stood at centre ice with wife Kaye while team officials hauled out the merchandise on four large carts. Master of ceremonies Michel Normandin announced the donors and what they had given: a television set; a radio-phonograph; a refrigerator; a freezer; a living room chair; a rowboat; a stetson; and more. His teammates presented a washing machine. Mayor Camillien Houde gave him a set of cuff links.

The lights went down, and a gleaming new automobile appeared, circled the ice and stopped at the faceoff circle. Toe Blake emerged, dressed as a chauffeur, and the crowd cheered wildly. Normandin handed the microphone to Lach. He cleared his throat, checked his emotions and began with "*Mesdames et messieurs* . . ." He spoke in French first and the fans responded with a roaring ovation.

Lach and the rookies led the Canadiens to second place. They met the Bruins in the playoffs and nearly let their old rivals steal the series, but prevailed in game seven when Maurice Richard scored one of his greatest goals.

Early in the second period, the Rocket raced up the ice—with his head down. Leo Labine, a ferocious checker, struck him shoulder to chest at top speed. The impact sent Richard face-first into the knee of a Bruin defenceman. Richard landed on the ice, bleeding profusely from a cut above his left eye. Reporters thought he'd broken his neck, and one later wrote that he was "knocked colder than a bailliff's heart." Two ushers arrived with a stretcher, but team doctor Gordon Young said: "You don't know this guy. He'd have to be dead before he'd allow himself to be carried off on that."

Dr. Young revived Richard. Teammates helped him to the clinic and laid him out on the table. Richard lost consciousness again. He didn't flinch as the physician cleaned and stitched his wound. When he finally came to, Richard brushed off the doctor and returned to the bench. He was so disoriented that he had to ask Elmer Lach the score (one–one) and how much time was left (a little more than over four minutes). Even so, Irvin sent him over the boards. Émile Bouchard picked up the puck deep in the Canadiens end. He passed to Richard. Richard blew past two Bruin forwards. He came in on defenceman Bill Quackenbush. The Boston defender steered him to the corner. Richard slipped around him. He raced for the net like a stone fired from a slingshot. He faked once. Goaltender Jim Henry hugged the left post and Richard shot to the far corner.

The red light went on. The fans leapt to their feet. They littered the ice with debris and they cheered for five minutes. Afterward, in the dressing room, Richard broke down and wept. When he regained his composure, he faced the sportswriters, who peppered him with questions. He recounted the goal, but drew a blank when they asked about the hit. "I don't remember a thing," Richard said. "Everything went black. I didn't know where I was."

The Canadiens played the Red Wings in the final. The Wings had won their fourth consecutive league championship. They had reached the hundred-point plateau for the second straight season. They had the league's top scorer in Gordie Howe and the best goaltender in Terry Sawchuk. They had swept the Leafs in four and they demolished the Canadiens with equal efficiency.

Sawchuk allowed a paltry five goals in those eight games, and a frustrated Richard said after one game: "He is their club. Another guy in nets and we'd beat them. They're just lucky."

When the series was over, the Canadiens lined up to shake hands, but Lach, Richard and Irvin went straight to the dressing room. "Have your fun," Irvin snapped at several fans who jeered him.

Frank Selke vowed that the Canadiens would not be humiliated again. He had plenty of prospects in the farm system, and some were ready to step up to the big club. The best of them was Jean Béliveau. The trouble was, Selke could not persuade him to sign.

The pursuit of Béliveau had begun two years earlier, in the spring of 1950. He had completed his first season with Quebec Citadelles, and Selke had this to say about him: "I'm going to make Jean Béliveau an offer he can't refuse. I know that he is only eighteen, but he is a big boy and other boys that age have broken into our league. I think he has demonstrated all the right qualities to be a star for a long, long time."

Béliveau attended his first Canadiens training camp in September 1950 and stayed three weeks. Selke did not offer him a contract directly. Instead, he sent emissaries to negotiate with his father, Arthur, in Victoriaville and with Citadelles owner Frank Byrne. Neither co-operated and, when the Montreal men had left, Byrne called Béliveau and said: "Whatever they offer you, Jean, we will match or better. Just don't sign anything."

Béliveau was the king of Quebec that winter. He was making six thousand dollars for playing hockey and another three thousand for public relations work with a local dairy—combined earnings that were higher than a typical NHL salary. He was packing Le Colisée—a new arena that sat more than ten thousand and was nicknamed Château Béliveau. He had a Saturday morning radio show for kids. He won the scoring championship and led the Citadelles to the eastern Canadian final, one step short of a berth in the Memorial Cup. On April 10, 1951, prior to one of Béliveau's final games as a junior, the fans gave him a brand new automobile, a Nash Canadian Statesman de Luxe.

He had also made his NHL debut that season. The Canadiens called him up on December 16, 1950. The Rangers were in town, and Béliveau had nine shots on net and was named the game's first star. He made his second appearance on January 27, 1951, and this time he scored.

Selke assumed that a taste of the big time would convince Béliveau to join the Canadiens in the fall of 1951. He was sorely disappointed when Béliveau signed for ten thousand dollars with the Quebec Aces, a senior team owned by the Anglo-Canadian Pulp and Paper Company. Selke was through with reason and persuasion. He proposed an amendment to the agreement between the NHL and the Canadian Amateur Hockey Association under which any player on an NHL team's negotiating list would be required to sign a contract with that club before playing in the QSHL. The proposal, quickly dubbed the "Béliveau rule," would allow an NHL club to assign an individual to a team—the Canadiens, in Béliveau's case. But the rule was never ratified.

The following season, 1952–53, the interest in Beliveau's services became so protracted that the provincial government of Maurice Duplessis intervened. In his autobiography, *My Life in Hockey,* Béliveau recounts how he and Jack Latter, the Aces' president and an Anglo-Canadian Paper executive, were summoned to a meeting with a senior Duplessis aide named Gérald Martineau. Béliveau had already agreed to a salary of fifteen thousand dollars. Martineau had a copy of the contract and, after a few minutes of small talk, said: "Jack, you're making money with Jean. Why don't you give him five thousand more?"

It was an order, not a request, since Anglo-Canadian held the rights to a timber concession near the community of Forestville and was seeking government approval to begin harvesting. Béliveau signed and, at age twenty, became one of hockey's highest-paid players, along with Rocket Richard and Gordie Howe.

He proved his worth when the Canadiens called him up for three games in mid-December 1952. Montreal was in second place—as usual, behind Detroit. Lach was out with a broken thumb, and Irvin used Béliveau on the first line with Richard and Olmstead. He scored three goals in a Thursday night home win over the Rangers, and sportswriters were effusive. "He is a neat player for such a big man and has an easy, effortless way of going," the *Montreal Star*'s Baz O'Meara wrote. "He has a wonderful shift, a great shot, either slap or straight, and he is able to carry the puck the distance."

The Canadiens played a home-and-home series with Boston that weekend. Prior to the game at Boston Garden, Irvin sent a telegram to the Bruins front office:

> "Convey to your fans that Montreal Canadiens play in your Garden Sunday with the world's greatest defence plus world's greatest goaltender. Will have on exhibition world's greatest amateur hockey player. . . . Expect you to have world's record attendance at your Garden. Regards, World's Greatest Coach, Dick Irvin."

The Boston papers promoted Béliveau's appearance, and almost thirteen thousand people, the Bruins' largest crowd of the season, attended. Béliveau scored twice in a four–three win and then returned to Quebec City. *The Hockey News* named him player of the week, even though Detroit's Ted Lindsay had scored his two hundredth goal. Maurice Richard said: "He's great. He's got the greatest shot I've ever seen in hockey and he's a fine man. He could help this team plenty and I wish he would change his mind."

The Canadiens challenged the Red Wings for first place for most of the season, but had to settle for second and opened the playoffs against Chicago. They went ahead by two games, but lost the next three. Facing elimination, Irvin pulled what one writer called "the biggest gamble in the history of the Stanley Cup playoffs." He benched three forwards and brought in replacements from the minor-league Buffalo Bisons and Victoria Cougars.

To complicate matters, goaltender Gerry McNeil suffered what was described as "a nervous crack-up" and needed a rest. Irvin turned to the Bisons' Jacques Plante, who was twenty-four and had played just three NHL games. Plante shut out the Hawks in game six and allowed just one in the seventh to lead the Canadiens into the final.

This time, Montreal caught a break. Boston had upset Detroit and, with Plante in net, the Canadiens rolled to an easy win in the opening game. Afterward, the young goaltender boasted: "They had twenty-seven breakaways on me in Buffalo before they scored. Gerry is a great goaltender, but he's so small that he has to move twice as fast as me to cover the same area."

The Bruins defeated the Canadiens four–one in game two. Irvin went back to McNeil, and Montreal swept the next three contests to win its first Stanley Cup since 1946. Irvin used four lines, an unusual tactic at the time, to wear down the Bruins. McNeil earned two shutouts. Lach scored the winner in the final game after a minute and twenty-two seconds of overtime. "Richard . . . threw his arms around Elmer in an uncontrolled joyful outburst," *The Hockey News* reported. "The Forum rafters rang with tumultuous acclaim for what seemed like hours and fans tumbled over the boards to get at their heroes."

A few nights after that resounding triumph, Frank Selke addressed his players, their wives and a roomful of Canadiens supporters at a celebratory banquet. "I am not going to preside over the disintegration of a Stanley Cup team," he declared.

Goaltending and defence had carried the Canadiens to the Cup, and they remained strong in those areas. But they had scored sixty-seven fewer goals than Detroit that season, and Selke needed to strengthen the offence. Not long after the banquet, Selke met Béliveau, who had won his second straight scoring title in the QSHL. They discussed his future and posed for a photo while examining a Canadiens contract. But the cagey Béliveau was in no rush to sign.

He remained unsigned when training camp opened in mid-September 1953, and still had not committed as the champion Canadiens prepared for a game on Saturday, October 3 against the NHL All-Stars. Around eleven o'clock that morning, Béliveau finally sat down with Selke to talk contract. The twenty-two-year-old player brought with him a financial advisor and a tax lawyer. Two hours later, a beaming Selke emerged and announced to a group of reporters and photographers, "You have not waited in vain."

As flash bulbs popped and reporters fired questions, Béliveau signed. Initially, the terms were not disclosed, but it later became known that the Canadiens had agreed to pay the rookie $100,000 over five years—the largest contract awarded to that time.

Injuries prevented him from playing to his potential, or contending for rookie-of-the-year honours, that season. On October 22, Béliveau cracked a bone in his ankle and was out till December 10. In his first game back, he crashed into a goalpost during a scramble and fractured his right cheekbone. He returned three weeks later, but played in the shadows cast by others. The first was Maurice Richard, who was again leading the NHL in goals and challenging Gordie Howe for the lead in the scoring race. But it was Richard's off-ice conduct that earned attention in early January of 1954. In a ghostwritten column that ran in the weekly newspaper *Samedi-Dimanche*, Richard accused league president Clarence Campbell of cheering for the opposition while attending games at the Forum and of imposing excessive fines and suspensions on Montreal players, especially the French-Canadians.

"Strange," he wrote, "that only Dick Irvin and I have the courage to risk our livelihood to defend our cause before such a dictator."

The league could not tolerate this assault on Campbell's integrity, and it fell to Selke to defuse the crisis. He summoned Richard to a meeting with the Canadiens board and convinced him to back down. Richard wrote to Campbell, apologizing "humbly and sincerely." He withdrew his remarks. He gave up the column and posted a thousand-dollar "good faith" bond with the league. His fans had the last word, though. They cheered him heartily at the next home game and booed Campbell when he took his regular seat.

In the final month of the season, Jacques Plante captured the attention of the hockey public. The Canadiens summoned the netminder from Buffalo to fill in for the injured Gerry McNeil. It was his third stint in the NHL, and this time he played the final seventeen games of the regular season and eight in the playoffs. The rookie netminder was extraordinary, as he had been at every stop in his career.

Plante grew up in Shawinigan Falls. He was the eldest of eleven children and his family was poor. He was asthmatic, and vigorous skating would bring on an attack, so he played goal. His father carved his first stick from the root of a tree and made him goal pads from potato sacks and slats of wood. Plante learned to play outdoors. A toque, pulled down to the eyebrows and below the ear lobes, provided essential protection against the Quebec winter. His mother had no time, so he knit his own toques—as well as socks, scarves and underwear.

One winter, he played for four different teams, all in different categories—midget, juvenile, junior and intermediate—and earned fifty cents a game tending net for a factory team. The Providence Reds of the American Hockey League tried to sign him at age fifteen, and in the fall of 1947, when he was eighteen, Selke offered Plante fifteen dollars a week to play for the Junior Canadiens. The Quebec Citadelles offered eighty-five, however, and that winter he recorded ten shutouts playing for a weak team. Plante had developed a unique style because he had learned goaltending on his own. He chased loose pucks in the corners. Sometimes he raced almost to the blue line. One night, he jumped over the net to get the puck. Two seasons in Quebec and he was off to play for the Montreal Royals. His next job, beginning in 1952–53, was with the Buffalo Bisons of the AHL, who were near the bottom of the standings. Plante allowed one goal in his first four games and quickly became a box-office attraction. Eight thousand fans a night were piling into Buffalo's Memorial Auditorium to witness the work of the goaltending sensation, whom the press nicknamed Jake the Snake.

He had left the Quebec winters behind, but he still wore a toque because he believed it made him play better. Dick Irvin put an end to the practice when Plante was called up to the Canadiens, but accepted his habit of wandering from the net.

"The fact is," Irvin told Elmer Ferguson, "Plante has revolutionized the art of goaling. He just slips around behind the net, blocks off a puck destined to make a complete circuit of the end, thus nipping a play in the bud. That play is the only new thing that has been introduced to goaltending in years."

Plante earned five shutouts in the seventeen regular-season games he played with the Canadiens in 1953–54, and his goals-against average of 1.86 was better than those of Detroit's Terry Sawchuk and Toronto's Harry Lumley, the two top goaltenders. The Canadiens finished second and swept

Boston four straight in the playoffs. Plante blanked the Bruins twice and held them to four goals in all.

His hot streak ended in the final against Detroit. The Red Wings skated to a three–one lead in games, and Irvin pulled Plante for McNeil. The Canadiens won the next two contests to force a seventh. A crowd of 15,792, the largest in Detroit history, packed the Olympia. Five hundred Montrealers made the trip, but couldn't get tickets and had to watch on television. Defensive forward Floyd Curry scored midway through the first. Detroit's Red Kelly tied it early in the second. The teams played fast, flawless hockey till the end of regulation time without scoring again.

The game ended strangely after four minutes and twenty-nine seconds of overtime. Red Wing forward Glen Skov picked up the puck in the Montreal end. He passed to Tony Leswick, a compact player who stood five foot six and had scored only six goals all season. Leswick was forty-five feet from the net. He swung wildly, and his high shot fluttered toward the net. Doug Harvey tried to bat it down, but it ricocheted off his glove, over McNeil's shoulder and into the net.

The Detroit crowd went wild and drowned out Clarence Campbell's Stanley Cup presentation speech. Hundreds of fans went over the boards, and most of the spectators refused to leave till the ushers began turning out the lights. The Wings were jubilant, the Canadiens stunned.

Sportswriters barged into the dressing room, but no one dared speak for a few minutes. Richard wept. Harvey seemed to be talking to himself. Irvin brooded and fiddled with an equipment bag. Pierre Proulx of *La Presse* was struck by the silence, a "silence like one has never witnessed in the Canadiens' room, even after the most bitter defeats."

In the fall of 1954, Maurice Richard began his twelfth season with the Canadiens. He was thirty-three years old. He was the most prolific offensive player the game had ever seen, though he had never won a scoring title. He held the single-season record for goals (fifty) and was the NHL's all-time leading goal scorer. Yet Richard had never been the fastest or smoothest skater. He had never possessed the hardest shot. And he was no longer the game's best right winger. Gordie Howe had laid claim to that distinction by winning an unprecedented four straight scoring titles. What separated Richard from all the others was style and temperament. "He's on fire inside all the time he's on the ice," Frank Selke once said. Former teammate Ken Reardon added, "His strength comes all at once like the explosion of a bomb."

No other player was as exciting to watch. None had Richard's ability to lift the fans from their seats. Few, if any, had endured as much physical and verbal abuse from opponents. He was hockey's biggest attraction, but in Quebec he had soared beyond stardom, as the novelist Hugh MacLennan wrote in *Saturday Night* magazine. "Richard has become more than a hero to millions of Canadiens. Owing to the way in which he has been (so they think) persecuted, he has imperceptibly become the focus of the persecution-anxieties latent in a minority people. Not even the fact that he is loved and admired almost equally by English-speaking Montrealers can modify the profound self-identification of loyal Canadiens with this singular man. They see in Richard not only a person who ideally embodies the fire and style of their race; they also see in him a man who from time to time turns on his persecutors and annihilates them. It sounds fantastic to say it, but . . . Richard has the status with some people in Quebec not much below that of a tribal god."

In 1954–55, French-Canadians had reason to worship Richard anew: he achieved yet another milestone. On December 18, 1954, in Chicago, he scored his four hundredth goal before a crowd of about six thousand. The entire team came over the boards to congratulate him. Several players hoisted him to their shoulders to carry him around the ice, but he wouldn't have it. He took no delight on scoring against a weak opponent like the Hawks. Afterward, in the dressing room, he wore a grim expression and told a throng of reporters, "It was just another goal."

Montrealers thought otherwise. Some five thousand adoring fans were waiting at the train station when the Canadiens arrived. They roared when Richard appeared. Several men lifted him above the crowd and carried him to the street, led by a fan decked out in a huge papier-mâché likeness of the Canadiens star. Mayor Jean Drapeau followed up with a reception at City

Hall and praised Richard as "an example to all the youth of the country with your spirit of fair play."

Two weeks later, in Toronto, Richard scored number 401 against Harry Lumley. He beat a defenceman and drove to the net with such ferocity that he wound up tangled in the mesh with his beaten opponent beneath him. The crowd of over fourteen thousand responded with a standing ovation. Toward the end of the evening, they were back on their feet—this time to denounce him. As the *Toronto Star*'s Milt Dunnell explained, "Hockey's smouldering volcano, Le Rocket Richard, erupted again last night, showering fire, ash and expletives all over the Gardens."

The trouble started when Leaf utility forward Bob Bailey, just up from Pittsburgh, nearly pasted Richard to the end boards. Richard pursued Bailey for fifty feet, crashed into him at top speed and high-sticked him in the face. Both went down. Bailey landed on top and began pummelling Richard. The linesmen pulled them apart. Richard rose, eyes blazing, and twice tried to attack Bailey with a stick. The officials attempted to restrain him, but Richard pushed them away, picked up a glove and slapped one of them across the face with it.

Five minutes after the initial hit, the linesmen managed to escort Richard off the ice. Referee Red Storey handed him a five-minute major and two ten-minute misconducts. League president Clarence Campbell subsequently fined him $250, which ran his career fine total to about $2,000.

His fervent followers quickly forgot the Bailey incident. For one thing, the Canadiens were having a great season. After years of rebuilding and adding talent, they finally appeared capable of displacing mighty Detroit atop the NHL and claiming their first league championship since 1947. And Richard was in the running for his first scoring title—battling point for point with teammates Jean Béliveau and Bernie Geoffrion—until the second-last weekend of the season.

The Canadiens played the Bruins at home on Saturday night and then travelled to Boston for a Sunday night game. Richard came out of the first game with a sore back, thanks to a stiff cross-check that laid him across the back of one of the nets. The Montreal *Herald*'s Vince Lunny asked him about the incident in the hotel lobby the following afternoon.

"How do you feel, Rocket?" he inquired.

"I had a bad night coming from Montreal," Richard replied. "Couldn't sleep at all."

"Your back?" Lunny asked.

"Yes," Richard said. "I had an ice pack on it all night. Didn't sleep a wink. I'm really beat."

The game that night was hard and chippy, with plenty of high-sticking and slashing. The Canadiens, who were just two points ahead of Detroit, trailed Boston with about six minutes to play. The Bruins took a penalty and Dick Irvin pulled Jacques Plante for an extra attacker.

Richard and Hal Laycoe fought for the puck along the boards just inside the Boston blue line. Richard barged past his opponent. Laycoe clipped him on the side of the head with his stick. Referee Frank Udvari raised his arm to signal a penalty, but let the play continue because Montreal had possession of the puck. By the time Udvari blew the whistle, Richard had circled the net and was near the blue line on the opposite side of the rink.

He felt his head. Blood seeped from a wound. Abruptly, he charged at Laycoe. The Bruin defenceman was waiting, with his fists up. Richard retaliated with what Lunny described as "a slaughterhouse stick swing" that struck Laycoe across the back and side of his face.

Linesmen seized the two players, but Richard broke free. He grabbed another stick and hit Laycoe twice with one-handed swings. Cliff Thompson, one of the officials, restrained Richard a second time. Again, he got loose, picked up a stick and whacked his opponent across the back.

Thompson wrestled Richard to the ice, but a teammate intervened. Richard sprang to his feet and, as Thompson rose, he punched the linesman twice in the face. His rage finally expended, Richard allowed the Montreal trainer to escort him from the ice. "The left side of his face looked like a smashed tomato," Lunny wrote. "As Richard skated the length of the ice, the rafters echoed with boos like thunder in a summer sky."

When the game ended, two officers from the Boston police department appeared outside the Canadiens' dressing room to arrest Richard on a charge of assault and battery by means of a dangerous weapon—a hockey

A critical moment during a game at the Westmount Arena on January, 14, 1911 between the Montreal Canadiens and the Renfrew Millionaires, as seen by an artist for the newspaper *La Patrie*. The Canadiens, in dark sweaters, defeated Renfrew four to one.

Canadiens goaltender and Chicoutimi businessman Georges Vezina, from a 1923–24 season booklet called *The Hockey Hour*. As cartoonist G.D. Lawrence's caption hints, Vezina was a quiet man.

GEORGES
VEZINA
HUMAN STONEWALL & SPHINX.

Aurel Joliat—a small man—as depicted in *La Presse*. The paper's artist attended a playoff game on March 8, 1924 between the Canadiens and the Ottawa Senators, and witnessed the jockey-capped Joliat executing one of his vertiginous moves.

Post-war, pre-season—and a boom time for speculation. John Collins's cartoon, from the *Gazette*, October 27, 1945, captures the mood of countless conversations between fans.

Canadiens General Manager Frank Selke, left, hams it up with Maurice (The Rocket) Richard, circa 1950. The star player is affixing his signature to a new contract.

Maurice Richard, left, and Hector (Toe) Blake were part of one of the most productive lines in NHL history.

Montreal natives Maurice Richard, born 1921, and his brother Henri (The Pocket Rocket), below, born 1936, had overlapping careers spanning 33 years.

The brothers played 2,547 games for the Canadiens and scored 1,033 goals. Banners bearing their numbers, 9 and 16, now hang from the rafters of the Bell Centre.

Goaltender Jacques Plante, seen here with Jean-Guy Talbot, 17, and Ton Johnson, wearing the A, was famous for leaving the net to chase loose pucks. During his junior days, Quebec fans nicknamed him The Rover.

Ab McDonald, Ralph Backstrom and Bernie Geoffrion celebrate the victory on April 16, 1959 that left the Canadiens one win away from their fifth straight Stanley Cup. Montreal fans took a dislike to McDonald and booed him so relentlessly that the Canadiens traded him to Chicago prior to the 1960–61 season.

Jean Béliveau's name appears on the Stanley Cup a record seventeen times, ten as a player and seven as an executive. Here he lifts his first Cup as captain on May 1, 1965, after the Canadiens beat the Chicago Blackhawks in the seventh game of the final. It was also a first for defenceman Terry Harper (left) and goalie Gump Worsley (right).

Yvan Cournoyer, pictured left, and Guy Lafleur, below, both played right wing and both were exceptionally fast. They helped maintain a Canadiens tradition, dating from the franchise's earliest days, of building speed and offence. Jack Laviolette and Didier Pitre, the first two players the Canadiens signed, were among fastest of their era.

Left: Serge Savard and Larry Robinson anchored a great Canadiens defence (along with Guy Lapointe) in the 1970s.

Ken Dryden pokechecks a Leafs forward as Serge Savard gives pursuit. In his first three seasons, Dryden won the Conn Smythe Trophy, the Calder Trophy, the Vezina Trophy and two Stanley Cups.

Les Canadiens sont…ummm…là

Cartoonist Aislin—Terry Mosher—of the *Gazette* summarizes the state of the Canadiens in the late 1990s, the darkest years in the team's history, next to the Great Depression of the 1930s.

For four decades, from the early 1940s to the early 1980s, fans expected the Canadiens to challenge for first place every year and make a run at the Stanley Cup. In the early years of the new century, as Aislin observes, fans were happy just to make the playoffs.

WE'RE #8!!!

KOIVU, KOVALEV, KOSTITSYN (1), KOSTITSYN (2), KOSTOPOULOS + KOMISAREK—IS IT TIME FOR AN UPDATED LOGO FOR LES CANADIENS?

Bob Gainey's Montreal Canadiens have a decidedly international flavour. Of the seven players cited by Aislin, only Tom Kostopolous, from Mississauga, Ont., is Canadian.

stick. Irvin barred the door, and a heated argument took place. The officers agreed to leave only after Bruins president Walter Brown and general manager Lynn Patrick assured them the league would handle the issue.

Campbell was in New York on league business and read about the incident Monday morning in the *New York Times*. He immediately called the game officials for a verbal report and scheduled a hearing for 10 a.m., Wednesday, March 16, at the NHL office on the sixth floor of the Sun Life building in downtown Montreal.

Richard arrived with Irvin and Reardon, the Canadiens' assistant manager, and walked past forty or more journalists—newspaper and radio reporters and television cameramen—who had taken over an outer office. The hearing lasted three and a half hours. The participants—Laycoe, Patrick, the game officials, referee-in-chief Carl Voss, and the Canadiens delegation—sat around a small table in Campbell's office. Afterward, the president reviewed his notes and began writing his decision. At 4 p.m. he addressed the newsmen.

"An incident occurred less than three months ago in which the pattern of conduct of Richard was almost identical," Campbell told the gathering. "Consequently, the time for leniency or probation is past. Whether this type of conduct is the product of temperamental instability or wilful defiance doesn't matter. It's a type of conduct that cannot be tolerated." Then, he delivered the verdict: "Richard is suspended from playing in the remaining league and playoff games."

The radio stations broadcast the ruling immediately. Irvin and Reardon were sitting around their offices at the Forum with Elmer Ferguson and Elmer Lach when the news hit. Richard arrived around 4:30 p.m.

"Is the ruling out?" he asked.

Irvin said: "Be prepared for a shock, Rocket. You're out for the season, including the Stanley Cup playoffs."

"You're kidding," Richard said. "Now tell me the truth."

"Sorry," Irvin replied. "That's the way it is, Rocket. No kidding."

The decision hit the city like a bomb. A French-speaking employee in the *Gazette* composing broke down and cried upon hearing the news. A bus driver was so distracted that he drove through a level railway crossing and nearly got hit by an oncoming train. Montrealers flooded the NHL office with phone calls. One said, "Tell Campbell I'm an undertaker and he'll be needing me in a few days." Another warned, "I'm no crank, but I'm going to blow your place up."

The French radio station CKAC invited the public to call, but the lines were quickly jammed. The next day's papers added their voices to the uproar. They all denounced Campbell's decision, none more vociferously than Jacques Beauchamp in *Montreal-Matin,* who described it as "simply revolting" and a "screaming injustice." He labelled one part of the ruling as "a flagrant lie" and another as "absolutely false." Mayor Drapeau didn't help matters when he said, "It would not be necessary to give too many such decisions to kill hockey in Montreal."

The Canadiens had a crucial game on March 17 against Detroit. Crowds of angry young men protested outside the Forum all day. Some carried signs bearing images of pigs and Campbell's name written beneath. Sensing trouble, radio station CKVL set up a mobile unit in a service station across the street and began broadcasting live late in the afternoon. At game time—8:30 p.m.—the Forum box office announced that the seats were all sold. Some six hundred demonstrators began chanting: "We don't want seats. We want Campbell."

The Canadiens played poorly from the start. They gave up two early goals. Midway through the first period, Campbell arrived with his secretary, Phyllis King, and took his usual seat at the south end of the rink, near one of the nets. The crowd forgot the game and began to roar: "Shoo Campbell. Shoo Campbell. *Va-t'en. Va-t'en"*—go away, go away. Fans seated above him hurled toe rubbers, programs and worse—tomatoes, eggs, vegetables and a pickled pig's foot.

Detroit scored twice more in the first to make the score four–one and with each goal another deluge came pouring down. Richard, seated inconspicuously behind the goal judge at the same end of the rink, turned to team physiotherapist Bill Head and said, "This is a disgrace."

It got worse. After the first period, Campbell remained in his seat, as did the fans around him. A young man approached and crushed two large tomatoes against Campbell's chest. Another talked his way past an usher, approached the NHL president and extended his hand. Campbell returned the offer and the man slapped him twice across the face. A crowd of angry young men gathered above and began to work its way down the stairs toward him. There were plenty of police on duty—nearly thirty inside the building and fifty outside—but none to protect Campbell. They were pre-occupied with the demonstrators on the street.

Campbell was nearly surrounded when an explosion occurred about twenty-five feet away. Someone had hurled a smoke bomb that landed near the ice surface. A thick plume of smoke rose toward the rafters. Everyone forgot Campbell. People coughed, their eyes filling with tears. They headed for the exits, and the Forum organist, in a loft high above the ice, played "My Heart Cries for You."

The police had maintained control of the street demonstration until the fans poured out of the Forum. Then pandemonium occurred. Young men began hurling bottles and chunks of ice at the windows. They tore a side door off its hinges. They tossed pieces of brick and concrete from a nearby construction site. They attacked businesses in and around the Forum. At 11 p.m., the mob outside the building still numbered about ten thousand. By 1 a.m., it had dwindled.

Forty police officers formed a line across Ste-Catherine Street and began pushing the crowd east, thinking everyone would disperse and go home. The move backfired. Youthful rowdies began breaking store windows and grabbing merchandise. They smashed windows on streetcars. They tore down signs. They marched fifteen blocks east on Ste-Catherine and looted fifty stores. The rampage lasted two hours.

"By 3 a.m.," Sidney Katz later wrote in *Maclean's*, "the last rock had been hurled, the last window had been smashed, the last blood-curdling shriek of 'Kill Campbell' had been uttered. The fury of the mob had spent itself."

The Canadiens were forced to forfeit the game to Detroit. Three nights later, they fell to the Wings again and finished two points behind their arch-rival. Richard lost the scoring title, by a single point, to Geoffrion. The team was defeated by Detroit in a seven-game Stanley Cup final.

There were other repercussions. Some observers saw the Richard suspension and riot as the first tremors in the upheaval that would be called the Quiet Revolution. Four days later, André Laurendeau wrote an article in *Le Devoir* that appeared under the headline, "They have killed my brother Richard."

"French-Canadian nationalism appears to have taken refuge in hockey," he wrote. "The crowds that vented their anger last Thursday night were not motivated solely by the passions of sport or an injustice committed against an idol. It was a frustrated people who protested against their fate. Their fate, in this instance, was called Mr. Campbell and he was the incarnation of all the adversaries, real or imagined, of this small people.

"Among those who were enraged at the decision of Mr. Campbell, there were certainly anglophones. But for this small people of French Canada, Maurice Richard is a sort of revenge. He is really the first of his order, which he proved again this season. A little of the astonishing adoration that surrounded [Sir Wilfrid] Laurier is concentrated in him.

"Then Campbell suddenly appears to stop his momentum. He deprived French-Canadians of Maurice Richard. He broke the momentum of Maurice Richard, who was going to establish more clearly his superiority. And this one speaks English. This one who decided against the hero.

"Well, he is going to see. We are suddenly tired of always having masters, of having for a long time been beaten down. Mr. Campbell is going to see. One does not have every day weak sorts between the hands; one cannot every day wring someone's neck without bad luck.

"The sentiments that animated the crowd Thursday evening, were assuredly confused. But is it deceiving oneself too much to see old sentiments resurfacing in a new and vibrant way, those to which [Honoré] Mercier appealed in old times when he travelled the province crying, 'They have killed my brother Riel.'

"Without doubt, the death today is symbolic. . . . But this brief flare-up betrays what lies behind the apparent indifference and long passivity of the French-Canadians."

1955–1964
A DYNASTY COMES AND GOES

FLORIDA IS WHERE THEY WENT TO HEAL THE WOUNDS—physical and emotional—of a long, roller-coaster season that was equal parts triumph, tumult and heartache. They left in mid-April right after losing the Stanley Cup final—Maurice Richard, Bernie Geoffrion, Doug Harvey, Butch Bouchard and Ken Mosdell and their wives—and they drove from Montreal to Miami, from slush and mud to sun and sand, and there they swam in the ocean, posed for photos on the beach, played shuffleboard, went deep-sea fishing and marvelled at Boom Boom's ability to devour a king-sized dessert, and sometimes two, at dinner every night. They returned tanned and refreshed in early May to learn that Dick Irvin was on his way out.

For twenty-five seasons, he had been one of the best coaches in pro hockey, an innovator. He had perfected the use of the short shift and the regular line change, was one of the first to use a fourth line, to pull his goalie for an extra attacker, to put someone up in the press box to keep detailed statistics and to assess his players' fitness at the start of training camp.

But Selke had concluded that his old friend had mishandled the team. The Canadiens were on the threshhold of greatness. They were young and fast and had so much flair and finesse that the sportswriter Andy

O'Brien invented a term to describe their style of play. He called it "firewagon hockey."

Selke knew this group could outskate anyone, Detroit included, and watched with dismay as Irvin pushed the players to pound the Wings into submission. He was convinced that his coach had contributed to the Rocket's periodic eruptions, that Irvin had kept his high-strung superstar emotionally riled and ready to snap at the slightest provocation.

It pained him deeply, but Selke decided Irvin had to go. He offered him a job for life with the Canadiens. Irvin turned it down. He moved on to Chicago, where his coaching career had begun, to take over the Black Hawks.

On the morning of June 8, 1955, the Canadiens announced his successor. Newspaper and radio reporters, photographers and TV cameramen packed the directors' room at the south end of the Forum. Shortly after 10 a.m., Selke walked in and said, "Gentlemen, here is our new coach," and Toe Blake appeared. They seated themselves at a table. Selke produced a contract, Blake signed it, and at that, bedlam ensued. As one journalist noted, "Flash bulbs popped and movie cameras began to grind while reporters dashed for phones to give their offices the green light to run pictures and stories already in type or on the wire."

Blake needed no introduction. He had been captain of the Canadiens through the lean years of the late thirties. He had been the cornerstone of the great team that Irvin and Tommy Gorman built in the early forties. He had continued to serve the organization after breaking his leg in January 1948. Selke sent him to Houston, with cast and crutches, to take over as coach of the Canadiens' affiliate in the United States Hockey League, and he led the team to the league championship. That fall, Blake started the season in Buffalo, playing eighteen games in a Bisons jersey. He became coach of the team, but couldn't get along with the general manager, Art Chapman, a meddler who tried to tell him how to run things. A rift developed between Selke and Blake. Selke expected the coach to stick it out in Buffalo. Blake, meanwhile, felt that Selke should get rid of Chapman. He quit in mid-January 1949, returned to Montreal embittered, and severed his ties with the Canadiens.

Blake was not unemployed long. He landed in Valleyfield, a small town on the south shore, west of Montreal, coaching the Braves of the Quebec senior league, and quickly produced a winner. His Braves won their league in 1950–51 and the Alexander Cup, awarded annually after a playoff between the champions of Canada's five semi-pro loops. Blake coached Valleyfield for five seasons, never producing another champion, but his teams were always competitive and fought hard. He was looking for his next job when the Montreal vacancy arose, but he was not an automatic choice for the position. He had done what he could to make life miserable for Selke and his colleagues, who tried to run the Quebec league for the benefit of the Canadiens. As well, there were two other serious candidates and Selke initially favoured one of them, former Canadiens defenceman Roger Leger, coach of the semi-pro Shawinigan Cataracts.

But two powerful voices advocated for Blake. The first was Maurice Richard. The second was Ken Reardon, then an assistant to Selke. Reardon held discussions with Blake to heal the breach between him and the Canadiens. When Blake and Selke met, they quickly put aside their differences and settled on a one-year contract.

"Everything happened so fast," Blake told Elmer Ferguson afterward, "that I haven't even begun to plan, except vaguely."

The new coach had inherited an extraordinarily talented group of players. In goal, he had Jacques Plante. On defence, he had two superb pairings: Doug Harvey and Dollard St-Laurent, and Tom Johnson and team captain Butch Bouchard. Up front, he enjoyed a potent combination of goal scorers (Richard, Jean Béliveau and Boom Boom Geoffrion). He had tough and tenacious wingers (Dickie Moore and Bert Olmstead) and smothering defensive forwards (Ken Mosdell and Floyd Curry). These players got along extremely well. On the road, they ate meals together and went out as a group after games. At home, they socialized with each other.

Blake's first challenge was to prevent Richard's occasional violent outbursts. That summer, he and Selke met with the Rocket. "You don't have anything to prove either to the players, the fans or us," Selke told Richard. "You carried the club during the lean years and now it's time for the younger players to help out, especially when it gets rough out there. Forget about the past. It's the future—and you—we're concerned about. Your heart is as young as ever, but you're now thirty-four years old. Remember that. We don't want you fighting a world of twenty-four-year-old huskies."

Blake's second challenge was to enrich his core group of players, and he had his pick of highly skilled young skaters at training camp that fall. Prospects from Montreal affiliates in Shawinigan, Cincinnati, Fort William, Victoria and elsewhere skated alongside the veterans in two-a-day scrimmages at the Verdun Auditorium. In the first four days, they scored 117 goals, and Blake later recalled: "I couldn't help but be amazed. The puck was flying around with such speed I thought I was in a shooting gallery."

The Canadiens signed three rookies that fall: Jean-Guy Talbot, who filled a role as the fifth defenceman; right winger Claude Provost, a high-speed checker who fit nicely with Curry and Mosdell; and Henri Richard, the Rocket's nineteen-year-old brother, who was still eligible to play another year of junior. Henri was small—five foot eight and 155 pounds. But he was fast, and when he had the puck he was magic.

In an interview with the author, Frank Selke Jr., who was the team's English-language public relations director, recalled a lunchtime conversation about Richard. His father had been working at the Forum for the morning. Reardon and Sam Pollock, the director of player personnel, ran the scrimmages in Verdun and reported back to the general manager at noon hour.

Reardon said, "You know, Mr. Selke, we've got to get that Henri Richard off the list."

"Why?" Selke asked.

"Well, he's spoiling the practices," Reardon replied.

"What do you mean he's spoiling the practices?"

"He's got the puck all the time. The pros can't get it away from him."

"Wait a minute—the pros can't get the puck away from him? He's nineteen and you want to get him out of the practices?"

"Yeah."

"I think I should have a look at him," Selke said.

The general manager gave Richard a three-game trial once the season started and signed him October 13. Two nights later, the rookie scored his first goal, at home, and according to one press box observer, "He heard a rafter-rattling ovation greet him as he retrieved the puck."

The younger Richard made a strong team even stronger. Blake played him with the Rocket and Dickie Moore, which became a high-scoring line. Béliveau, Geoffrion and Olmstead formed a second powerful offensive unit. The Canadiens opened with four wins and a tie. After they lost in Boston on October 21, Montreal's sportswriters learned something about Blake: he hated to lose. While his players changed, he brooded in the corridor outside the dressing room.

"You can't win them all," one writer ventured.

"Why not?" snapped Blake.

The Canadiens enjoyed a ten-game undefeated streak in November and won eight in a row in December. They faltered only once that season, losing four of five over a two-week period in January. They clinched first on February 25, three weeks before the end of the season, and finished with 100 points, twenty-four ahead of second-place Detroit.

Béliveau won the scoring championship. Plante took the Vézina. Harvey was awarded the James Norris Trophy for a second straight season. The Canadiens swept aside the Rangers in five games and eliminated the Red Wings in five as well.

During the final, Blake told a journalist: "I've been in this league since 1934, but I've never known a hockey club as intensely serious as this Canadiens team. All season long, they've set their goal as the Stanley Cup. When we clinched the league championship, there wasn't a ripple of excitement. They all said: 'So what. The big one for us is the Stanley Cup.'"

Montrealers were thirsting for victory as well. Mayor Jean Drapeau organized a Stanley Cup parade, the first in the city since the Wanderers won the Cup in 1907. The celebratory march was held on a chilly Saturday in late April, four days after the final game. There were bands, floats and thirty-five convertibles for players and team officials. Those with players aboard had placards taped to the side bearing the individual's name and number.

The parade began near the Forum shortly after 9 a.m. It travelled through eleven districts, covering thirty miles. One newspaper said 250,000 people, a quarter of the city's population, turned out. Another paper put the estimate at 500,000. Crowds repeatedly besieged the cars, bringing the whole thing to a halt. It was supposed to take four hours, but lasted six and a half, and by the time it was over the placards had been ripped from the cars, Tom Johnson's overcoat had been swiped, and grasping fans had torn the buttons off the Rocket's jacket.

Montreal's special teams completely outplayed the opposition during that 1955–56 season. The Canadiens' two top defensive players, Floyd Curry, a veteran centre, and Donnie Marshall, a second-year centre, surrendered just twelve goals in 300 penalty kills. And the power play could not be stopped. The top unit had Doug Harvey on left point, Boom Boom Geoffrion on the right and Jean Béliveau, Maurice Richard and Bert Olmstead up front. Olmstead was the digger, Béliveau the playmaker and Harvey the quarterback who could pass with extraordinary accuracy to the left, the slot or to the other side, where two ravenous goal scorers, Richard and Geoffrion, were always waiting to strike. League rules stipulated that a player serve an entire two-minute penalty regardless of how many goals were scored, and these five frequently put a game out of reach during a single power play. They so disrupted the competitive balance that league president Clarence Campbell mused publicly at mid-season about amending the rule.

Two other executives, Boston general manager Lynn Patrick and his brother Muzz, the GM in New York, suggested the same to Frank Selke while attending a Stanley Cup final game in Montreal. Selke blew up.

"You might outvote me on that one," he said. "But you'll never convince me of its justice. In all the years of Detroit's dominance and their almighty power play, there was no suggestion of such a change. Now Canadiens have finally built one and you want to introduce a rule to weaken it. Go get a power play of your own."

Selke was outvoted, and henceforth a penalized player returned to the ice after the opposition scored. It hardly mattered, though. Montreal's general manager had built a team capable of dominating every aspect of the game. The Canadiens won the league championship in four of five seasons between 1955 and 1960 and were crowned Stanley Cup champs in each of those years. They compiled a playoff record of forty wins against nine losses and never fell behind in a series.

Bobby Hull was an emerging star with the Chicago Black Hawks at the time. "They were an awesome group," Hull told the author. "They just kept coming at you. Five after five, right down to their so-called third and fourth lines. They'd come back in their own end and they wouldn't stop. They'd turn, and that Harvey would just thread the puck up to them. He was fantastic. Going into Montreal, if we could keep the score under double figures we considered ourselves lucky. We were chasing red shirts all night."

The danger for a team like the Canadiens was that people would begin to believe that success was inevitable—and some had come to that conclusion in the fall of 1956. Someone even boasted that Montreal would rule hockey for a decade. "It's not a good thing," Selke fretted during training camp. "Mind you, it's not so much the players; it's everybody associated with the organization. Even I've been quoted as saying that we'd finish first and win the Stanley Cup easily. But I say this: nobody has the right to delegate teams to first or second or third or anywhere else. Yet I hear our club officials telling everybody that we can't lose. In time the players will start believing that nonsense. It's dangerous and I wish it would stop."

The team faltered in 1956–57, largely owing to injuries. Plante, Geoffrion, Béliveau, Olmstead and the Richard brothers all missed action. Detroit clinched first place at the Forum on March 17, and Jack Adams remarked that the Canadiens' reign had been "the shortest ten years of my life."

The Canadiens finished second, but they were healthy, and unstoppable, during the playoffs. They beat the Rangers in five games, and Maurice Richard scored the overtime goal that eliminated New York. Three nights later, Montreal routed Boston five–one in the opening game of the Stanley Cup final, and Richard put four pucks past Bruin goalie Don Simmons. Afterward, the rattled netminder said, "It's a strange sensation to see Richard coming in with his eyes popping like headlights."

The Bruins managed to steal one from the Canadiens. They forced a fifth game in Montreal, only to be trounced five–one. A good part of the credit for Montreal's second straight Cup went to the third line. Blake had his choice of players—Curry, Marshall and Provost, as well as rookies Phil Goyette and André Pronovost. They shut down Boston's offence, protected leads late in the third period and contributed timely goals. More importantly, they gave the Canadiens depth to go along with extraordinary talent.

Maurice Richard celebrated his thirty-sixth birthday in August 1957, making him the oldest player in the league, and a few weeks later he began another campaign. He had scored 493 regular-season goals. From opening night, the fans and their surrogates in the press box began a countdown to number five hundred.

Richard reached that milestone on October 19. The Canadiens played the Black Hawks that night before a capacity crowd of 14,405. Near the sixteen-minute mark of the first period, Dickie Moore carried the puck into the Chicago end. He was forced to the corner, but passed to Jean Béliveau near the side of the Hawk goal. Béliveau spotted Richard cruising into the slot, twenty-five feet out, and fed him the puck. Glenn Hall, the Chicago goalie, anticipated a shot from Béliveau and had no chance when the Rocket unloaded.

At the flash of the red light, fans sprang to their feet and roared. The Forum organist played a high-volume rendition of "Il a gagné ses epaulettes" (He's earned his stripes). The announcer waited two minutes before the din subsided and then proclaimed, "Canadiens goal scored by Mr. Hockey himself, Maurice Richard." That triggered another ovation. All told, the game was delayed ten minutes.

Richard was playing that fall like a man ten years younger. By mid-November, he had accumulated twenty-three points and was tied with brother Henri for the scoring leadership. But his hopes of winning the title were dashed by a fluke injury November 13 in Toronto. During a pile-up in front of the Leaf net, a Toronto player accidentally stepped on Richard's right foot and nearly severed his Achilles tendon.

The wound required fifteen stitches, and doctors encased the foot in a cast to provide stability. Richard missed three months and was out till February 15, 1958. By then, the Canadiens were closing in on another league championship. Linemate Moore was leading the scoring race and brother Henri was a close second.

Moore had also suffered an unusual injury that season. He got the worst of a scuffle with Detroit defenceman Marcel Pronovost during a game in early February and damaged his left wrist. He had it X-rayed. Doctors saw no signs of a fracture, but the arm remained tender and the injury did not heal. A second X-ray at the end of February revealed that he had broken a small bone between the wrist and the hand. His doctor recommended surgery, but Moore refused. An operation would have cost him the scoring title.

Instead, the physician wrapped the injured limb in plaster from the palm of the hand to the elbow. The cast severely impaired Moore's shooting ability, but he could still score on deflections, rebounds and tip-ins. He finished first in scoring with eighty-four points, four better than Henri Richard. He led the league in goals (thirty-two) and game-winners (eight) and played superb defensive hockey, allowing wingers opposite him just three goals all season.

When the Canadiens arrived home from their final game of the season, several hundred admirers from Moore's old Montreal neighbourhood, Park Extension, were at the station to greet him. They held up signs reading "Our Hero Dickie Moore" and "Park X Is Proud of Dickie" and draped a large floral horseshoe around his neck. Then he and wife Joan rode in a thirty-car motorcade to a reception and dinner organized by childhood friends and acquaintances.

Moore wore the cast during the playoffs and accumulated eleven points, but the post-season belonged to Maurice Richard. Montreal swept Detroit in the semifinal. The Rocket scored seven times and left his fans in a swoon. "It is very easy to choose the star of the Canadiens–Detroit series," Roger Meloche wrote in *La Patrie*. "It is always the same: the unique, the inimitable Maurice Richard. It seems the same story repeats itself, but becomes more fantastic each year because the Rocket should have disappeared from the game long ago. Imagine, at thirty-six, he still has the vitality to score seven goals in four games."

Richard contributed another four in the final against Boston, including the goal that turned the series Montreal's way. The teams split the first four games. For the fifth, the Forum was packed and the crowd noisy from start to finish.

One writer described the contest as "Stanley Cup hockey at its fiercest." Another said it was "a bitterly fought, high-speed, hard-shooting battle."

The score was tied two–two at the end of regulation time, and the Rocket hadn't seemed himself. "He had been a weary, exhausted figure most of the night," Red Fisher wrote in the *Montreal Star*. "Passes had eluded him and he missed others. But seventeen times in years past, he had scored over-time goals and now the clock passed the five-minute mark and his line tumbled over the boards. Richard moved slowly along the left wing, strange territory for him, and suddenly the puck was at his feet. He cut sharply, fired, and the puck was a blur over the leg of goalie Simmons. It was Richard's 80th playoff goal."

Three nights later, the Canadiens finished off the Bruins in Boston. They had become the second team in the NHL's forty-year history to win three straight Stanley Cups, and the players were jubilant. "They leapt over the boards, hugging and backslapping and pounding each other," Fisher wrote. "Coach Toe Blake was mobbed and jostled and pushed by the players and nearly a hundred giddy, hysterical Montrealers who swept onto the Boston ice in a mass display of devotion."

Maurice Richard suffered another serious injury in 1958–59, a broken ankle that kept him out of action from mid-January till the Stanley Cup final in April, but even without the Rocket the Canadiens rolled over their opponents like a relentless, marauding army. They finished first, eighteen points ahead of the Bruins. Dickie Moore, with an NHL-record ninety-six points, won the scoring championship again, Jacques Plante captured the Vézina Trophy, Tom Johnson took the Norris, and Ralph Backstrom was named rookie of the year.

The Canadiens met the Leafs in the final, and prior to the opening game Toronto coach and general manager Punch Imlach boasted: "I couldn't care less if Richard's back. I hope they have Béliveau too. I hope they have all their big guns. But it won't be enough. We're going to beat them in six games." That proved to be a silly bit of braggadocio. The Canadiens demolished the Leafs in five games and became the first team to win four consecutive Cups.

They were the team to beat again in 1959–60, and demonstrated as much in the annual all-star game, played Saturday, October 3 in Montreal. The Canadiens faced a collection of the league's top talent, coached by Imlach, who had learned nothing of the perils of boastfulness. "We're going to win," he bellowed at a press conference. "I've got the best players going for me and I didn't come down here for a social trip."

The league's best were no match for the Canadiens. Montreal's shooters pumped six goals past Terry Sawchuk while Jacques Plante held the all-stars to one goal. Afterward, Imlach's assistant King Clancy noted: "That Plante's all by himself as a goalkeeper. I've heard all the stuff about him having a great team in front of him, but he's one of the reasons the team is great. The Canadiens are a goal-hungry bunch and they're up there trying to score. They often leave Plante alone, but he makes saves the others don't."

Plante had been the league's premier netminder for four seasons, but he was beginning to suffer from the same malady that had afflicted his predecessors Bill Durnan and Gerry McNeil. Bad nerves, brought on by too many serious facial injuries, had ended their careers prematurely, and Plante had been struck often by errant pucks, sticks and skate blades. His nose had been broken four times. He had fractured both cheekbones and his jaw. He had taken more than two hundred stitches to his face.

Some of the worst injuries occurred during the Canadiens' high-speed practices. In 1954, left winger Bert Olmstead fired a shot that struck Plante in the cheek, broke a bone and put him out for five weeks. The following year, Butch Bouchard deflected a shot from Don Marshall that broke Plante's nose.

Eventually, Plante began to wear a plastic mask at practice, one sent anonymously by a fan. It provided protection, but was heavy and cumbersome, and come game time it remained in the dressing room. The hockey world wasn't ready for masked goaltenders, despite the inherent dangers of playing the position.

By the fall of 1959, Plante had a mask that was suitable for actual competition. Light, unbreakable and a snug fit, it was the work of another fan, a Montrealer named Bill Burchmore, who had been involved in hockey as a player and coach all his life. Burchmore was the director of sales and promotion at Fibreglas Canada and had seen Plante take a puck in the face during the 1958 playoffs. That summer, he wrote to the goaltender and offered to design a fibreglass mask.

Plante waited a year before taking up Burchmore's offer. During the summer of 1959, he allowed technicians at Montreal General Hospital, under the supervision of team doctor Ian Milne, to make a mould of his face. Burchmore used the plaster likeness to produce a fibreglass mask coated in polyester resin and baked in an oven. It was durable enough to withstand the rigours of NHL competition, where shooters like Bobby Hull were firing hundred-mile-an-hour slap shots, and Plante wore it throughout training camp.

But Toe Blake and others discouraged him from using the mask in games. Some believed it would impede his vision no matter how snugly it fit. Others thought that a little fear kept a goaltender sharp and quickened his reflexes. Blake offered another line of reasoning: "If you start the season wearing a mask and you let in a few shots that looked easy to stop, the fans are going to hassle you and blame the mask."

Playing without the mask, Plante was as good as ever in the first month of the season and suffered only one minor injury: a cut to the chin that took five stitiches. On November 1, a Sunday, the Canadiens played the Rangers in New York. Madison Square Garden was filled to capacity. Three and a half minutes in, Andy Bathgate fired a hard backhand from close range. The puck smashed into Plante's face, opening an ugly gash between the upper lip and the nostril on the left side of his face. He collapsed, and blood spewed to the ice.

Plante rose slowly. He was dazed and unsteady. He held a towel to his face and leaned on teammates Maurice Richard and Dickie Moore as he left the ice. Blake crossed the playing surface and followed his players to the first-aid clinic. He had to decide, within a twenty-minute limit set by league rules, whether Plante could continue or he would have to find a substitute.

Plante lay on a medical table while a doctor worked on him. He looked at his coach and declared that he was going back in—with the mask.

"We'll see," said Blake, stalling for time. "We'll see."

He left to look for Muzz Patrick, the Rangers' general manager. There were two goaltenders in the building, Patrick said. One was Arnie Knox, a thirty-three-year-old usher who used to play in a New York men's league and occasionally practised with the Rangers. The other was a junior, Joe Shaeffer, who hadn't skated yet that season.

Blake was in a bind. The Canadiens couldn't win with either of these men. He returned to the clinic. By this time, the doctor had applied seven stitches and covered the wound with bandages. Plante was back on his feet and he was adamant: he was going to play, but his face would be protected. He returned to the ice in his blood-stained sweater. The crowd welcomed him with warm applause and the organist played "For He's a Jolly Good Fellow." Plante skated to the other side and went to the dressing room. When he came back, he was wearing the mask.

He was unbeatable most of the night. Moore opened the scoring late in the first period. André Pronovost and Bernie Geoffrion added to the Canadiens' lead. Plante shut out the Rangers till midway through the third, when Camille Henry tapped in a rebound.

After the game, a pack of New York reporters surrounded Plante. "The injury was extremely painful," he told them. "It even cut my nostril. I think I have proven once and for all that I can see clearly with my mask. I am ready to wear it regularly, but will make a decision in Montreal. All that matters now is to take care of my injury."

Plante's performance had convinced one of the skeptics. "He proved to me this evening that his mask does not impede his work in the slightest," Blake said. "He was sensational and I have no objection if he wants to wear the mask all the time."

Others were less receptive. Ranger general manager Patrick believed that masks, as well as helmets, would rob players of their individuality. "We start out with goalies wearing masks," he argued. "Every club has a defenceman or two who goes down to smother shots. Soon they'll want masks. All the forwards will wear helmets. Players will become faceless, headless robots all of whom look alike."

Patrick's own goaltender, Lorne Worsley, also rejected the mask. "Why all of a sudden, after hockey has been played for seventy years, do they decide we should wear masks?" Worsley wondered. "Plante may make a pot full of money on that idea. He can have it. I don't want the thing."

Plante showed the critics. He played with greater confidence and without fear, and for the next month the Canadiens were invincible. They won nine and tied one before losing to the Leafs on December 2. Plante's stand also convinced other goaltenders to follow his lead. Boston's Don Simmons announced that he would begin wearing the mask, and Terry Sawchuk disclosed that he was using one in practice.

Nevertheless, fresh questions arose later in the season when Plante performed poorly for a stretch of several games and wound up in a tight race for the Vézina with Chicago's Glenn Hall. Blake even persuaded him to drop the mask for a game against Detroit in early March, but the Canadiens lost three–nothing.

Plante pulled out of his tailspin before the regular season ended. He won his fifth straight Vézina. The Canadiens finished first, thirteen points ahead of Toronto and twenty-three better than Chicago, whom they met in the opening round of the playoffs. They put the Hawks down in four and advanced to the final for the tenth consecutive time, once again against the Leafs.

Imlach appeared at the Forum on the day of the first game with four-leaf clovers attached to his suit, shirt and the new fedora he was wearing. That got a laugh from the media, but didn't help his cause. The Leafs couldn't take a single game from Montreal. The Canadiens won their fifth Cup in a row and a resigned Conn Smythe said, "We lost to the greatest team of all time."

In a separate interview, Frank Selke offered his view of what had made this team so powerful: "It's the greatest team because it has more great players than any one team ever possessed. Some players that we use only occasionally would be stars with other clubs. Then there's team spirit, and the strength that comes from two or more racial units on the club, each with a different approach mentally to the game. The player of English or German or Polish descent has the inborn urge to drive right in, to smash his way along. On the other hand, there's the Gallic spirit of our French-Canadian players. They like to set up plays in almost dramatic fashion by passing the puck. They're the artists of the game."

———

Training camp opened at the Forum on September 12, 1960, and before anyone set foot on the ice, Selke laid out his expectations for the upcoming season. He stood at the centre of a room, a small man surrounded by lean, muscular players—forty-two veterans and prospects, all told. "There is no valid reason," the general manager said, "why we should not win the Stanley Cup for the sixth consecutive season."

Selke's sprawling farm system had produced the usual number of promising young players, including J.C. Tremblay, Jacques Laperrière, Terry Harper, Bobby Rousseau, Jim Roberts and Gilles Tremblay, all of whom were trying out that fall and would eventually become core members of the team. For the moment, though, attention was focused on the oldest player in camp. Maurice Richard had turned thirty-nine that summer. He had played eighteen seasons, accumulated over a thousand points and held fifteen scoring records.

But age had caught up with him. He had missed eighty-nine games over the previous three seasons due to serious injuries: first, a nearly severed Achilles tendon; next, a broken ankle; then a fractured cheekbone. During the playoffs the previous spring, he had said in a post-game interview: "I've felt awful for the last three years. It's not that I'm sick, but I've been hurt so often. I just can't keep up the pace anymore. Some of the younger fellows can skate all night. I can't."

He had scored just once in eight playoff games—a meaningless goal that padded an already comfortable Montreal lead in the third match of the final. Nevertheless, he retrieved the puck from the net. The next day's sports pages were filled with speculation that Richard was about to retire, and such articles continued to appear in the Montreal press during the off-season.

The Rocket still had not declared his intentions when he arrived at training camp, but he promised a decision before the season began in the first week of October. Selke wasn't prepared to wait. He summoned Richard to a meeting after the morning scrimmage on September 15—a scrimmage in which the Rocket had scored four goals and assisted on three others.

The *Star*'s Red Fisher happened to be seated in the corridor outside Selke's second-floor office when Richard strode in, looking grim and accompanied by his agent. Half an hour later, he stormed out.

"What's happening?" Fisher asked.

"They want me to retire," Richard snapped and kept walking.

Selke had been direct and unequivocal. He told Richard he had no options. It was time to quit. He had gained weight. He wasn't as fit as he needed to be. He would be risking even more serious injury if he were to play. A poor season would tarnish his magnificent reputation. Besides, there was a job waiting as a team ambassador, at full salary for the first year, to ease the transition to retirement.

Richard begrudgingly accepted Selke's offer. A press conference was held that evening at the Queen Elizabeth Hotel. About fifty media representatives were present. Richard spoke for four minutes, first in French, then in English, and was given a standing ovation.

The Canadiens were deep enough in talent to remain the league's top team even without Richard. By the end of November, Dickie Moore had scored twenty-one goals and was in the running for a third scoring title till he was hit by injuries and a slump. Jean Béliveau took the lead after Moore fell from contention.

Then, in March, a surging Bernie Geoffrion charged past Béliveau. Geoffrion also overtook Toronto's Frank Mahovlich in the goals department. Both players were chasing Richard's record of fifty in a season. They went head to head in a Thursday night game at the Forum on March 16. Geoffrion had forty-nine goals, Mahovlich forty-eight, and their teams were fighting for first place. The contest drew the biggest crowd of the season, 15,011, and 2,500 were turned away when the last standing-room ticket was sold.

The score was tied one–one at the start of the third period. Then Montreal's offence broke loose. Billy Hicke, Henri Richard and Ralph Backstrom scored. The fans showered the ice with debris after each goal. The biggest demonstration occurred late in the game, when Geoffrion fired a fifteen-footer past Johnny Bower.

"The building vibrated with a tremendous roar," Dink Carroll of *The Gazette* wrote, "and the exultant Boomer jumped on his linemate Béliveau and both fell to the ice. Then the whole Canadiens team seemed to be on top of the Boomer."

Seated in the dressing room afterward, his face flushed with sweat and tears, Geoffrion addressed a mob of reporters, cameramen and well-wishers. "Last night my wife kept telling me to go to sleep, that she was sure I'd score against Toronto, but it didn't do much good. I was nervous out there and missed a couple of chances before getting that big goal. Gee—fifty goals— it's like a dream come true."

The following Tuesday, the Canadiens began their pursuit of a sixth Stanley Cup. They played the Chicago Black Hawks, who had finished seventeen points back in third. The Hawks had four great players—Bobby Hull, Stan Mikita, Pierre Pilote and Glenn Hall—and a solid supporting cast led by six ex-Canadiens—Murray Balfour, Dollard St-Laurent, Ed Litzenberger, Red Hay, Reggie Fleming and Ab McDonald.

The teams split the first two games at the Forum. The third, played at Chicago Stadium, proved to be the turning point. Balfour scored for Chicago in regulation time; Henri Richard replied for the Canadiens. The two sides then played forty minutes of scoreless overtime. Montreal scored twice, but referee Dalton McArthur disallowed both goals. At 12:12 of the third period of extra play, Balfour scored again. Toe Blake was livid. Montreal was shorthanded, thanks to what he viewed as a dubious tripping call against Moore. While his players headed for the dressing room, Blake charged across the ice and managed to slug McArthur before the linesman intervened.

Clarence Campbell fined Blake a record two thousand dollars, but did not suspend him, and the Canadiens coach was behind the bench for game four. Montreal outshot Chicago sixty to twenty-one and beat them five–two. That tied the series at two apiece, and the teams returned to Montreal for the fifth game. There, the big guns of the Canadiens went silent, and they lost three–nothing—an "inexplicable defeat," according to Blake.

The Hawks had gained the upper hand by outhustling the Canadiens, by checking them closely and hitting ferociously. Maurice Richard, who watched every game, said he had never witnessed such a dirty series. Geoffrion, Hicke, Ralph Backstrom, Phil Goyette and Don Marshall all went down with injuries. Geoffrion injured a knee, and team doctor Larry Hampson put on a cast and pronounced Boom Boom through for the series.

Geoffrion accompanied the team to Chicago for game six. During the overnight train trip, he and Doug Harvey borrowed a knife from a porter and retired to a women's washroom. Harvey spent ten minutes removing the cast, and the next morning Geoffrion declared himself fit to play. He took a few shifts in the first, but spent the rest of the night on the bench.

The Hawks skated to another three–nothing victory and 16,666 Chicago fans roared themselves hoarse. The players were elated, and afterward their coach, Rudy Pilous, was at a loss to explain his club's triumph. "We simply cannot believe it," he said. "We have beaten a famous team, the champions."

Blake was despondent and untalkative, but Selke spoke his mind after digesting the defeat. "I can tell you one thing," he said on the train trip back to Montreal, "the Canadiens are going to be a lot tougher next season. We have been playing nice, clean hockey a little too long. The Hawks deliberately racked up five of our best players and not one of the Canadiens put a hand on them in retaliation."

On May 1, 1961, the league announced that Harvey had won the James Norris Trophy as the NHL's top defenceman yet again—the sixth time in the eight years since it was created. A few days later, he left on a two-week goodwill tour of western Canada, and Selke made his first off-season move. He called Muzz Patrick of the New York Rangers and told him that Harvey was available. The perennial all-star was thirty-six. He had played fourteen seasons. He was both a mentor and a leader, the veteran who stayed after practice to work with the rookies and the player chosen by his teammates to succeed Maurice Richard as captain. Age had hardly slowed him, and he remained a commanding presence on the ice.

His behaviour was the problem. Harvey was different. He once attended a formal event in a tuxedo and running shoes. On another occasion, he skipped a team dinner at a golf and country club to drink with a caddy he had just met. Teammates worried about his fondness for drink, and management wondered what he would do next.

"He was always the last guy on the train, always the last guy on the bus," recalled Selke's assistant Ken Reardon. "You always had to wait for him, but maybe he was just hiding around the corner and coming at the last second. As a front office man, you didn't want him as captain."

Frank Selke Jr., the team's English-language public relations manager at the time, says his father and other senior managers had decided that Harvey had no future with the organization once he was finished playing. So, they decided to trade him while he still had some value in the market.

Selke Sr. and Patrick quickly concluded their negotiations. Harvey would go to New York as a playing coach, an idea Selke proposed in order to help the defenceman make the transition to an off-ice career. Lou Fontinato, a tough, hard-hitting blueliner of average skill, would come to Montreal.

They announced the deal while Harvey was in Vancouver. But his exit was protracted and difficult. Harvey met with Selke on May 12, a Friday, and later that day flew to New York to meet Patrick and Admiral John Bergen, chairman of the company that owned the Rangers. They offered him a two-year contract at $25,000 annually. Harvey asked for the weekend to think it over, caught a flight home and went fishing at Lake Mephrémagog in the Eastern Townships. On Monday, he informed both parties that he was staying in Montreal.

Four days later, Selke announced that he had given New York permission to resume negotiations, and Patrick flew to Montreal. The Rangers sweetened the offer. They increased the salary to $27,000 per season and added a year to the contract. Harvey still didn't want to go.

"Money isn't the big thing," he told Red Fisher. "I'm happy here. I've always lived here and I lose all this if I go to New York. I know they want me down there, and for what? Money? Living alone?"

He phoned Senator Hartland Molson, co-owner of the Canadiens, to plead his case. The senator told him Selke was responsible for all hockey decisions. At that point, Harvey had nowhere to turn. He signed with the Rangers on June 1, and Patrick told the New York media, "This is the beginning of a new era in Ranger hockey."

Harvey won the Norris again in 1961–62. He also led the Rangers to the playoffs for the first time in three seasons. The Canadiens, meanwhile, finished first for the fifth straight year. Seven players scored twenty goals or more, and the team racked up 259 goals to establish a new league record.

Jacques Plante won the Vézina—his sixth in seven seasons—and the Hart Trophy, while winger Bobby Rousseau was named rookie of the year.

But the Canadiens faltered again in the playoffs. They met Chicago in the opening round and were heavily favoured, having finished twenty-three points ahead of the Hawks. They won the first two games at home, then lost four straight. "I never thought for a minute that we would lose," Toe Blake said as the Canadiens gathered for a team photo two days after being eliminated. "The only reason I can see for our defeat is that not enough of our men played well while every one of the Hawks managed to get up for the series."

The Canadiens were in transition. The great team of the 1950s was finished, and a new one was emerging. The rebuilding would be done largely through Selke's farm system, in which Selke had an unshakable faith. "As long as hockey is played," he said in an interview, "we'll be up there because our player well will not run dry. Player development is our strength, now and in the future."

Newcomers from the minor-league affiliates filled some big holes that developed due to injuries during the 1962–63 season. Tom Johnson's year ended when he and Rousseau collided in practice. The winger went down. One skate came up and struck Johnson on the left side of his face, fracturing his cheekbone and opening a wound that took nine stitches to close. A week later, in a game against the Rangers, Fontinato crashed headfirst into the end boards. He was carried off on a stretcher, and doctors determined that he had broken his neck.

Terry Harper of the minor-pro Hull-Ottawa Canadiens replaced Johnson, while teammate Jacques Laperrière took over for Fontinato. Laperrière made an immediate impact with his big shot. "Jacques is about the first fellow we've had all season who really fires that puck from the blue line," Blake noted.

Laperrière and Harper made their NHL debuts during the tightest race for first place in seven years. And they joined a Canadiens team that had been hot and cold all winter, winning the big games while losing to weaker rivals like Boston and New York.

The Canadiens finished third, three points behind the Leafs, whom they met in the semifinal. They had won only three of fourteen games against Toronto and were no match for the hard-hitting, tight-checking Leafs, who were defending Stanley Cup champions. They lost the first two games at Maple Leaf Gardens and suffered another defeat at home. They won the fourth contest, but endured a humiliating five–nothing defeat back in Toronto.

Blake was so distraught after being eliminated that he initially barred everyone, including team officials, from the dressing room, but later admitted a reporter from the Canadian Press. The players showered and dressed in silence. Blake, always a poor loser, had never seemed so low, according to the CP man.

"Well, Toe," the journalist asked. "What about next year? What will you have to do to get back in there?"

"What these guys need is a lot of prayers and a change in attitude," Blake snapped.

Outside the room, Selke addressed the rest of the media. "Sure I'm disappointed," he said, "but I'm not taking anything away from the Leafs. They have a great club."

"Do you have any plans for next year?" someone shouted.

"I sure have," he replied with a smile and walked away.

Jacques Plante and a teammate spent the morning—a Tuesday in early June—playing a round of golf at a Montreal country club. Shortly after noon, Plante headed for downtown and the Queen Elizabeth Hotel, where general managers and player representatives from all six NHL clubs had gathered for the league's annual meeting. He had the radio on and was listening to music when the station interrupted its programming for a news bulletin.

"Ladies and gentlemen," a newsreader said, "the Montreal Canadiens have just signed the most spectacular agreement in the history of the NHL. They have traded seven players, including their star goaltender Jacques Plante, to the New York Rangers.

"The man that many experts have called the greatest goaltender in modern hockey is going to Rangers along with centre Phil Goyette and winger Don Marshall. In exchange, the Canadiens are getting goaltender Lorne 'Gump' Worsley and forwards Dave Balon, Léon Rochefort, and Len Ronson, all players from the minor leagues."

Plante pulled over. Shaken, he needed a moment to collect his thoughts. He considered going home, but decided to continue and was swarmed by reporters when he reached the Queen Elizabeth. He had always been open with the press, but this time he was tongue-tied, saying only that he was surprised, not shocked. In a separate interview that day, his wife Jacqueline told *La Presse*, "The news hit our house like a bomb."

The Canadiens had unloaded Plante because, like Harvey, his behaviour had become disruptive. He frequently blamed defencemen for goals scored against him. He told a reporter that Boom Boom Geoffrion's shot had lost its zip. He complained that the Canadiens were suffering from a lack of leadership following the departures of Maurice Richard and Doug Harvey—a dig at Jean Béliveau, who had succeeded Harvey as captain. He had missed fourteen games the previous season due to asthma attacks, illness or soft-tissue injuries—usually pulled muscles that were hard to diagnose. He also insisted on a room at the Westbury Hotel when the Canadiens played in Toronto, rather than at the Royal York, where the team stayed.

Still, he had his defenders. *Montréal-Matin* sportswriter Jerry Trudel charged that the Canadiens had long tried to suppress Plante's colourful character. "When Irvin was coach, Plante accepted everything without saying a word," Trudel wrote. "But as the years passed, and he proved himself as an extraordinary goaltender, Jacques refused to merely accept everything he was told."

But Toe Blake was fed up with Plante, and so was Frank Selke. "Jacques Plante is an extrovert who can't put his personal interests aside for the benefit of the team," Selke told a French-Canadian journalist. "In the circumstances, no matter how brilliant a goaltender he may be, it was better that he left. You can put that in your paper."

Plante's replacement was affable and even-tempered. Playing behind New York's often-lamentable defence—and without a mask—Worsley routinely faced forty-five shots a night and nearly a hundred in a pair of weekend games. "The number of shots doesn't bother me as long as I stop 'em," he once told the Montreal *Gazette*.

Appreciative Ranger fans called him Captain Courageous. Otherwise, he was Gump—a nickname he had acquired at age ten because of his resemblance to a popular comic strip character named Andy Gump, who was short, portly and wore a crew cut. Worsley stood five feet, seven inches and often carried a few extra pounds on his stocky frame. Once, though, his weight surged to 185 pounds and Ranger coach Phil Watson accused him of having "a beer belly."

"Watson doesn't know what he's talking about," Gump responded. "I never had a beer in my life. I'm strictly a whisky drinker."

Worsley was thrilled with the trade. At age thirty-four, he was coming home. He had grown up in the Montreal suburb of Pointe-St-Charles, the son of an ironworker, had played junior for the Verdun Cyclones, a Ranger affiliate, and in 1949 joined the New York Rovers of the Quebec Senior Hockey League. Worsley made stops in New Haven, Connecticut, St. Paul, Minnesota, and Saskatoon before joining the Rangers in 1952–53. He won the Calder Trophy as the NHL's best rookie, but lost his job to Johnny Bower the following season and played for Vancouver of the Western Hockey League. He returned to New York in 1954–55 and stuck for nine years.

A reporter once asked him which team gave him the most trouble. "The Rangers," Worsley replied. "Just the other night I looked up and there was the opposition coming at me—three on nothing."

Worsley's homecoming proved short-lived. In the eighth game of the 1963–64 season, he pulled a hamstring muscle. While recovering, his weight shot up to 210 pounds. Blake sent him to the Quebec Aces of the AHL to regain his form, and Worsley was stranded there till midway through the following season.

Selke reached into the farm system and replaced Worsley with Charlie Hodge, another diminutive Montrealer. Hodge stood five foot six and weighed only 150 pounds. He was thirty years old. He had played a total of fifty-nine games for the Canadiens over the previous decade, always as a substitute for the injured Jacques Plante—and he always returned to the minors after Plante had recovered.

Hodge had worn the colours of the Montreal Royals, Cincinnati Mohawks, Buffalo Bisons, Providence Reds, Seattle Americans, Rochester Americans, Shawinigan Cataracts, Hull-Ottawa Canadiens and Quebec Aces. The low point in this odyssey occurred in the spring of 1961. The Canadiens left him unprotected in the annual intra-league draft and no team would pay the twenty thousand dollars necessary to claim him. Hodge told Selke he was quitting, but the Montreal general manager put his arm around Hodge's shoulder and told him, "Plante can't go on forever."

When he finally got the call in October 1963, Hodge was in Quebec City. He anticipated another abbreviated trip to the NHL and packed only his shaving kit, his pyjamas and an extra shirt. But this time he stayed. In sixty-two games that season, he earned eight shutouts. He posted a 2.26 goals-against average and won the Vézina Trophy.

He also had a remarkable effect on morale. "Something about the little guy's all-out effort fired the team," Andy O'Brien wrote in *Weekend* magazine. "That and his relaxed, almost boyish good nature in the dressing room worked wonders."

The Canadiens had been picked in most pre-season polls to finish fourth or lower. They surprised the hockey world by landing atop the standings in March 1964. Hodge played a major role in the turnaround, but he had had plenty of help. Montreal had improved at every position: Jacques Laperrière, who won the Calder Trophy as 1963–64's rookie of the year, added a booming slap shot and playmaking ability to the defence corps. Terry Harper, a graduate of the Regina Pats and Hull-Ottawa Canadiens, brought toughness and a knack for belting opponents. Dave Balon proved to be the surprise acquisition in the Plante trade. He scored twenty-four goals, more than doubling his output the previous season. Perhaps the most important addition was John Ferguson, who contributed energy and ferocity.

Ferguson made his NHL debut October 8, 1963, at Boston Garden. He started on a line with Jean Béliveau and Boom Boom Geoffrion and made an immediate impact. Twelve seconds into the game, he squared off against one of the most feared fighters in the league, Bruin defenceman Ted Green.

"As I listened to the final strains of 'The Star-Spangled Banner,'" Ferguson later wrote in his autobiography, *Thunder and Lightning*, "I peered over at Green and said to myself 'John, you might as well start at the top.' No sooner had the puck been dropped for the opening faceoff than he came after me . . . and POW, I landed one right on Green's kisser. And another and another."

Ferguson delivered two messages that night. First, he could fight. Second, he could score. He put one past Bruin goalie Eddie Johnston in the first and added another in the second as the Canadiens earned a four–four tie. Furthermore, his value was quickly recognized. *The Hockey News* named him the first player of the week for the 1963–64 season, saying: "When Ferguson came to training camp, there were some skeptics who said he wouldn't make the grade. Ferguson has happily proved them wrong."

Selke acquired Ferguson from the Cleveland Barons of the AHL. There was nothing slick about this twenty-five-year-old native of Vancouver, who had only taken up hockey at age twelve. He was a choppy skater who tended to barge over opponents rather than whiz around them. He played three seasons with the Melville Millionaires of the Saskatchewan Junior Hockey League, one with the Fort Wayne Komets of the International Hockey League and another three in Cleveland. At each stop, Ferguson demonstrated that he could score and throw punches. Without both, he wouldn't have made the Canadiens.

"As far as muscles and hitting power are concerned," Blake told *The Hockey News,* "we're glad he has them but they're of secondary importance. We don't bring men to this team just because they're bashers."

Ferguson was the NHL's top-scoring rookie that season with eighteen goals and twenty-seven assists. He came close to beating Laperrière for the Calder Trophy, and he had a positive impact on Béliveau. The Canadiens' captain had had two poor seasons. He had been injured. His offensive output had dropped sharply. On a few occasions, Forum fans had booed him, and the sportswriters suggested he was finished. With Ferguson on his wing, Béliveau regained his touch, came third in scoring and won his second Hart Trophy.

The rejuvenated Canadiens met the Leafs in the opening round of the 1964 playoffs. They demonstrated conclusively that they were no longer the fast, slick, but soft team that had been pushed around by tougher opponents over the previous three seasons. The two old rivals pounded each other. Referee Frank Udvari called sixteen penalties in the first period of game one, a new record, and thirty-one over the full sixty minutes, another record.

There were twelve penalties in the second contest, fourteen in the third and thirty in the fourth, including six majors and three misconducts. The total for the first five games was 102 infractions, surpassing the old mark for a post-season series.

At that point, the Canadiens led three games to two, but the Leafs shut them out in the sixth to force a seventh at the Forum. Dave Keon scored twice in the first period. The second was scoreless. The Canadiens fired seventeen shots at Johnny Bower in the third, but only put one past him, and Keon finished it with an empty-net goal in the final minute.

The Canadiens had come a long way that season, and this was a painful defeat. "One had the impression of mistakenly opening the door and having entered the chapel of a funeral home," Louis Chantigny of *La Patrie* wrote of the post-game scene in the dressing room. "The players were all seated on the wooden benches, which form a large U around the room, shoulders slumped, heads down, fixed in the timeless pose of the vanquished."

Chantigny and the rest of the journalists were so cowed by the silence that they dared not break it till Selke entered and addressed the players. "You have nothing to be ashamed of," he told them, his own voice choked with emotion. "I'm proud of all of you. You fought courageously to the end."

Chantigny visited Selke the following afternoon at his office and was surprised by the change in demeanour. "I expected to meet a discouraged, old man, crushed by misfortune," he told his readers. "I saw in front of me a man ready to resume the fight."

Selke was full of vigour and excited about the prospects then playing in the farm system. Yvan Cournoyer, star of the Junior Canadiens, was the best of them. The talk was that he could pass like Béliveau, shoot like Geoffrion and score impossible goals like Maurice Richard. Selke knew that Cournoyer was ready—he had played five NHL games that season and scored four goals—and several others were on the cusp. "Next season, the Maple Leafs will not beat us," he said. "Next season, they will pursue us because our club is going to be much stronger."

The Canadiens' manager was ready to go back to work. A few days later, he left Montreal, accompanied by his son Frank Jr., to take in the final between Toronto and Detroit. The Leafs were playing the Wings in Detroit. The Selkes took a hotel room across the river in Windsor, Ontario. They had scarcely arrived when Frank Sr. received a call from Senator Hartland Molson, co-owner of the Canadiens with his brother Tom since 1955.

The senator told him to catch the next train back to Montreal. When he arrived, Selke learned that the Molson brothers were turning over control of the team to their younger cousins David, Peter and Bill. "Part of the deal," Senator Molson said, "is that you are going to retire and Sam Pollock is going to become general manager."

Selke was seventy-one years old. He had been managing the Canadiens for eighteen years and had been a hockey executive for thirty-five, since joining the Leafs as assistant manager in 1929. He was a superb organizer and a shrewd judge of talent, and he wanted to experience the thrill of victory one more time, but Senator Molson had decided to entrust the organization to younger hands.

Selke was a loyal employee and a gracious individual. He accepted the decision without protest. On May 15, 1964, the senator formally announced that he and Selke were making way for a new management team. "This occasion is a time of sadness and rejoicing," he told media representatives who gathered at the Forum. "Sadness because the old must give way to the young after having devoted many years to the cause of the Club de Hockey Canadien. And rejoicing because the men succeeding us will know how to pursue their task and lead the *Tricolore* to success after success."

Then Selke spoke: "You know my favorite slogan: 'The Kids Go Marching On.' If it applies to others, it naturally had to catch up with me." He reminded his audience of all that had been achieved under his watch. "We built a hockey empire which brought three Memorial Cups, one Allan Cup and six Stanley Cups to the Forum, plus many league championships. Since 1956 we have finished first or second every year, except 1963 when we were three points out of first place. . . . Our affiliates won league championships in Shawinigan Falls, Montreal, Ottawa, Hull, Regina, Fort William, Cincinnati, Peterborough, Winnipeg and Omaha."

Before concluding, Selke offered a word of advice to the new team. "No victory," he said, "is important enough to justify the loss of the respect of your friends or to damage the good name of the Club de Hockey Canadien."

1964–1971
SAM POLLOCK TAKES CHARGE

ANYONE WHO FOLLOWED THE CANADIENS closely in the late 1950s and early 1960s knew the name of Sam Pollock. He was the team's director of player personnel. He had started with the organization in 1947 and made his reputation as a win-at-all-costs coach. Pollock's Junior Canadiens had won the Memorial Cup in 1950, his Hull-Ottawa Canadiens in 1958. A Pollock team was usually scrappy, a reflection of his combative personality. Pollock was always arguing with someone—fans, officials, opposing coaches and players, even rink attendants. Or, when words failed, he would throw things onto the ice—folding wooden chairs were a favourite. But for all that, scarcely anyone, colleagues included, really knew the man.

"What kind of person is Sam Pollock?" mused Louis Chantigny in *La Patrie* after the management changes of May 1964. "A tyrant? A genius?" Chantigny couldn't say for sure. Pollock was too tight-lipped to come across as either. "He is not a man of long speeches and grand declarations," the journalist wrote. "In official meetings and press conferences, where Frank Selke is in the spotlight, Sam Pollock stands at a distance, in a corner where he attracts no attention. He is an enigmatic personality who exercises power in the shadows, behind the scenes."

Pollock's journey to the top had begun years earlier, when he was a boy in Notre-Dame-de-Grâce, the same English-language suburb where Doug Harvey grew up. Harvey was from the south end and competed for Oxford Park. Pollock was from Snowdon, a north-end neighbourhood, and as a kid was crazy about sports. He played hockey, but was better at baseball. He read the New York papers to stay current with the major leagues and aspired to a pro career, but realized quickly that he didn't have the talent to be a ballplayer. Instead, he began organizing and managing.

In 1943, at age eighteen, Pollock put together the Snowdon Stars, a men's team that competed in the Snowdon Fastball League. It was the city's best senior circuit, and crowds of three to five thousand attended Sunday afternoon games. Pollock played shortstop and surrounded himself with high-calibre talent. Bill Durnan pitched for the Stars; Toe Blake played second base; Elmer Lach moved between the infield and outfield. Ken Reardon joined the team after completing his military service, and several members of the Montreal Royals senior hockey team were also members.

By the time he formed the Stars, Pollock already had plenty of experience. He had begun coaching hockey in Notre-Dame-de-Grâce in 1940, when he was fifteen, and worked at three levels, bantam, midget and juvenile. His teams won nine provincial championships, and he sent so many good prospects to the Junior Canadiens that he caught the attention of Wilf Cude, the former NHL goalie who ran the team.

In 1944, Cude rewarded Pollock by affiliating his teams with the junior club and renaming them the Snowdon Canadiens. The following season, Cude made Pollock his manager and put him in charge of scouting and recruitment. Pollock was just twenty, but he was extremely dedicated. He spent every weeknight, as well as Saturdays and Sundays, watching kids on outdoor rinks, looking for the rare ones who might someday be able to play professionally.

Selke hired Pollock to coach the Junior Canadiens in the fall of 1947, and the two men worked together for the next seventeen years. Pollock came to know the Canadiens' vast farm system better than anyone, including Selke, and was the natural choice to succeed him.

After his appointment, Pollock granted media interviews at his office in the Forum, which was small, sparsely furnished and poorly decorated—hardly in keeping with the position of general manager of the Montreal Canadiens, according to Chantigny. Pollock sat in a wooden armchair, behind an imposing, but almost empty, wooden desk. The walls were bare, except for a map secured by pins. There was a photo of his fiancée on a shelf, a single, straight-backed chair for visitors and, in one corner, a metal filing cabinet painted brown.

"The Sam Pollock who welcomes journalists into his office is affable and courteous," Chantigny wrote, "but little inclined to make confidences and even less likely to reveal a secret. One has the impression of stumbling into a wall, of forcing the door of a mysterious room to which he denies you access, politely, but firmly."

Pollock made the same impression on colleagues. Frank Selke Jr., who also started with the Canadiens in the fall of 1947, told Chantigny: "His files on our clubs do not contain a hundredth of what he keeps in his head. He tells us only what he wants to tell us. He knows all the players who belong to us, all the players who belong to the other teams in the NHL, their names, their ages, their strengths, their weaknesses. It is a living encyclopedia . . . but, I repeat, nobody other than him has access to this knowledge."

Pollock had made himself indispensable to the organization. If he left, he took everything with him. He had been approached by two other NHL clubs, but had turned them down. This, at least, he was prepared to talk about. "It didn't appeal to me to leave Montreal," he said, "where I was born, where I grew up and where I've always lived, in order to exile myself in a strange city. My loyalty was to Mr. Selke and the Canadiens. And finally, my chances of moving up the ladder and getting to the top were excellent in Montreal."

Pollock's commitment was evident to all who observed him. "He has devoted himself body and soul to our farm clubs for many years," Selke Jr. said. "He works day and night without ever complaining. I have never seen a man dedicate himself to something with such enthusiasm and relentlessness. Our system of farm clubs is in large part his work."

Some former players and associates, speaking anonymously, described Pollock as ruthless and tyrannical and charged that he had ruined more prospects than he made, but Chantigny had no trouble finding admirers. "It is true that he was very tough with us," Jacques Laperrière said. "Sam demanded of each one of us that we work together perfectly. He wouldn't accept mediocrity and insisted that we always give the best of ourselves. But he was at the same time a man who knew how to be understanding and fatherly. When it wasn't going well, he would come and see us in our rooms or sit beside us on the bus or train and give us advice and encouragement."

At game time, Pollock had only one objective: victory. Sportswriter Lionel Duval knew him from his days as coach of the Hull-Ottawa Canadiens and was struck by his intensity. Once, he and Duval paced up and down a corridor beneath the stands while Pollock's players were getting dressed. They didn't exchange a word for a long time—almost an hour, according to Duval. Then Pollock stopped abruptly and exclaimed: "We absolutely have to win this game. We need it at any price."

Winning was uppermost in Sam Pollock's mind as he prepared for his first training camp as general manager. As he saw things, the Canadiens would win the league championship in 1964–65. They would win their round of the Stanley Cup semifinals. And then they would triumph in the final and bring the big silver trophy home to Montreal after its pit stop in Chicago and three-season sojourn in Toronto.

Pollock had inherited a very good team. "The Canadiens club we have today isn't unlike the powerful teams we had during our Cup years," he told a member of the press shortly after his appointment.

Unlike their counterparts of the late fifties, the Canadiens of the mid-sixties did not have a superstar at every position, but they did have a potent mix of established and emerging stars, backed by better-than-average players at every position. They had a Vézina Trophy winner—Charlie Hodge—in goal. Young, but proven defencemen—Jacques Laperrière, a strong skater and solid hitter with a booming shot; J.C. Tremblay, a forward whom the Canadiens had moved back to take advantage of his exceptional skill with the puck; Terry Harper, a pound-them-in-the-corners, clear-the-front-of-the-net type; and Jean-Guy Talbot, whose speed had kept him in the lineup for ten seasons and five Stanley Cups.

Up front, they had two of the league's best defensive forwards in Claude Provost and Gilles Tremblay. Both could skate and score and inspire teammates with hard work, and each had a role: Provost shadowed Bobby Hull, while Tremblay contained Gordie Howe. Pollock's Canadiens had finesse and ferocity on the wings in Bobby Rousseau and John Ferguson, and they were strong down the middle. Ralph Backstrom was a good third-line centre. Henri Richard, the number two centre, was swift and tenacious and had scored an average of twenty-two goals per season in his nine years with the team. Their leader was the graceful and regal Jean Béliveau, the most prolific centreman in history.

The Canadiens started the season with two new faces in their lineup. Defenceman Ted Harris had come late to the NHL. He was twenty-seven and had spent eight seasons with the Springfield Indians of the American Hockey League. He was big for his day—six foot two, 185 pounds—and added toughness at the blue line. The other newcomer, Yvan Cournoyer, was no ordinary rookie. He was replacing Bernie Geffrion, who had retired, and came highly touted—the next Rocket, according to many.

A stocky, baby-faced whirlwind, Cournoyer shot left, but like Maurice Richard he played the right side and scored stunning goals. He had prepared himself for professional hockey from an early age. As a boy in Drummondville, he was a rink rat who pushed a four-foot-wide wooden scraper to clear the ice and strengthen his legs. In his teens in the Montreal suburb of Lachine, he cut pucks from iron bars at his father's machine shop, fired them for hours against the wall of the family garage, and acquired a blazing wrist shot that spooked all but the best opponents.

Cournoyer established himself as a prospect at age sixteen, when he accumulated sixty-eight points in forty-two games with the Lachine Maroons of the Montreal Metropolitan Junior Hockey League. The following season he moved up to the Junior Canadiens and in his third and final year exploded for 111 points in fifty-three games. That's when the hype began.

"From the red line to the net," his coach, Claude Ruel, said, "he is without any doubt the most dangerous scorer I have ever seen in my life. He has everything he needs to succeed in the NHL: speed, stickhandling, the shot, the intelligence and this instinct for scoring which is a gift, a thing that one has and no one can teach you."

He had scored four times in a five-game trial with the Canadiens the previous season, including two sensational goals against Toronto that had lifted Montreal fans from their seats. "He is ready to make the jump," Frank Selke said afterward. "Cournoyer is wasting his time and his talent in junior. The National Hockey League is where he belongs."

For those who adored the Canadiens, a new saviour had arrived. "Since the retirement of Maurice Richard," Louis Chantigny wrote in November 1964, "thousands of fans from one end of the province to the other, and in some cases the country, dreamed of the day when a young man, preferably a French-Canadian in the uniform of the Canadiens, would perpetuate the exploits and glory of the incomparable, the unique and the immortal Rocket."

But Cournoyer fizzled as a rookie. He had a hard time putting the puck in the net, scoring only three times in the first two months of the season, and defensively he was a liability. By the end of November, he was being used strictly on power plays. "Yvan Cournoyer is worried and questioning himself," *La Patrie* reported, and things did not improve. In early February, the Canadiens scratched him for a night, and he was sent to the minors for seven games. Cournoyer finished the season in Montreal, but was good for only seven goals.

The team experienced other problems as well. Hodge, who had been shaky at training camp and through the month of October, injured his back in early November, so the team summoned Gump Worsley from Quebec City. Worsley got the call at 6:30 a.m., after playing the night before. He drove three hours to Montreal, caught a flight to Chicago (despite his morbid fear of flying) and led the Canadiens to a victory that night. Worsley and Hodge shared goaltending duties, but both were far from the best. They finished behind their peers in Chicago and Toronto (where Johnny Bower and Terry Sawchuk won the Vézina), not to mention Detroit's dazzling rookie, Roger Crozier, who won the Calder.

Among the forwards, there were both slumps and injuries. By mid-December, Béliveau was in a prolonged scoring drought and, a few days before Christmas, Gilles Tremblay broke his right leg. He was finished for the year, and Pollock traded for a replacement, sending Bill Hicke to New York for Dick Duff, a twenty-eight-year-old left winger.

Duff, a small player at five feet, nine inches and 166 pounds, was a product of the Leaf system. He grew up in Kirkland Lake, a northern Ontario mining town, played junior at St. Michael's College and spent nearly nine full seasons in Toronto. He averaged twenty-seven goals in his three best years, and scored most of them by fighting for rebounds, tip-ins or deflections while taking a pounding from defencemen. Duff was a leader in the dressing room and a venomous adversary—hitting, taunting and agitating—especially when the Leafs played the Canadiens.

The Leafs traded him to New York in March 1964 after his offensive output sagged, but he played poorly because he had left a big piece of his heart—and most of his game—in Toronto. "The Montreal guys revived me," Duff said in an interview with the author. "I always wanted to play the way they played. They were smart. They were always on the attack. They had an innate desire to play. They played to win every game. They put an end to losing streaks quickly."

The Canadiens finished second that season, beat the Leafs in the semifinal and played the Black Hawks for the Stanley Cup. The final lasted seven games, but neither team won on the road and some unusual heroes emerged. Claude Provost held Bobby Hull to one goal and two assists. Montreal's goaltenders also shone. Worsley allowed only three goals in three games before pulling a muscle in his left leg. Hodge played games four through six, allowing two goals per night. Everyone expected he would finish the series, but Blake had a hunch that Worsley would better handle the pressure of a winner-take-all showdown.

"I wasn't supposed to play," Worsley recalled later. "I was sitting in a coffee shop at the Forum a couple of hours before game time with my wife and Toe Blake's wife. Larry Aubut, who was our trainer, comes into the restaurant and says, 'Hey Gumper, you better get in there. You're playing tonight.'"

Worsley's teammates relieved the pressure early. An errant Chicago clearing pass on the first shift of the game caromed off Béliveau's leg and past Glenn Hall into the Hawk net. The Forum crowd cheered, sang, blew horns and rang bells for nearly five minutes, by which time Duff had scored Montreal's second. Worsley made three sensational short-handed saves midway through the first to give his side a lift. With less than five minutes remaining, Duff spotted Cournoyer in full flight, made a rink-wide pass, and the rookie zoomed past Elmer Vasko and beat Hall. Henri Richard added a fourth goal before the end of the first to complete the scoring.

When the final buzzer sounded, Worsley bolted for the blue line and met J.C. Tremblay in a mid-air embrace. The rest of the players leapt over the boards in a celebratory rush. After shaking hands with the Hawks, the Canadiens gathered at centre ice. Clarence Campbell presented the newly created Conn Smythe Trophy to Béliveau, the most valuable player in the playoffs, and then lifted the Stanley Cup from a table and passed it to the team captain. Béliveau led his teammates around the ice with the Cup aloft, with the Forum fans on their feet and applauding rapturously as organist Léo Duplessis played an extra-exuberant version of "Happy Days Are Here Again."

Teammates sometimes said of Henri Richard that he was "puck lucky." It was their way of explaining why he seemed to have the puck more than anyone else when he was on the ice. Toe Blake said luck had nothing to do with it. "He's smart enough to be where the puck is all the time," Blake once told a journalist. "He's almost uncanny that way. He sizes up how a play is going to go and then he gets there, and the first thing you know he's got the puck. When he doesn't have things figured out in advance he's so fast he gets there anyway."

Despite his speed and instincts, Richard had never been as prolific as his brother Maurice or the Canadiens' other big offensive stars. Still, in his third season, he had scored twenty-eight goals and finished second in scoring, with eighty points. Two years later, he registered a career-high thirty goals and tied for fifth in the NHL in goals (with teammate Geoffrion) and points (seventy-three, with Gordie Howe). He had earned fifty points or more per season, except for his first, and was chasing his six hundredth point as the 1965–66 campaign began.

Richard achieved that objective in early November 1965, and at the end of January 1966 picked up his four hundredth assist. Several other players reached milestones that season as well. Jean Béliveau played his eight hundredth game, became the first Canadien to register five hundred assists and recorded his nine hundredth point. Claude Provost scored his two hundredth goal, and both he and Jean-Guy Talbot played in their seven hundredth game.

Bobby Rousseau had the best season of his career. He scored thirty goals, added forty-eight assists and tied Chicago's Stan Mikita for second in the scoring race. Jacques Laperrière won the James Norris Memorial Trophy as best defenceman. Gump Worsley and Charlie Hodge shared the Vézina Trophy, and the Canadiens finished first with ninety points, eight ahead of the Black Hawks.

The Canadiens swept the Leafs in four games, then had to wait ten days before starting the final against Detroit. They ran into a hot goaltender in Roger Crozier and lost the first two games at home. Faced with an embarrassing defeat, they rebounded in Detroit and won both contests.

"It was Canadien pride and nothing else that stirred the team to find itself," Blake told Elmer Ferguson on the train back to Montreal. "The Canadiens are a great hockey team. They are a proud hockey team. Defeat does not rest lightly on Canadien shoulders. You could feel it as we journeyed to Detroit. There was no joking, no laughing on the trip, none in the motel where we were staying. This was a grim, even bitter team that felt it had been pushed around by an inferior team and determined that it wouldn't happen again."

The Canadiens beat the Wings in six, but the series ended strangely. Montreal took a two–nothing lead in the sixth game. Detroit tied late in the third. Two and a half minutes into overtime, the Canadiens were on the attack. Léon Rochefort passed to Richard, who relayed the puck to Dave Balon on his left. A Detroit defenceman checked Balon, who threw the puck to the front of the net. Richard charged at it, but was tripped from behind. He slid into the net and carried the puck with him.

Two days later, on a Sunday afternoon, Montreal honoured the Canadiens with another enormous victory parade. Half a million people attended. The route was eleven miles long and the celebration lasted three and a half hours. Then the players attended a civic reception for three hundred. Mayor Jean Drapeau told the team that this was just a warmup. Next year was Canada's centennial, and Montreal was to host the world's fair—Expo 67—but that wouldn't be enough for Montrealers. The party wouldn't be complete without the Stanley Cup.

Mayor Drapeau and the fans almost got their wish. The Canadiens finished second in the spring of 1967 and eliminated the Rangers four straight. The third-place Leafs upset the heavily favoured Hawks, who had finished nineteen points ahead of them. That set up a Montreal–Toronto final—the eleventh post-season clash between the teams since the spring of 1944.

Such high-octane competition had enflamed passions on the ice, in the stands and in the living rooms of the nation. Fans from coast to coast embraced one side or the other, and feelings were especially raw and hot in Canada's two largest cities. These sporting contests reflected other struggles—between French and English, Catholics and Protestants, Toronto and Montreal. In the post-war years, Toronto had begun to challenge Montreal's pre-eminence as Canada's metropolis. Its population was growing rapidly and becoming more diverse. It became a centre of commerce and a home to more and more corporate head offices. By 1967, Toronto was poised to overtake Montreal.

On the ice, though, those trends were reversed. The Leafs were old and in decline while the Canadiens were young and in possession of a bright future. Toronto's starting goaltender, Johnny Bower, was forty-two, while his backup, Terry Sawchuk, was thirty-seven. In all, five Leafs were over the age of thirty-five, ten were over thirty, and coach Punch Imlach had endured some stinging criticism for sticking with aging veterans.

By comparison, Pollock and Blake were quick to make changes when veterans faltered. Charlie Hodge had performed inconsistently that season and Gump Worsley was injured. The Canadiens turned to their farm system and came up with Rogatien Vachon, the only newcomer of note on the Canadiens.

He was twenty-one and had had an undistinguished junior career, most of it with the Thetford Mines Canadiens of the Ligue de Hockey Junior A du Quebec. He had played thirty-four games with the Houston Apollos of the Central Professional Hockey League before getting the call from the Canadiens. Vachon appeared in nineteen games for Montreal, won eleven of them and posted a goals-against average of 2.48, right behind Vézina Trophy winner Denis DeJordy of Chicago.

It was a good start for the rookie, but the Leafs' Imlach was unimpressed. Prior to the opening game, he sat with a cluster of reporters in the stands at Maple Leaf Gardens and watched his team practise. The journalists peppered him with questions about Toe Blake, but Imlach responded by throwing a barb at Vachon: "You can tell that Junior B goaltender he won't be playing against a bunch of peashooters when he plays the Leafs. We'll take his head off with our first shot."

The series turned on the performances of the goaltenders. Sawchuk played poorly in the opening game and the Canadiens won six–two. Bower shut out Montreal in the second. At one point, he took a stick across the nose and blood trickled down his face. Leaf trainer Bob Haggart sprinted across the ice with a towel, thinking Bower might need stitches. "I'm hot," the netminder snapped. "Hot. Leave me alone. Don't bother me."

Bower sizzled again in game three. The Leafs won, and Imlach's confidence soared. The following morning he spotted a Montreal reporter in the coffee shop at Maple Leaf Gardens. "How's your team?" Imlach shouted. "Ask them if they want to be humiliated any more."

"For crying out loud," snapped assistant manager King Clancy, who was seated next to Imlach. "Will you cut that out."

Imlach couldn't resist another jab at the Canadiens and Vachon. "There's no way we can lose to them," he said. "He's up to Junior A now. He's graduated from Junior B to Junior A."

The Canadiens caught a break when Bower pulled a muscle in the warmup for game four. Sawchuk took over and Montreal put six past him to tie the series. Two nights later, the Canadiens faced a different Sawchuk. This time, he stopped all but one shot. His teammates scored four and Blake pulled Vachon in favour of Worsley.

Sawchuk barred the door again in game six, allowing just one goal in fifty-nine minutes of play. The Leafs had scored twice and made a last stand on a faceoff in their end with under a minute to go. Blake pulled Worsley for an extra attacker, and Imlach defied all those who had criticized the Leafs for being too old. He put his five oldest players on the ice: Bob Pulford; George Armstrong, Red Kelly, and the defence partners Tim Horton and Allan Stanley. He instructed Stanley to take the faceoff, something the defenceman hadn't done in four years. Worse still, Jean Béliveau lined up opposite him.

"Defencemen always used to take the faceoffs," Stanley explained years later, "because the centremen were usually a little smaller. The ref would drop the puck and you'd run the centreman right out of there. That was before they brought in the faceoff interference rule.

"I'm watching the referee, and when he drops the puck I played Béliveau so he couldn't get his stick on it, and I ran the son of a bitch right out of there with my stick between his legs. The puck came back to Kelly, who threw it up to Pulford, who threw it to Armstrong. Armstrong put the puck in the net and Béliveau was chasing the referee around hollering, 'Faceoff intereference! Faceoff interference!'"

It was a painful defeat for the Canadiens and their followers. "The Stanley Cup final was a nightmare," *La Patrie* declared afterward, and the pain lingered, especially for the players. "Of all the years that I lost, 1967 is still the one that hurt the most," Béliveau recalled later. "And I know it hurt my teammates because we had a good team and we had no reason to lose."

In twenty-three seasons, the Canadiens and Leafs had met six times in the semis and five times in the final. The Centennial-year playoff was the rubber match and the rivalry was never the same again. The Canadiens continued to win, but the Leafs declined and would not be a genuine contender for twenty-five years. The old grudge was robbed of oxygen—high-stakes games and playoff series—and it lived on more in the minds of the fans than the hearts of the players.

Sam Pollock faced the biggest challenge of his managerial career in the spring of 1967. The league had admitted six new franchises, doubling its size to twelve teams. The newcomers were to fill their rosters with players selected at an expansion draft, held in early June at the Queen Elizabeth Hotel in Montreal. Pollock's job was to protect the deep, rich pool of talent he had inherited from his predecessor, Frank Selke, and he received some unexpected help from NHL president Clarence Campbell, who turned to him to help draw up the rules of the draft.

Under their plan, the six established teams were each allowed to protect one goaltender and eleven skaters. Each time an old club lost a player, it was allowed to add one to its protected list. New teams could select the twelfth player, but the thirteenth became protected. The fourteenth was available, the fifteenth protected, and so the draft continued until each expansion club made eighteen choices. Players who had turned pro in 1966–67 but were still eligible for junior hockey were excluded from the draft, as were those who had played professionally for the first time that season.

Montreal lost eighteen players, four of them veterans (Charlie Hodge, Jean-Guy Talbot, Dave Balon and Jim Roberts). The balance were minor leaguers. But Pollock had preserved the core of the team that, six weeks earlier, had competed for the Stanley Cup. He had also held on to the organization's top prospects—Rogatien Vachon, Serge Savard, Carol Vadnais and Jacques Lemaire—as well as its junior talent.

That fall, while others struggled to assemble competitive teams, Pollock and Toe Blake were blessed with abundant talent. "I am in my twenty-sixth year of professional hockey," Blake told *La Patrie*, "and I tell you sincerely that I have never seen so many players who have a chance at earning a place on the team."

Midway through training camp, a headline in the paper declared, "Our rookies have too much talent," and a columnist wrote: "Players of the calibre of Carol Vadnais and Serge Savard would not even have to fight for a regular position with any of the six new clubs. They would be considered untouchable." Both had played the previous season in Houston. They were one of the top defence pairs in the CPHL, but in the fall of 1967 they were competing for fifth spot on the blue line. Savard won the job and spent his rookie season filling in for injured veterans, killing penalties and, like most Canadien newcomers, watching from the bench.

Savard had been Montreal property since his early teens. The team's scout in the Abitibi region of Quebec spotted him around 1960, playing for the village of Landrienne, more than three hundred miles northwest of Montreal. Savard, was just a big kid who revered the Canadiens. He stood six foot three, weighed a little over two hundred pounds and could play either defence or forward.

The Canadiens brought him to Montreal at age fifteen to try out for the Junior Canadiens, but he began the season with an affiliate that represented Rosemont, an east-end neighbourhood, in the Montreal Metropolitan Junior Hockey League. The coach, Tony Demers, a former NHLer, sat him on the bench. The owner took over from Demers, and he thought even less of Savard—he sent him to a Junior B team in the Montreal parish of Immaculate Conception. That nearly ended his hockey dreams.

The Junior Canadiens didn't bother to send him an invitation to their training camp the following autumn, but Savard returned to Montreal anyway, registered for school and called Cliff Fletcher in the player development department. "They always claimed it was a mistake, but I don't think it was," Savard would later say. "I guess they figured they were stuck with me, so Fletcher told me to show up. They put me with a team called the Notre-Dame-de-Grâce Monarchs of the Metropolitan league."

By Christmas, he was an all-star, and the following season he made the Junior Canadiens—as a defenceman, because the team thought he was too big to play forward. At age twenty, with a year of junior eligibility remaining, the Canadiens sent him to Houston, where he was named the CPHL's rookie of the year. Savard soon impressed fans and opponents in the NHL with daring rushes, effortless puck handling and dramatic goals.

"I've never seen a man of his size who could stop and turn so quickly," the Leafs' Dave Keon said of Savard. "He's strong and very hard for a fellow my size to handle. In most of their games against us, he showed up as their best defenceman."

Savard was one of six rookies in the Canadiens' lineup in 1967–68. Vachon still qualified as a first-year player. Vadnais was called up during the season. The new forwards included Peterborough Petes graduates Mickey Redmond and Danny Grant, and a quiet Montrealer named Jacques Lemaire.

Lemaire was a centre, but no rookie was going to start ahead of Jean Béliveau, Henri Richard or Ralph Backstrom, so he played left wing, killed penalties and took occasional turns on the power play. Lemaire was a handsome man of moderate stature and was awestruck by the famous names around him, which reinforced his natural reticence. Although he hardly spoke in the dressing room, on the ice, he was a dynamo—a powerful skater and a dogged checker who possessed one of the hardest shots in hockey, a skill he had acquired by firing steel pucks against a wall as a youth. After thirty-five games, he had scored twelve goals and inadvertently triggered an explosion that reverberated for weeks.

In early February 1968, Blake benched Henri Richard for two games and used Lemaire in his place between Claude Provost and Dick Duff. Richard had been injured four times that season. He was playing poorly and hadn't scored ten goals. But he was enraged and humiliated and quit the Canadiens. Fans were shocked. The Montreal newspapers and radio and TV stations treated the story like a grave national crisis.

Richard tried to sit out the tempest at a retreat in the Laurentian mountains north of the city. Reporters tracked him down, and the normally reserved Henri told them exactly how he felt. "I was going crazy," he said in an interview with *La Patrie*. "I couldn't sleep. I couldn't eat. I would rather be a garbageman than sit on the bench.

"I told Toe Blake and repeated it to Sam Pollock. I am incapable of warming the bench. If circumstances don't permit Blake to play me, then trade me."

That was not an option. The Canadiens had had a Richard in their lineup for twenty-five years. One was a god, the other a prince. Pollock massaged the bruised ego of his fiery star and soothed everyone's nerves, though Lemaire confessed to a reporter that he had been deeply shaken by the commotion.

Richard returned to a team rampaging through the second half of the schedule. The Canadiens had been in last place in their division at Christmas, but lost only eight times during the balance of the season and finished first overall. They eliminated Boston in four games, Chicago in five and advanced to the final against Scotty Bowman's St. Louis Blues.

Bowman's club kept things close with fine defensive play. Each contest was decided by a goal—two of them in overtime—but the Montrealers had desire, discipline and pride on their side, and one of hockey's greatest coaches to motivate them.

The Canadiens won four straight and claimed their fifteenth Stanley Cup at home on May 11, 1968, a Saturday. Immediately afterward, Blake announced that he was retiring. He was fifty-five. He had coached the Canadiens for thirteen seasons, finished first nine times and won eight Stanley Cups.

He was a stern and forbidding figure behind the bench, a man in a suit and a fedora with a permanent scowl on his face. But the players respected and admired him. He was adept at handling the competing egos and conflicting personalities that comprise any team. He was demanding, but treated his charges with dignity and never berated anyone publicly.

Blake expected to win every night, and his competitive zeal was contagious. "Toe Blake hated to lose so much that he made us the same way," defenceman J.C. Tremblay said in the dressing room, which became subdued after the players learned of the coach's decision. "He was the heart of this team and I'm happy he was able to quit after we won everything."

Blake left the Forum shortly before midnight. A young photographer named Denis Brodeur captured him from behind as he walked alone toward an exit. He was without his fedora. He had an overcoat draped over his left arm and a briefcase in his right hand. His shoulders were stooped, his head down and he appeared tired and emotionally drained. The competitive fires that had inspired his players had finally consumed him.

He had conveyed his distress in a long conversation with Béliveau one afternoon during the playoffs. Blake summoned the team captain to his hotel room. He was pacing the floor like a man possessed when Béliveau arrived. At one point, Blake confided: "Jean, I don't know what's wrong with me. Something's going to snap here." Then, placing his hands on his head, he said it again: "Something's going to snap."

The Canadiens announced Blake's successor—chief scout Claude Ruel—on Monday, June 10, 1968, the day before the NHL's annual player draft began at the Queen Elizabeth Hotel in downtown Montreal. Ruel was twenty-nine. He had become the property of the Canadiens as a child, had worn their colours as an adolescent and had worked his entire adult life for the organization.

Ruel had been a promising player with the Junior Canadiens in the mid-fifties, under coach Sam Pollock and alongside Henri Richard, Ralph Backstrom and J.C. Tremblay. He seemed destined for a pro career, but his dreams ended during an exhibition game in Belleville, Ontario in September 1957.

"I clearly remember the incident," former teammate Tremblay would later say. "We had begun a five-man attack. I picked up the puck in the corner and made a long pass to Claude. He attempted to avoid an opponent, then suddenly fell to the ice bleeding badly."

The other player had butt-ended Ruel. The shaft of the stick struck Ruel's left eye and destroyed it. The following season, at nineteen, Ruel replaced Pollock as coach of the Junior Canadiens. He guided the team to the Ontario Hockey Association Junior A title in 1961–62 and to second place the following season before becoming a scout in 1964. By then, he had coached the Tremblays (J.C. and Gilles), Yvan Cournoyer, Bobby Rousseau and Jacques Laperrière.

Observers inside the organization and out applauded Ruel's appointment. "Claude was selected because he loves hockey," said former player and team executive Floyd Curry. "He has given body and soul to the job. He is the most conscientious employee you could find and is dedicated to the cause of the Canadiens."

"In its choice of a coach for next season," Marcel Desjardins of *La Presse* wrote, "the management of the *Bleu Blanc Rouge* has shown yet again one of the reasons for its glorious history. Why choose Claude Ruel? Becuse he is dedicated to hockey and the Canadiens like his predecessors Toe Blake and Dick Irvin."

Ruel acknowledged he was stepping into big shoes, but had no hesitation. "Maybe I'm young," he told the media, "but age doesn't mean anything as long as I get my team ready mentally and physically for each game. I can't expect to do what Toe Blake did—he's the greatest coach ever—but somebody has to take the job and I feel confident."

Pollock had made Ruel the youngest coach in NHL history. His players made him a winner in his first season behind the bench. "I told him that all we needed were good practices and a little direction," Dick Duff later recalled. "We knew why we were there."

The Canadiens won forty-six games in 1968–69, lost nineteen and tied eleven. They finished first overall with 103 points, three better than the Boston Bruins, who had become a new power in the NHL thanks to the presence of Bobby Orr, Phil Esposito and Gerry Cheevers. Three Canadiens were named to the second All-Star team: Jean Béliveau, Ted Harris and Yvan Cournoyer—who had scored forty-three goals, added forty-four assists and was sixth in total points.

The Canadiens beat New York four straight in the opening round of the playoffs. They eliminated Boston in six tough games, three of them decided in overtime, and they swept the St. Louis Blues in four. The NHL sportswriters awarded the Conn Smythe Trophy to Serge Savard, the first defenceman to win it, and Montrealers gave their Canadiens a riotous welcome when they arrived at Dorval Airport with the Stanley Cup. Hundreds packed the terminal hoping for a handshake, an autograph or perhaps even a word or two with a favourite player.

The rookie coach, who had shed tears of joy when the siren sounded to end the final game, was on the brink of nervous exhaustion. "I am dead tired," Ruel told a reporter from *La Patrie*. "I just want to find a tranquil place where I can think of nothing and sleep in peace."

After such a promising start, Ruel scarcely enjoyed a moment of calm as coach. The Canadiens were a team in turmoil the following season. First, there were injuries. In late October, J.C. Tremblay hurt his wrist and missed seventeen games. On December 6, Jean Béliveau fractured an ankle. A week later, John Ferguson broke his big toe. Just before Christmas, Henri Richard injured an ankle. At the end of the month, rookie Christian Bordeleau went down with a separated shoulder. Early in February, Ferguson suffered a deep gash under his right eye. In mid-March, Savard crashed into a goalpost and fractured his left tibia in three places and required surgery.

There were suspensions to Ferguson and Jacques Laperrière, and other distractions. Duff was preoccupied with personal problems—financial setbacks from a failed business venture. He played poorly in training camp, and Sam Pollock traded him to Los Angeles after seventeen games.

Ruel clashed with Gump Worsley. He disapproved of the goalie's indifferent approach to practice, while Worsley disliked Ruel's coaching techniques. One night, between periods, Ruel exhorted his players. "You've got to work hard. You've got to skate, skate, skate."

"Does he ever knock it off?" Worsley groaned from his corner, just loud enough for Ruel to hear.

Worsley played only six games for the Canadiens that season. On November 29, 1969, after playing in Chicago, the forty-year-old veteran quit the team and caught a train back to Montreal. He was on the brink of a nervous breakdown due to his fear of flying, a phobia he had acquired on his first commercial flight twenty years earlier, when an engine caught fire. The pilot made an emergency landing and Worsley clutched the armrest, his eyes fixed on the flames and smoke outside his window.

"I just can't take it anymore," he told the sportswriters before leaving the team. "Los Angeles one day. Boston the next. The trip to Chicago took two hours and fifteen minutes and we were strapped in for two hours. Montreal must make some arrangements for me."

Worsley spent a month at home. By Christmas, he was ready to return, but Pollock insisted he play his way into game shape with the Montreal Voyageurs of the American league. When Worsley refused, Pollock suspended him. Two months later, at the trade deadline, Pollock dealt him to the Minnesota North Stars.

By then, the defending Stanley Cup champions were fluctuating between third and fifth and had no chance of catching the league leaders, Boston and Chicago. The fans were restless, the media were growling and Ruel was withering under the heat. He complained to Pollock that the players had stopped listening and told *La Presse*, "If someone else can do the job better than me I am willing to step aside."

Ruel stayed to the end, and it was a bitter one. The Canadiens played their final game on a Sunday evening at Chicago Stadium. They had ninety-two points. The Rangers had pulled even with them in fourth place that afternoon by thrashing the Red Wings nine–five, a suspect outcome since Detroit coach Sid Abel sat Gordie Howe, Alex Delvecchio and Frank Mahovlich, his top line, for two periods, ostensibly to rest them for the playoffs.

Montreal needed a win or a tie to move ahead of the Rangers. If they lost, fourth place would go to highest-scoring team on the season. Things did not go well for the Canadiens that night. Midway through the third, they trailed the Hawks by three and were two back of the Rangers in total goals. A tie was unlikely, a win less so. Ruel took a desperate gamble. He began pulling Rogie Vachon for a sixth attacker after each faceoff. The Hawks put five into the empty net, and the roiling Chicago crowd booed and jeered each goal.

The Canadiens lost ten–two. They finished fifth and missed the play-offs for the first time in twenty-one seasons. "A year of frustration," Ruel told reporters on the bus ride to the airport. "A year of frustration from start to finish. I never thought that one day I would live through such a disappointment."

The team's supporters were equally morose, a mood captured by a front-page headline in the next day's Montreal *Gazette:* "R.I.P—A Stanley Cup playoff dynasty: Canadiens (1949–1970)."

John Ferguson retired on October 6, 1970, four days before the season opened, but was coaxed back in mid-November because the team was losing, because there were injuries and because word was spreading among the league's bruisers and brawlers that they could take liberties with the Canadiens and go unpunished. Ferguson returned in time to witness the meltdown of Claude Ruel.

The players were fed up with their coach, and by early December there were press reports of turmoil within the dressing room. Ruel was a yeller, at least when the team was winning. Advice, encouragement and line changes were all delivered at high volume. Then he became sullen and subdued when the Canadiens fell behind. After each road game, he called Sam Pollock, who seldom travelled, and the players wondered: Who's in charge?

They didn't like Ruel's practices or his motivational talks prior to games or between periods, and Ruel didn't like coaching. He had never sought the job and was pleading with Pollock to let him go back to scouting. The general manager relented in the first week of December, and Ruel told the media: "I have my deliverance. I am a happy man today. I am very happy. I will go to the Forum and I will be the Canadiens' best fan. I hope they win fifty games."

The team's new coach was Al MacNeil, a thirty-five-year-old native of Sydney, Nova Scotia, and the first Maritimer to coach in the NHL. MacNeil was a quiet man. He had played defence in the NHL for eleven seasons, beginning with the Leafs. They dealt him to Montreal in 1960. The Canadiens sent him to their minor pro Hull-Ottawa team, where he played for Pollock, who was impressed with his understanding of the game and thought he would make a good coach. MacNeil moved up to the Canadiens in 1961–62, but was traded to Chicago before the end of the season.

Pollock reacquired him in June 1968, this time from the Pittsburgh Penguins. The Canadiens needed someone to run their Houston Apollos farm team and MacNeil went there as player-coach. He served in the same dual capacity with the Montreal Voyageurs in 1969–70. In the fall of 1970, he became Ruel's assistant—the final stop in his coaching apprenticeship.

MacNeil inherited a third-place team. The Canadiens were well behind the front-running Bruins and Rangers, and one month later were in the same position. That's when help arrived unexpectedly. On a Saturday morning in early January, Pollock received a long-distance call from Detroit. Ned Harkness, the Wings' newly appointed general manager, was on the line.

"I'm in charge now," Harkness said. "Are you interested in Mahovlich?"

"Is the Pope a Catholic?" Pollock replied.

So began a negotiation that lasted till Wednesday afternoon, January 13, when the Canadiens were gathering at Dorval Airport for a flight to Minnesota. They were about to receive boarding passes when Pollock's assistant, Ron Caron, arrived.

The reporters knew something was up and swarmed Caron before he could address the players. "We've made a trade," Caron announced. "It's three for one. Bill Collins, Mickey Redmond and Guy Charron are going to Detroit for Frank Mahovlich."

The Canadiens had given up two good, young forwards in Redmond and Collins, as well as a minor-league prospect, for a premier player in his fourteenth season. Mahovlich had been a key member of Toronto's four Stanley Cup teams in the sixties. The Leafs traded him to Detroit in March 1968, where he played with Gordie Howe and Alex Delvecchio, a powerful forward unit that was seen as the second coming of Detroit's famous Production Line—Howe on the right, Ted Lindsay on the left and Sid Abel at centre. Mahovlich had scored 134 goals with Detroit, and Pollock believed he had some punch left in him.

"I know he's thirty-three," Pollock told a columnist. "But he should give us three or four great years. That's what we need to keep us moving. We have draft choices and promising kids. Until they arrive, Mahovlich gives us a proven man of superstar status."

The big left winger accumulated forty-one points in thirty-eight games, and the Canadiens went on a tear. Jean Béliveau scored his five hundredth regular-season goal in a game against the Minnesota North Stars in February. That month, the Canadiens had the best record in the league. They left behind the Toronto Maple Leafs, who had challenged them for third place, and they clinched a playoff spot by beating the Red Wings in Detroit March 7 with twelve games and nearly a month left in the schedule. But despite all that, they gained no ground on the two teams ahead of them. The Canadiens finished with ninety-seven points, twelve behind the Rangers and twenty-four back of the Bruins, whom they would face in the opening round of the playoffs.

The Bruins were the defending Stanley Cup champions, and they appeared unstoppable in 1970–71. They had won more games, scored more goals, earned more points and set more records—thirty-seven all told—than any team in league history. Boston had taken five of six regular-season games against Montreal. Twice in the final week, they had beaten the Canadiens soundly—and they had rubbed it. In one of those games, the 200-pound defenceman Rick Smith nearly ran Montreal's Bobby Sheehan, a 155-pound centre, through the end boards. Bobby Orr viciously slashed J.C. Tremblay, and laughed about it.

As the teams prepared for the series, two questions loomed. How could the Canadiens conceivably withstand the whirlwind of muscle and fire-power that would hit them on the ice at Boston Garden? And who would play goal? Would it be Rogie Vachon, who had been in net for the two late-season losses; his backup, Phil Myre, who had scarcely done better against the Bruins; or the twenty-three-year-old newcomer Ken Dryden, who had started and won six games in the final month of the season?

Dryden did not expect to get the call. "It's no secret that Rogie is going to start," he told the Montreal *Gazette*. "But I'm looking to get some action. I wouldn't be telling the truth otherwise."

Pollock saw things differently. Dryden was fresh because he had spent most of the winter playing part time with the Voyaguers and attending law school at McGill University. He had allowed only nine goals in the six games he played with the Canadiens. He had performed superbly in two wins over the Rangers and another against Chicago. Most importantly, he hadn't faced the Bruins.

"We weren't going to have any chance against them with Rogie or Phil in net," Pollock said in an interview with the author. "We thought we would try another goalie who hadn't been shell-shocked by the Orrs and Espositos."

The Canadiens started Dryden in game one. He faced forty-two shots and was beaten three times, but gave his side a chance to win. "For a while," Pat Curran wrote in *The Gazette*, "it seemed that Dryden's superb goaltending might help steal the opener."

The trouble was, Boston's Gerry Cheevers was even better. He allowed just one goal, and the Canadiens expected to see him in the second game. So did most of the reporters covering the series. But Bruin coach Tom Johnson had other plans, which he shared with the *Montreal Star*'s Red Fisher.

"I'm using Eddie in the nets tonight," he told Fisher. "Johnston is playing."

"Are you nuts?" Fisher asked incredulously. "Didn't you watch Cheevers last night? He had to stand on his head for your team to win."

"If I don't use Johnston, I'll lose him, " the coach replied. "I promised before the series I'd use him in game two."

For the first forty minutes that night, it didn't matter who was in the Boston net. Yvan Cournoyer opened the scoring. Orr tied it. Ted Green put

Boston ahead. John McKenzie, Wayne Cashman and Derek Sanderson padded the lead. Late in the second, Henri Richard beat Johnston, and the period ended with Boston in front, five–two. Richard's goal gave the Canadiens a lift, but hardly prepared anyone for what followed.

Béliveau scored twice in the first five minutes of the third. Jacques Lemaire stole the puck from Orr at the Montreal blue line, raced in alone and tied it. Then Béliveau won a skirmish behind the Boston net and, while pinned to the boards, flipped a pass to a red sweater out front. Ferguson was there to bat it in and the Canadiens were ahead. Mahovlich added a late goal to complete one of the most remarkable comebacks in Stanley Cup history.

That changed the dynamic of the series. It planted an idea in the minds of the Canadiens—we can win—and sowed doubt among the Bruins. The two old rivals split the next four games and played the seventh on a Sunday afternoon in Boston Garden. The Bruins scored first, but Montreal refused to wilt. Mahovlich tied the score, and the rookie Réjean Houle gave the Canadiens a lead they never relinquished.

They won four–two and arrived home to a tumultuous welcome. A crowd estimated at ten thousand packed the terminal and spilled out of the building onto sidewalks and roadways. They cheered as the players appeared one by one or in pairs. Then a chant went up: "*On veut Dryden. On veut Dryden.*" We want Dryden. We want Dryden.

The victory had been a team effort. Béliveau launched the big comeback in game two. Henri Richard shut down scoring champion Phil Esposito. Lemaire set up three goals in game seven. Mahovlich averaged a goal a game. But Dryden was the brightest star. Twenty-six shots eluded him, but he had stopped 260.

The Canadiens met the Minnesota North Stars next and rolled over them in six, but internal discord nearly derailed their pursuit of a seventeenth Cup. MacNeil had been no more successful than Ruel at managing the talents and temperament of this prodigious group of athletes. His coaching methods bugged many of the players, especially the veterans. He constantly juggled the lines, sometimes using twenty to twenty-five combinations in a single game. The French-language papers were critical, and the players were talking among themselves. They had named a combination sandwich at a favourite downtown eatery the MacNeil special. And some said they felt like participants in the TV game show *What's My Line?*

The discontent percolated below the surface until the second game against Minnesota. The Canadiens had fallen behind five–two after forty minutes. In the third, MacNeil benched Ferguson and used little Bobby Sheehan on the Béliveau–Cournoyer line. Three times the coach called Sheehan's name, and each time the fiery veteran seethed. Upon hearing it again, Ferguson snapped. He unleashed an obscenity-laden tirade at the coach. A few minutes later, the North Stars scored. Ferguson smashed his stick, punched the stick rack and headed for the dressing room with twenty-one seconds on the clock. He ducked into the team training facility to avoid the media and exhausted his rage by booting the whirlpool bath hard enough to puncture its base.

Ferguson left the Forum without granting interviews, but his outburst made headlines the following day. "Ferguson Tosses Tantrum as Habs Lose," declared one paper, while another said, "Fergy Keeping His Own Counsel; MacNeil Says Issue Closed."

A tight, tense final against Chicago deepened the rupture between coach and players and led to another blow-up after the fifth game. It was played in Chicago. The series was tied at two. Richard was serving a minor late in the first when Dennis Hull opened the scoring. The thirty-five-year-old Montreal veteran, as fierce and proud a competitor as ever wore the sweater, scarcely saw the ice for the rest of the game, even though MacNeil tried seventeen different forward combinations in the first two periods and another eight in the third. Nothing worked. The Canadiens lost two–nothing and Richard spoke his mind.

"I've never played for a worse coach," he snarled at the pack of French-speaking reporters who rushed to interview him. "I'm paid to play. I give one hundred per cent and I think it's time somebody said something. We won in Montreal with three sets of lines. Then we come in here and he mixes them all up. How can you win with him? He's incompetent."

Richard's outburst exposed the fissures within the team. It also brought out the worst in some of the fans. Several phoned the Forum and issued death threats against MacNeil. The Canadiens hired security guards to protect their coach at home and work. Two guards kept watch from the Canadiens bench during the emotionally charged sixth game, played on a Saturday afternoon at the Forum. The teams traded goals in the first. Peter Mahovlich put Montreal ahead early in the second. Chicago scored twice in the last three minutes of the period. At the intermission, the Hawks were twenty minutes from the Stanley Cup. But they couldn't hold the lead.

Frank Mahovlich tied it five minutes into the third, and a thunderous ovation shook the Forum. Midway through the period, brother Peter scored and, with Dryden in net, Montreal's lead was iron-clad.

Game seven was played May 18, a Tuesday. Chicago Stadium was like a steam bath. The ice was soft. The Hawks got off to a roaring start and won the first period. Dennis Hull scored with under a minute to go, and Danny O'Shea put the Hawks ahead by two early in the second. They remained in control until the fourteen-minute mark, when Lemaire carried the puck out of the Montreal end, stepped over centre and fired a slap shot. Chicago goaltender Tony Esposito immediately fell to his knees, but the puck kept rising and sailed over his right shoulder.

"The goal stunned the Chicago crowd and the players as well," Ferguson later observed. "You could almost feel the confidence draining out of them."

With less than two minutes remaining in the period, Richard tied the score on a feed from Lemaire, and the Canadiens took control. Early in the third, Richard struck again. He swooped into the Chicago end and around a sprawling Keith Magnuson, cut across the front of the net and fired the puck past Esposito.

Dryden made several game-saving stops, and when the siren sounded the score remained three–two. The Canadiens had mounted another remarkable comeback. They swarmed Dryden and lifted him to their shoulders, then raised their bruised and beleaguered coach and carried him to centre ice. There, under the glare of the stadium lights and the disappointed Chicago crowd, Clarence Campbell presented the Conn Smythe Trophy to Dryden and the Stanley Cup to Béliveau.

Afterward, in the champagne-soaked dressing room, reporters surrounded Richard. "The best," said the jubilant veteran. "The best of all the ten Stanley Cups I've won. It's the best, better than the other nine because we were so much the underdogs it wasn't funny."

The celebration continued on the flight home. The players guzzled champagne and sang the fans' old war chant: "*Halte là! Halte là! Halte là! Les Canadiens sont là.*" They arrived home late, but were up early because Mayor Jean Drapeau had planned a parade and civic reception. It began at the Forum at noon and ended in mid-afternoon at City Hall. The route, mostly along Ste-Catherine Street, was just over four miles long. Police estimated that six hundred thousand people, a quarter of the city's population, attended. The crowds were so thick that the cars carrying the players could barely move, and it was hot—ninety degrees Fahrenheit.

Montrealers barely had time to digest the team's latest triumph when the post-season changes began, changes that marked the end of one era and the start of another. Ferguson retired for good after eight seasons, 145 goals, 1,214 penalty minutes and five Stanley Cups. Béliveau, the team's thirty-nine-year-old captain, whose hair was showing flashes of grey, announced that he, too, was finished. Teammates urged him to reconsider. Hundreds of fans phoned or sent letters pleading with him to play another year. A crowd of twenty thousand packed Jarry Park when the Montreal Expos held a Jean Béliveau Night in early June. "They came," as one sportswriter put it, "to worship the superstar they have idolized for close to two decades."

Béliveau had played eighteen seasons, scored 507 goals and accumulated 1,219 points. He had won a scoring title, the Conn Smythe Trophy, was twice named the NHL's most valuable player and had ten Stanley Cups to his credit. But he would be remembered for his integrity, his dignity and the unparalleled elegance he brought to the bear pit of professional hockey.

And prior to the annual player draft, held at the Queen Elizabeth Hotel in the second week of June, MacNeil told Pollock he was prepared to step down and go back to coaching the Voyageurs. He had coached the Canadiens for fifty-five regular-season games (winning thirty-three, losing fifteen and tying nine) and twenty playoff games that culminated in the team's seventeenth Stanley Cup.

MacNeil was a good man. He had endured the Richard and Ferguson incidents with "courageous silence," as the columnist John Robertson wrote, and he would demonstrate over the next decade and half that he was a good coach. But MacNeil, like Ruel before him, was cursed by circumstances. He had been handed a team that still belonged to Toe Blake. He had not been able to step out of Blake's enormous shadow and take the players with him.

In the spring of 1971, the Canadiens needed a fresh start behind the bench and on the ice. They needed a coach who could make the players forget the past and focus on the future. And they needed a vibrant young talent who had the potential to bridge the chasm created by Béliveau's departure. And Pollock had candidates ready to fill both openings.

1971-1979
SCOTTY'S TEAM

A NEW ERA IN THE HISTORY of the Montreal Canadiens began on the evening of September 18, 1971, a Saturday, when the reigning champions played their keenest rival, the Boston Bruins. This was the first of ten pre-season exhibition games each would play, so there was nothing on the line except pride. But that was enough to ensure that both teams used their best players. Gerry Cheevers, Bobby Orr and Phil Esposito were in the lineup along with the rest of Boston's big names—Ted Green, Ken Hodge, Wayne Cashman and Derek Sanderson. The Canadiens countered with Ken Dryden, Jacques Laperrière, J.C. Tremblay, Henri Richard, Yvan Cournoyer, Jacques Lemaire, the Mahovlich brothers and their top prospect, twenty-year-old Guy Lafleur, the slender, fair-haired, goal-scoring dynamo who was expected to be Montreal's next French-Canadian superstar.

Lafleur's debut drew the Forum's biggest crowd for a hockey game up to that time. Eighteen thousand, nine hundred and six fans attended, and they got more than their money's worth. Lafleur started the game at centre between Cournoyer and Frank Mahovlich. He won the opening faceoff from Esposito. He stole the puck from Hodge in the Bruins' end, passed to Mahovlich and, at the forty-one-second mark, had set up his first goal at the

NHL level. Lafleur earned three assists that night. Mahovlich scored twice. So did Cournoyer.

Referee Bill Friday handed out 116 minutes in penalties. The linesmen broke up four fights, all in the third period. Dryden tangled with Sanderson. Peter Mahovlich went at it with Cashman. Orr punched out Phil Roberto and Bruin rookie Terry O'Reilly hammered the veteran Claude Larose. When the game finally ended, the scoreboard read Canadiens seven, Boston five, and Esposito told a reporter, "The hockey season is off to a helluva start."

Everyone, except perhaps some of the Bruins, went home happy: the fans, who had witnessed a game with playoff-like intensity; the rookie Lafleur, who admitted afterward that he'd had the jitters before the opening faceoff; and Scotty Bowman, Montreal's new coach, who had turned thirty-eight that day and had fulfilled a dream by taking his place behind the Canadiens bench.

The game was a homecoming for the native Montrealer and the end of an apprenticeship begun a decade and a half earlier in the trenches of junior hockey. Bowman was born in Verdun, a few miles west of the Forum, and grew up in a neighbourhood called The Avenues, a series of numbered thoroughfares lined with sixplexes where working-class French- and English-speaking families resided.

He was the second of four children of Scottish immigrants, had learned French on the streets before he began grade one, and spent his youth on the playing fields of Verdun. Hockey, mostly played outdoors, was his favourite sport. He was a quarterback in high school, a sprinter on the track team and in the summer he played baseball and softball.

Bowman's athletic abilities carried him as far as the Junior Canadiens. He played left wing for parts of two seasons (1951–52 and 1952–53) under coach Sam Pollock and then moved on to the rival Royals. His playing days ended, uneventfully, in the spring of 1954.* That fall, Bowman enrolled in a

---

* Bowman has always maintained that his career ended during a playoff game against the Trois-Rivières Reds on March 6, 1952. According to the oft-repeated story, Bowman had a breakaway in the final minute and Reds defenceman Jean-Guy Talbot clubbed him with his stick, fracturing

business program at Sir George Williams College and afterward took a job in the stockroom at a Sherwin-Williams paint plant on Atwater Avenue, a few blocks south of the Forum.

Hockey was never far from his mind, though. He often walked to the Forum at lunch to watch the Canadiens practise, and he stayed in touch with Pollock, who made him director of the bantam, midget and juvenile teams the Canadiens sponsored in Verdun. In 1955–56, Pollock gave him a Junior B team to run, the Park Extension Flyers, and the following season offered him a paid position as assistant general manager and assistant coach of the Hull-Ottawa Canadiens.

Bowman spent the next decade working under Pollock, either as a junior coach or an amateur scout. They took their Canadiens to the Memorial Cup final in 1956–57, but lost. The following year they won the national title. In the fall of 1958, the Canadiens sent Bowman to Peterborough to coach their Ontario junior team, the Petes, and in the spring of 1959 he led them past Claude Ruel's Junior Canadiens to a berth in the Memorial Cup. He was coaching the Junior Canadiens in 1965–66 when Lynn Patrick, the newly appointed general manager of the St. Louis Blues, offered him a position as his assistant.

Patrick and Bowman had a year to prepare for the June 1967 expansion draft, and they used the time wisely. Bowman scouted pro teams across the continent. He concluded that the Blues could not acquire the offensive talent necessary to compete with the likes of Montreal, Boston and Chicago, so he and Patrick built a team that was defensively solid. Patrick coached the first sixteen games of the 1967–68 season before turning over the Blues to his assistant—an inspired decision. Bowman inherited a last-place club and guided them to the Stanley Cup final against Montreal in the spring of 1968.

His Blues advanced to the final in each of the next two seasons before things turned sour in St. Louis. Sid Salomon III, the owner's son, who

---

his skull. However, while researching his unauthorized biography, *Scotty Bowman: A Life in Hockey*, writer Douglas Hunter read the newspaper accounts and found that the vicious slash opened a four- to five-inch wound that required fourteen stitches. Bowman missed one game.

claimed to know men even if he didn't know hockey, began meddling in personnel decisions. Bowman objected, and the Salomons dumped him after the Blues were eliminated in the opening round of the 1971 playoffs.

Pollock welcomed his old friend and understudy back to the Canadiens fold. He had put two men behind the bench—Claude Ruel and Al MacNeil—and neither had worked out. Pollock had to get it right the third time around. He met privately with Bowman in Chicago during the Stanley Cup final, and introduced him as the team's new coach on the eve of the June 1971 player draft in Montreal.

Bowman was a trim, muscular man, youthful enough to pass for a player, though no player ever mistook him for one of them. He was more a tyrant than a chummy coach who tried to be one of the guys. He had told the recruits at the first Blues training camp: "Not one of you deserves to be here. If the league hadn't expanded, you'd all still be in the minors where you belong. So the twenty of you who make the team will be the ones who work the hardest. Let's get at it." It was indicative of Bowman's blunt and abrasive way of getting the most out of his players, which was always his objective. He was a shrewd judge of character. He understood that a dressing room is full of different personalities. He treated his players as individuals, masterfully manipulating them to keep them on edge, to drive out complacency and to extract the best possible performance.

He rarely divulged much publicly about his methods, but once told a journalist: "A big thing is to know your players. Some guys come to play under all circumstances. Others have to have somebody prodding them all the time. Yelling at them does not work. Instead, make them miss a shift. Put them out under a tough situation. Or put them into an easy situation if you think if you think they need to regain their confidence. You've got to know how to motivate them. Some guys respond to the whip. Others don't."

Bowman had another skill that set him apart from most of his peers. He coached according to the game rather than a game plan. "You have to have a feel for the game," he explained. "When you feel things aren't working, you have to make changes. Use a fourth line. Change the makeup of your lines. Play some guys more than you have been. Sit a guy out for a shift or two."

But no coach can turn brass into gold, or low cards into high ones, a point he made in his first season in St. Louis. "There are twenty guys in here who probably have twenty different ways to make out the lineup," he told his players on one occasion. "I suppose you all have a better way to shuffle this deck and come up with a winning hand. But let me tell you this gentlemen: you can't shuffle deuces and threes."

A coach needed two things to be a winner. First, he had to have good goaltending, and the Canadiens had dealt him a pair of aces in Dryden and Rogie Vachon. A coach also required a general manager who could supply him with raw talent that could be moulded into a team, and Bowman's GM in Montreal would prove spectacularly successful at that task.

Sam Pollock knew that the Canadiens had to make changes every year if they were to remain a contender or win championships. Renewal was relatively simple when he became general manager in 1964. The Canadiens owned a bigger and richer network of sponsored teams than any of their rivals. The system extended from peewees to minor pros. It produced bright prospects and potential stars every winter.

But professional hockey was at a crossroads in the mid-1960s. Expansion was imminent, and that forced the NHL to abandon the sponsorship system in favour of the universal player draft. Kids would play for unaffiliated teams until age twenty, which was later lowered to eighteen. The best would be placed in a pool, and the NHL teams would take turns selecting them based on their position in the league standings at the end of the previous season.

The Canadiens opposed the new system because they had the most to lose. They also argued that the universal draft would ultimately erode the French-Canadian character of the team. The league responded by passing a bylaw allowing the Canadiens to draft the top two prospects from Quebec for a period of three years, starting in 1967. This turned out to be more a liability than a benefit, according to Pollock. In an interview some years later, he pointed out that the Canadiens got only two good players—Réjean Houle and Marc Tardif—who were taken first and second respectively in the 1969 draft. But they had to pass on many other talented prospects in those three years in order to select French-Canadians.

As well, the rules of the draft were amended from time to time, as new teams were admitted to the NHL. Pollock recalled that under one set of revisions, the established clubs were allowed to protect fourteen skaters—four defencemen, nine forwards and one spare—going into the draft. The new clubs were allowed to select up to three unprotected players from their older rivals, though each selection would cost thirty thousand dollars.

"This was a real problem for us," Pollock recalled years later in an interview. "We had a championship team. Our fifteenth, sixteenth and seventeenth players were very desirable. We had to make sure we weren't going to lose players just for cash. The trick was to make trades."

Pollock traded older players who were past their prime and younger players who were not likely to be better-than-average NHLers. In doing so, he made room on the Canadiens' protected list for the team's best prospects and acquired the draft picks necessary to build another champion. He and Wren Blair of the Minnesota North Stars moved about forty-five players between their franchises. Pollock dispatched Gump Worsley, Ted Harris, Danny Grant, Jude Drouin and Claude Larose to the Stars for additional draft choices, and the deals helped both sides, as Blair later told an interviewer from *Reader's Digest*. "In 1968, we gave Sam our first-round draft choice for 1972 in order to get Danny Grant," Blair recalled. "Grant was twenty-one years old and in the next four seasons scored 115 goals for us. So in 1972 we didn't have a first-round draft choice, but in the meantime we'd got 115 goals. What's wrong with that?"

At one time or another, Pollock dealt with almost all the expansion clubs. His most controversial trade occurred on January 26, 1971, when he sent centre Ralph Backstrom, a thirteen-year veteran, to Los Angeles for two minor leaguers and the Kings' second-round pick in 1973. At the time, Los Angeles and Oakland were the NHL's two worst teams. Backstrom scored twenty-seven points for the Kings and led the team out of the basement and into the playoffs, while the Seals finished dead last. That meant Oakland should have drafted first in 1971, except that the team had surrendered its pick to Montreal. The media, and some general managers, cried foul. They accused Pollock of unfairly influencing the NHL's West Division standings, an allegation he always denied. "Somebody put out the story that we traded Backstrom so Oakland would finish below Los Angeles and everybody else repeated it," Pollack said in an interview some years later. "It was pure luck the way things turned out.

"Backstrom was getting older. He wasn't getting played. He was going through a divorce and needed a change. He came in and asked to be traded. He wanted to go to a west coast club. The first team we tried was Oakland, because we'd made a lot of deals with them in the past, and they said no. We tried Vancouver and they weren't interested. We weren't particularly interested in making this deal, but we did."

In any event, Pollack's let's-make-a-deal approach provided Bowman with the talent he needed to build another champion. The Canadiens owned four of the top twenty picks in the 1971 draft. They chose Murray Wilson, a lanky, high-speed left winger from the Ottawa 67's; Chuck Arnason, a tough, goal-scoring right winger from the Flin Flon Bombers; and defenceman Larry Robinson from the Kitchener Rangers. But on draft day, June 10, these young men were swept into the shadows by Montreal's number one pick.

The proceedings began shortly before 10 a.m. in the big ballroom at the Queen Elizabeth Hotel. "First choice . . . Golden Seals of California," league president Clarence Campbell announced.

"California regretfully defers its number one choice to the Stanley Cup champion Montreal Canadiens," replied general manager Gary Young.

"Canadiens' turn," said Campbell.

"Time, please, Mr. Campbell," Pollock shouted for effect. Then, smiling broadly, he said, "Mr. Campbell, Montreal Canadiens choose Guy Lafleur of the Quebec Remparts."

Guy Lafleur had trouble sleeping in the final days of August and the first days of September, so excited was he about training camp, his first as a member of the Montreal Canadiens. He had dreamed of wearing the team's famous colours since he was a boy growing up in Thurso, a pulp and paper town of about four thousand people on the Ottawa River, twenty-five miles downstream from the nation's capital.

His father, Réjean, was a welder with the James McLaren Company, which owned the pulp mill that made the air in Thurso reek of sulphur. Réjean Lafleur bought skates for his only son when Guy was five. He built a backyard rink and made a net of old pipes welded together.

From the moment he learned to skate, Lafleur lived for hockey. He sometimes slept in his equipment so he could be on the ice quicker in the morning. When he outgrew the small rink behind the family home, he would get up before sunrise on winter mornings, sneak into the town's aged and rickety arena, turn on a single light and skate and shoot all by himself while other boys his age were climbing out of bed and getting ready for class. Frère Léo Jacques, the coach of his school team, cut a hole in a board so the kids could practise shooting on the outdoor rink in the yard, and Lafleur did until he developed a pinpoint shot to go with his mesmerizing speed.

For three straight winters, starting in 1962 when he was ten years old, Lafleur competed in the famous Quebec peewee tournament that attracted teams from across the continent. He scored twenty-five goals the first time, more than any other player. TV and radio stations interviewed him, and a newspaper reporter predicted that he was "the young French-Canadian most likely to inherit the nickname Boom Boom."

The Quebec Aces, a Junior B team, took note of the prodigy. Club executive Paul Dumont introduced himself to Réjean Lafleur during the 1964 tournament and offered his son a tryout when he turned fifteen. In the fall of 1966, Lafleur left home to play for the Aces. He spent three seasons with them, and two with the major junior Quebec Remparts. He wore sweater number four, the same as his boyhood idol, Jean Béliveau. He taped a large picture of Béliveau to his Remparts locker and he became as big a star in Quebec City as Béliveau had been two decades earlier. He scored 388 goals in 286 junior games and accumulated 675 points. He led the Remparts to the Memorial Cup championship in his final year. He filled the ten-thousand-seat Colisée night after night, and the fans showed their appreciation by buying him a burgundy Buick Riviera.

By the time the Canadiens drafted him, Lafleur was famous in Quebec. His hometown held a parade and threw a party to celebrate his ascension to the NHL. He worked that summer as a goodwill ambassador for Molson Breweries, touring the province, attending fairs, softball tournaments and powwows and signing autographs everywhere. Béliveau introduced him to his agent, Gerry Patterson, who negotiated a two-year, $105,000 contract, making him the highest-paid rookie in Canadiens history. Béliveau's wife, Elise, found him an apartment in suburban Longueuil, a few blocks from their home, and helped him pick his furniture.

Throughout that whirlwind summer, Lafleur never lost sight of hockey. He jogged three miles daily or rode several miles on an exercise bike. But no amount of training could prepare him for his rookie year. He shook like a leaf when he lined up to start his first game of the regular season. Everyone—the fans, the media and his opponents—expected so much.

Away from the rink, he was lonely. He lived by himself. He didn't have friends or family in Montreal. His friends were all in Quebec City, and on days off he would drive 180 miles to the capital to see them. On occasion, he would go there just for a haircut.

Despite the stress and loneliness, he had a good season. His numbers—twenty-nine goals, thirty-five assists and sixty-four points—were better than those of any of the highly-touted prospects of the past. Better than the Rocket's or Béliveau's or Geoffrion's. But they weren't good enough to satisfy expectations. Other rookies in 1971–72 were more impressive. Marcel Dionne, drafted right behind him by the Detroit Red Wings, had twenty-eight goals and a record seventy-seven points. Richard Martin, another Quebecker, scored forty-four goals for the Buffalo Sabres.

Lafleur that season was just a swift and promising newcomer on a powerful club stacked with veteran talent. The team leaders were Henri Richard, who succeeded Béliveau as captain; Frank Mahovlich, who scored forty-three goals and finished sixth in scoring; and Yvan Cournoyer, who had forty-seven goals and placed eighth. The Canadiens won forty-six games, earned 108 points and finished third behind the Bruins and Rangers. By any yardstick, 1971–72 was a good season, but it ended prematurely. They met the Rangers in the first round of the playoffs and went down in six.

———

One evening in the summer of 1972, Sam Pollock received a phone call from Larry Pleau, a twenty-five-year-old centre from Massachusetts who had played parts of the previous three seasons with the Canadiens. Pleau had bounced between the farm team in Halifax and Montreal. He hadn't played much when he was with the Canadiens and he wanted out. He had already asked for a trade and been refused. Now, he had an offer from the New England Whalers of the recently formed World Hockey Association, and the Whalers wanted him to sign the following morning.

"Mr. Pollock," Pleau said, "if you'd just tell me you'd trade me, I'd stay in the league. . . . That's what I want to do."

"Larry," Pollock replied, "I'm not going to trade you and there's not going to be a WHA tomorrow and there's not going to be one ever."

Pollock hung up. The next day, the Whalers held a press conference and Pleau affixed his signature to a contract. He became the first player to jump leagues and, in so doing, broke the monopoly that the NHL had enjoyed since 1926, when pro hockey collapsed in the west.

As the summer waned, dozens of others received offers. Some were extravagant, some outrageous, and they shook the game to its foundations. About eighty NHLers bolted to the WHA prior to the start of the 1972–73 season. The new league poached the famous (Bobby Hull) and the obscure (Gerry Odrowski) and gravely damaged the Stanley Cup champion Bruins by signing goaltender Gerry Cheevers, defenceman Ted Green and forwards Derek Sanderson and John McKenzie.

In the first wave of defections, the Canadiens lost only Pleau and J.C. Tremblay, a thirteen-year veteran and two-time all-star who joined the Quebec Nordiques. By mid-September, when training camp opened in Kentville, Nova Scotia, Pollock was over the shock and all smiles. "The best camp we've had in the last eight or nine years," he told reporters. There were openings at each position and there were eager draft picks fighting for the jobs. Wayne Thomas and Michel Plasse competed for the backup goaltender's job. There were two spots available on defence and three good candidates: Bob Murdoch, Pierre Bouchard and twenty-one-year-old Larry

Robinson. The prospective forwards included Dave Gardner and Steve Shutt, Toronto Marlboro graduates who had played together on one of the highest-scoring offensive units in junior hockey history; big, tough Yvon Lambert, the Voyageurs enforcer who looked like a young John Ferguson, according to Pollock; and the tall, lean, exceptionally fast left winger Murray Wilson, who reminded Pollock of Frank Mahovlich with his ability to burst around the outside of defencemen with great gusts of speed.

The Canadiens threw a formidable mix of youth and experience at their opponents that winter. They won fifty-two games, lost ten and tied sixteen. They finished with 120 points, thirty-two up on Buffalo, whom they met in the opening round of the playoffs. They never lost two games in a row and they had remarkable depth, as *The Gazette*'s Ted Blackman noted. "The fourth-line left winger scored eighteen goals," he wrote. "That's Murray Wilson. The fifth-line left winger scored eight. He's Steve Shutt. The backup goalie and assistant backup had goals-against averages of 2.54 and 2.42 respectively and can't get into a game."

There was just one cloud on the horizon that threatened to undo the magnificent team that Pollock and Bowman were building: the WHA. The Quebec Nordiques were trying to steal Guy Lafleur, whose two-year contract was about to expire. In January 1973, Lafleur's agent, Gerry Patterson, met with two members of the Nordiques board, including Roger Barré, whose daughter Lise was engaged to Lafleur. The following month, the Quebec group offered a three-year deal worth $320,000. Lafleur dismissed it as insulting because others had received much more lucrative packages from WHA teams.

Patterson met three more times with representatives of the Nordiques and stipulated that Lafleur wanted a fully guaranteed long-term contract. In March, Quebec presented a second offer. It was valued at $465,000 over three years. By then, the season was winding down and Patterson was also negotiating with Pollock.

The Canadiens general manager put together a package that addressed Lafleur's demands. It was competitive with the WHA money, yet it would not completely distort the team's salary structure. The offer was worth a guaranteed one million dollars over ten years, and could be renegotiated at the end of years three and six. Pollock presented it on April 4. He wanted a decision within the next twenty-four hours because he had had difficulty convincing the owners and directors to approve it. Besides, he knew the Nordiques remained interested. In fact, Roger Barré left Quebec City for Montreal on April 5 with a new offer. It would make Lafleur a millionaire even faster than the Canadiens deal. Lafleur skated with his teammates that morning. He attended a team luncheon. Then he huddled with Pollock and Patterson while the rest of the players departed for a Laurentian resort called La Sapinière to prepare for game two of their playoff series that evening against the Buffalo Sabres.

Lise Barré phoned La Sapinière repeatedly, hoping to tell her future husband not to sign until he had talked to her father. She never reached him, and Roger Barré never got a chance to make his pitch. Lafleur signed that afternoon. An hour before the opening faceoff, Pollock appeared in the Forum media lounge and announced that Lafleur would be a Montreal Canadien for the next decade.

The contract was the richest in team history, even though Lafleur was still an emerging talent who played in the shadows of his rivals, Dionne and Martin, as well as Montreal's offensive leaders—Frank Mahovlich, Jacques Lemaire and Yvan Cournoyer.

In the playoffs that year, Cournoyer finished first among scorers with twenty-five points, Mahovlich was right behind him with twenty-three and Lemaire had twenty. The Canadiens eliminated the Sabres in six, the Philadelphia Flyers in five and then met the Chicago Black Hawks in the final. Montreal took control in game four, played on a Sunday afternoon in Chicago. The Stadium was packed from rinkside to the rafters with raucous and vociferous Chicago fans howling for a victory that would tie the series at two games each. NBC and CBC's *Hockey Night in Canada* broadcast the game and 150 journalists covered it.

Montreal won four–nothing and the Hawks barely touched the puck. "They are too fast for us," a subdued Billy Reay, the Hawks' coach, murmured to a group of reporters who cornered him in his office. "It's absolutely unbelievable. What more can we do?"

The Canadiens prepared to celebrate their eighteenth Stanley Cup after game five at home. They rented the ballroom at the Queen Elizabeth. They had champagne ready. Mayor Jean Drapeau had a parade planned for the next day. And the Hawks did the impossible: they upset the Canadiens eight–seven in a game that was more like shinny than play-off hockey. Back home two nights later, the Hawks ran out of miracles. The Canadiens prevailed by a score of four–two. Cournoyer, who had set a record for playoff goals, won the Conn Smythe Trophy. Clarence Campbell presented the Stanley Cup to Henri Richard—his first as captain, his eleventh as a Canadien. Two thousand Montrealers hailed the champions when they arrived home, and the following morning the mayor had his parade.

Kids skipped school. Factories halted production. Downtown office towers emptied. The city took the day off. Five hundred thousand Montrealers packed the usual route, east on Ste-Catherine Street from the Forum toward City Hall. They tossed confetti. They thrust pens and paper at the players for autographs. They sang the decades-old chant: "*Halte là! Halte là! Halte là! Les Canadiens sont là.*" And they smiled through rain showers that dampened the city, but not their spirits, on a warm and joyous spring day.

Four days later, general managers, coaches and scouts from each of the NHL's sixteen teams gathered at the Mount Royal Hotel in Montreal for the league's annual player draft. The event had been moved ahead by almost a month to beat the WHA in the pursuit of talent. The Canadiens began with four first-round draft picks, but Sam Pollock traded three of them—to Atlanta, Vancouver and Los Angeles in exchange for first-rounders in 1974. The Canadiens still had the fifth pick overall, but dealt it to the St. Louis Blues, who were anxious to move up in order to choose goaltender John Davidson. Pollock used the eighth selection, obtained from St. Louis, to select forward Bob Gainey—a decision that puzzled many Montrealers.

"Who did the Canadiens take?" Red Fisher asked a colleague in the *Montreal Star* newsroom.

"A kid named Gainey," the co-worker replied. "Bob Gainey."

"Never heard of him," Fisher said.

The name drew a blank with Yvon Pedneault of *La Presse* as well. "Who among us has ever heard the name Bob Gainey?" he asked his readers. "I consulted the statistics to see if they had got the name correct. I expected to find a fifty-goal scorer, at least a centreman—in short, a logical choice for the big team."

Pedneault could only tell his readers that Gainey was nineteen, that he played left wing, that he had scored twenty-two goals and added twenty-one assists in junior that season, that he weighed 184 pounds and stood six foot one, though head scout Claude Ruel insisted that Gainey was six–two.

"Only forty-three points!" Pedneault exclaimed. "Must we believe that Ruel has made a mistake?"

Gainey had come recommended by Ron Caron, who scouted the Ontario Major Junior Hockey League for the Canadiens, and Roger Neilson, Gainey's coach with the Peterborough Petes, who doubled as a Montreal scout. Pollock never saw his number one pick play junior. He got his first glimpse during an exhibition game that fall. The Canadiens were playing the Bruins.

Pollock watched as Bobby Orr picked up a loose puck in his own end and took off. Past one player. Then another. Across centre ice. Over the blue line. His mind focused on the play in front of him and completely oblivious to the strapping young man in the red sweater who had given chase, gained steadily and then slammed into hockey's reigning superstar, sending him sprawling and snuffing out the attack. Pollock looked at the number on the sweater, then at his roster. It was Gainey.

The tall, reserved rookie had made an audacious debut, though he had felt uncertain and slightly starstruck during the pre-game warmup. Each time he passed the end boards he gazed at his reflection in the glass and wondered, *What am I doing in this famous sweater?* But once the puck was dropped, he did what he had always done, as a Peterborough church league all-star, as a Peterborough Junior B Lion and as a Peterborough Pete: he outskated everyone on the pond.

And he quickly skated his way onto the big club. After five games as a Halifax Voyageur, he joined the Canadiens and was a pleasant surprise in an autumn filled with discord and disruption. Réjean Houle and Marc Tardif had deserted the team for the Quebec Nordiques. "Quebec paid them two or three times as much as we would have," Pollock recalled in later years. "They didn't even try to renegotiate. They just left."

Then Ken Dryden quit. He had a year to go on a contract that was paying him eighty thousand per season, but he wanted more and, after winning the Conn Smythe, the Calder, the Vézina and two Stanley Cups in three seasons, he was undoubtedly worth more. But the Canadiens' position was straightforward: they would not renegotiate contracts— unless agreed upon in advance, as in the case of Guy Lafleur—and Pollock would make no exceptions.

Dryden departed just as training camp opened. He held a press conference in Montreal and said: "I can name six goaltenders who are higher paid than me. That bothers me and I can't see why this should be the case." He went to work as a law clerk with a Toronto firm. He earned $135 a week and in his spare time played defence for Vulcan Packaging in the Toronto Industrial League.

With Dryden gone, Montreal's goals-against total rose by fifty-four. Coincidentally, the team's offensive output dropped by thirty-six and Lafleur, having lost linemates Houle and Tardif, scored only twenty-one goals. Late in the season, he fell into a dreadful slump and connected only twice in twenty games. Bowman reduced his ice time and, one day, Pollock told a group of reporters: "We consider Guy Lafleur an ordinary player. Once in a while he shows something exceptional, but we're no longer expecting much from him."

The Canadiens finished behind Boston, Philadelphia and Chicago. They lost to the Rangers in the opening round of the playoffs and, in some quarters, Scotty Bowman got blamed for the debacle. "[H]e was the root of the major failings which dragged so many players down to mediocrity this season," *Montreal Star* columnist John Robertson wrote. "Loss of pride. Loss of desire. Loss of togetherness. Lack of leadership. Inability to deal with the shirkers and malcontents in his midst. This is what he is paid handsomely to do.'

———

Frank Mahovlich left the Canadiens at the end of the 1973–74 season—his seventeenth in the NHL. He was thirty-six. He had played three and a half winters in Montreal and contributed 310 points. Sam Pollock offered him a new short-term deal at $135,000 annually, but it was no match for the Toronto Toros of the WHA, who signed Mahovlich for five years at $225,000 per season.

The team lost two other veterans as well—one to retirement, the other to injury. Jacques Laperrière retired at age thirty-two because he and Bowman couldn't get along. Their worst run-in occurred between periods during a humiliating blowout in St. Louis in February 1974. "You're finished," Bowman snapped at the veteran defenceman. "Take off your skates. Don't ruin your life, and don't try to ruin mine."

A few days later, Laperrière told the sportswriters: "Don't think I want to leave. I've been here eleven years, but if we hate each other it's no use. If things do not get better between him and I, there's no way I can play here next year."

Team captain Henri Richard started the 1974–75 season—his twentieth as a Canadien. He was thirty-eight. His hair was going grey and he was tiring of the grind. "I don't enjoy hockey as much anymore," he confided to a reporter one day in the dressing room. "I used to look forward to practice the day after a game. Now I just can't go through it. My body aches too much." Richard dressed sixteen times before fracturing his left ankle on November 13, 1974, in a game against Buffalo. He returned to the Forum before the end of the third period—he hobbled in on crutches, his leg in a cast—but would not return to the ice till the following spring.

With Mahovlich and Laperrière gone and Richard nearly finished, a new version of the Canadiens was emerging, one forged by the hand of Scotty Bowman. The on-ice leadership passed to Yvan Cournoyer, Jacques Lemaire and Serge Savard, the veterans who had joined the team during Toe Blake's final years. The balance of the lineup, with the exception of Peter Mahovlich and Jim Roberts, were young players, draftees just beginning to make their mark, and two more graduating juniors—Mario Tremblay and Doug Risebrough—made the team that fall.

The Canadiens were further strengthened by the return of Ken Dryden, who signed a new three-year contract worth nearly half a million dollars. And Guy Lafleur finally had the breakthrough that the team and its fans had hoped for. He started slowly, scoring his first goal late in October, eight games into the season, and then he went on a tear. He put six pucks past opposing goaltenders in the next two weeks and quickly earned the praise of his teammates.

"The kid has had a helluva start," Savard told the Montreal *Gazette*. "He's playing just like he was with the Remparts."

"He's got more confidence," Cournoyer added. "More confidence up and down, left and right."

Asked to explain, Lafleur shrugged. He acknowledged that he did feel more confident and was hitting more often, but could not account for the sudden change. The fans noted that he had shed the helmet he wore in his first three seasons, and some speculated that maybe the impending birth of his first child or the purchase of a country property for his wife's horses had somehow made a difference. Whatever the reason, Lafleur had found his scoring touch.

By February 12, when he broke his left index finger, he had accumulated forty-four goals and ninety-six points in fifty-four games. He was challenging Bobby Orr and Phil Esposito, the NHL's top scorers. Lafleur returned early in March and promptly lit up the Forum. He picked up four points in his first game back and hit the hundred-point plateau. The crowd responded with a roof-raising ovation and littered the playing surface with toe rubbers and programs.

Three weeks later, on a Saturday night, Lafleur scored his fiftieth at home against the Kansas City Scouts. The crowd gave him another ovation and showered debris on to the ice. His teammates mobbed him and, between periods, Maurice Richard phoned. "Guy seemed very happy that I called," said Richard, who watched the game on TV, "and I was very happy to congratulate him. He really deserves it, especially after the troubles he's had in his first three seasons in the league."

Lafleur scored his fifty-first the following evening in Boston to break the team record held jointly by Richard and Bernie Geoffrion. He finished with fifty-three goals and 119 points, two better than linemate Peter Mahovlich. They placed fourth and fifth respectively in scoring.

Montreal, Buffalo and Philadelphia each ended the season with 113 points. The Canadiens eliminated the Vancouver Canucks in five games, but fell to the Sabres in six. Buffalo's checking line—Craig Ramsay, Don Luce and Danny Gare—stopped Montreal's big scorers while Montreal's checkers proved unable to contain Gilbert Perreault, Richard Martin and René Robert, Buffalo's fabulous French Connection line. "One hundred and thirteen points during the regular season," Peter Mahovlich muttered after playoff-ending game, "and all down the [expletive deleted] drain."

In the wake of that painful defeat, Scotty Bowman mused that the Canadiens had to adopt a more structured style of play to keep pace with the changes occurring in the NHL. "We tried to go open and full out against the Sabres and it didn't work," he said. "All the emerging teams are resorting to systems. The big new player fits well into a system, and with this team I know it will be difficult, but we are going to have to resort to a system ourselves."

Bowman was thinking about the Sabres and, even more so, the Philadelphia Flyers, who had achieved great success with a system built on hard work, punishing checks and physical intimidation. The Flyers had humbled weak opponents and stared down or knocked down those who dared stand up to them. Their system had carried them to a Stanley Cup victory over the Boston Bruins in 1974 and another in 1975, when they beat the Sabres in six.

The Flyers had just two bona fide superstars. One was goaltender Bernie Parent, who led the NHL in shutouts and goals against in both Cup-winning seasons. The other was their captain, Bobby Clarke, who possessed a maniacal will to win. And they had three top-notch forwards in Reg Leach, Bill Barber and Rick MacLeish. Otherwise, the Flyers were mostly average players who would never be household names anywhere but Philadelphia.

Their coach, Fred Shero, had turned them into champions, and they were deeply grateful. "We won because of Freddie," Clarke told a Montreal reporter after their first Cup. "We don't have a bunch of stars, that's for sure. He's given us a system that's made us winners. Look at guys like Ed Van Impe. He used to ice the puck every time he got it because he never knew where anybody would be. Now the guys are in position and Eddie looks like an all-star. Same with Joe Watson."

Shero had apprenticed in the minors, where his teams finished first or second eleven times in thirteen seasons. He was a quirky character who wore "Photogray bifocals, a Fu Manchu moustache and early–American Bandstand clothes," according to a *Sports Illustrated* writer, and he had a fondness for motivational aphorisms, which he posted on the blackboard in the dressing room.

Shero was a disciple of Anatoli Tarasov, who had made the Soviet Union a hockey power, and he borrowed some of the Russian master's techniques. The short shift, for one. Shero's players were on and off in forty-five to sixty seconds and were consistently fresher than opponents who remained on the ice longer. The Flyers played their positions. They made short passes. They picked up their man on the backcheck and they finished their checks.

Shero had a way of making the game simple. "There are four corners in a rink," he would tell his players, "and there are two pits, one in front of each net. To win a game, you've got to win in the corners and in the pits. You give punishment and you take it."

The Flyers gave more than they ever took. They were a muscular team, dominated by players drafted from the Western junior league for their size and toughness, and they put fear into the minds of many opponents. In the championship years, no Flyer came close to leading the league in goals or points, but Dave Schultz led in penalty minutes in both Cup-winning seasons, each time establishing new records for minutes served. André Dupont was never far behind. And they had one of hockey's best fighters in Bob "The Hound" Kelly, who, according to Clarke, had usually thrown three or four punches before the other guy had even dropped his gloves.

The Flyers were the team the Canadiens had to beat to reclaim the Cup and, by the time training camp opened in September 1975, Bowman had some ideas on how to do that. But they did not include a system. As Ken Dryden later wrote in is his book *The Game,* "No one has ever heard of a Bowman system as they have a Shero system."

Instead, the Canadiens' game was predicated on speed. Bowman ran high-velocity practices and, during games, he urged his players to "throw speed at them." Relentless speed that confused opponents, made them hesitant and dismantled their system. In a game of skating and speed, the Canadiens could outrun and outscore anyone, including the Flyers. But to dethrone the champions, they would need the will and the courage to win the battles in the corners and the pits.

In back-to-back exhibition games in September 1975, they removed all doubt about their determination. The first was played at the Forum on a Saturday night, the second at the Spectrum twenty-four hours later. The Flyers won in Montreal, the Canadiens in Philadelphia. Both were hard-hitting contests. There were twenty-four penalties in the Saturday game. Schultz scored the winner and he decided to deliver a message the Canadiens wouldn't forget. Twice, he roughed up Yvan Cournoyer, who had succeeded Henri Richard as captain. On the second occasion, sophomore centre Doug Risebrough stepped in and wrestled the penalty king to a standstill without an exchange of punches.

The following evening, it was Risebrough who sent a message. With one minute and thirty-five seconds to go and the game out of reach, he went after Clarke, and the rest of the Flyers came unhinged. Those who were on the ice charged to their captain's aid. Risebrough's linemates piled on. Then the Philadelphia benched emptied, with the Canadiens were right behind them.

The brawl lasted ten minutes. Nobody kept track of who fought whom or how many punches were thrown. Referee Bruce Hood called the game. The next day, Bowman phoned Clarence Campbell and told him, "I'm not proud to be a coach in a league which tolerates this type of hockey."

It may have been ugly, but the free-for-all changed the competitive dynamic between the teams. The Canadiens had demonstrated that they had no fear of the Flyers. Henceforth, their games would be settled on the basis of skill rather than skulduggery.

The Canadiens and the Flyers were the two best teams in the league that year. Montreal set a record for points with 127, while Philadelphia had its best season ever with 118. Both advanced to the Stanley Cup final, and in this playoff there was more at stake than a trophy. Many said the future of the game hung in the balance. If the Flyers won, mayhem would prevail. If the Canadiens triumphed, speed and finesse would rule.

The series opened at the Forum. The Canadiens emerged with a three–two victory and, according to *The Gazette*'s Tim Burke: "It was one of the great hockey games I've witnessed in this decade. . . . The chances on goal were a bonus. What really piqued my interest was the marvellous free-wheeling style of both teams."

The Flyers played clean, high-quality hockey, and they were good enough to test the Canadiens. But they did not have the depth of talent necessary to win. Montreal won the second game and the series shifted to Philadelphia. The third contest was pivotal, as Dryden told a reporter: "In every game we've ever played in Philadelphia, we've let the Flyers set the tone and pace of the play. It's like saying, 'Okay, you dictate the rules and we'll follow them.'"

The Canadiens had not won in the Spectrum in two and a half years, and had been humiliated at least once. That occurred on March 3, 1974, when Philadelphia trounced Montreal six–nothing and some of the Flyers who were injured that night and watching from the press box urged their teammates to make it "ten–nothing against the froggies," according to Burke. "Gales of laughter swept through the Spectrum," he wrote, "as the apprehensive red sweaters threw up banks of snow in efforts to avoid their oppressors."

This time, it was the Flyers who had the jitters, and they reached for their favourite talisman—Kate Smith's rendition of "God Bless America," which was played at full volume over the public-address system prior to the opening faceoff of the third match. When they were revved up by Smith's powerful singing and an energized home crowd, the Flyers had tied one, lost three and won thirty-six over a five-year stretch.

But it didn't work this time. In the first minute of play, Canadiens defenceman Rick Chartraw flattened Joe Watson along the boards with what

Burke described as "a shattering check." That ignited both sides and "triggered twenty of the most furious minutes you'll ever see in a hockey game."

Montreal's depth made the difference that day. Bowman played twelve forwards almost equally, whereas Shero was overly reliant on the line of Clarke, Leach and Barber. Bowman also used two defensive centres—Risebrough and the rookie Doug Jarvis—against Clarke. As the game wore on, the Flyers wilted while the Canadiens maintained a consistent pace, or got stronger.

Still, the final score was close: three–two for Montreal. Afterward, the Canadiens began thinking about the next game. "We were up three–nothing in the series and you'd have thought everybody would just be doing cartwheels," recalls former left winger Murray Wilson. "But the dressing room was stone silent because we wanted to take it to them in their building four straight. It became an issue with us. It was never broadcast outside the dressing room. It was closed door. This is what we want to do. It was quiet, quiet, quiet. We hadn't lost focus on what we went there to accomplish."

Three nights later, hoping to save their season, the Flyers brought out Kate Smith herself and the ploy nearly worked. The teams were tied at three with a little over five minutes left in the third when Guy Lafleur scored his second game-winner of the series. Seventy seconds later, Peter Mahovlich put the Canadiens ahead by two and dashed all hope of a Flyer comeback.

The Spectrum was quiet afterward, except for the visitors' dressing room, where the jubilant Canadiens celebrated. They laughed, shouted, sprayed each other with Champagne and gathered around the Stanley Cup singing their own raucous version of "God Bless America."

The games had been tight and the hockey excellent. The Canadiens had won with what Burke called "a superbly balanced machine of talent, toughness, speed and poise." This new team was strong in so many ways that a question inevitably arose: Was this the start of another Montreal dynasty?

"Dynasties have a way of being short-lived," Dryden responded coyly when asked. "But I'll say that this will be a very competitive team for an indefinite period. We have so much versatility. We have such depth that we can play any type of game: offensive, defensive, wide open, rough. Any way we prefer."

After three seasons with the Quebec Nordiques of the World Hockey Association, in which he had scored twenty-seven, forty and fifty-one goals, Réjean Houle rejoined the Canadiens in the fall of 1976 and Harry Neale, coach of the New England Whalers, told a Montreal newspaper: "If I had to pick the single best player in our league last year it would be Houle. He does everything and he has a lot of guts. The Canadiens are getting a player who is infinitely better than when he left."

And Houle was returning to a team that had become exponentially stronger. In the 1976–77 season, the Canadiens lost three games in October, one in November, one in December, two in January and one in March. They set records for wins (sixty) and points, (132) among other things.

The team that Sam Pollock built and Scotty Bowman coached had hockey's best goalie in Ken Dryden and the sport's top defence corps, which was anchored by the "Big Three," Serge Savard, Guy Lapointe and Larry Robinson. The checking line (Bob Gainey, Doug Jarvis and Jim Roberts) could smother the most potent offensive unit, while the high-energy third line (Yvon Lambert, Doug Risebrough and Mario Tremblay) could shake any opponent's composure. The five or six spares could have been regulars with most other teams, and the highly capable Houle served as a utility forward who played all three positions and brought mirth to the dressing room.

They had two scoring lines, the second of which comprised Peter Mahovlich at centre, Yvan Cournoyer at right wing and a changing cast of characters at left. They were good, but the first line was unstoppable. Guy Lafleur, Steve Shutt and Jacques Lemaire combined for 150 goals and 316 points. Lafleur scored fifty-seven goals, his third consecutive season of fifty or more, and he won the scoring title for the second straight year.

He had become the most exciting player in hockey and attained the same exalted status in Quebec as his French-Canadian predecessors

Rocket Richard and Jean Béliveau. Whenever he launched one of his lightning-quick sprints toward the opposing goaltender, with his sweater billowing and blond hair rippling, an ear-splitting chant filled the Forum: "Guy! Guy! Guy!"

Wherever he went in Quebec, people wanted a piece of him. "You can see it when he eats in a downtown Montreal restaurant," journalist Dan Proudfoot wrote in a magazine profile. "The waitress arrives with his order of sliced London broil, bends as low as her low-cut blouse will allow, and whispers, 'The extra piece is from the chef.' Lafleur's eyes flick to the open window in the kitchen. A little guy topped with a chef's hat is waving frantically, shaking his head up and down in exaggerated support.

"At the next table two young men are ordering beer. They're quiet, but only until they see who sits beside them. 'Guy Lafleur!' one shouts. 'You're fantastic!'

"They reach out to touch him. That is the essential thing: to touch, to have actual contact, perhaps even to chat. A businessman stops at the table and declares that he is buying Guy Lafleur's next beer. The offer is refused . . . and the man leaves, satisfied at least that he has shaken Lafleur's hand.

"They are touching Lafleur physically because it is the only way they have of paying him back for the way he has touched them."

If he wanted to see a movie, Lafleur had to arrive just before show-time and leave before the credits rolled. His phone number was unlisted. Nevertheless, wife Lise changed it every three months and distributed it only to their closest friends. He once took his son Martin, then a pre-schooler, to a shopping mall at Easter to see a toy display, but a mob of autograph hunters assembled around them and he headed for the exit.

Lafleur was a solitary individual. The rink was his sanctuary. He arrived for games three to four hours before the opening faceoff. He dressed, taped his stick, fidgeted with his equipment, smoked cigarettes, drank Coke. He was always on the ice, alone, an hour before practice.

"Like a kid on a backyard rink," Dryden wrote in *The Game*, "he skates by himself . . . shooting pucks easily off the boards, watching them rebound, moving skates and gloved hands wherever his inventive instincts direct them. Here, far from the expedience of a game, away from defenders and linemates who shackle him to their banal predictability, alone with his virtuoso skills, it is his time to create."

He had done this as a boy in Thurso and as a teenager in Quebec City. "It was when he got older and nothing changed that his story became special," Dryden concluded. "In the whirl of more games, more practices, more off-ice diversions, more travel and everything else, other players gave up solitary time as boring and unnecessary. Lafleur did not."

Only one player in the NHL scored more goals than Lafleur in 1976–77, and that was his linemate Shutt. He finished with sixty, eclipsing the great Bobby Hull as the most prolific left winger in history. His career had followed a trajectory similar to that of Lafleur's. He had been a great junior player with the Toronto Marlboros, and a high draft pick (first round, fourth overall) in 1972. And then there followed a three-year apprenticeship.

As a rookie, he was fourth and sometimes fifth on the depth chart, and his linemates constantly changed. He appeared in only fifty games and scored eight goals. The following year, his output rose to fifteen, but he was still not part of a regular line. In his third season, he got a break when Frank Mahovlich and Marc Tardif left for the WHA and Bowman combined him with Lafleur and Peter Mahovlich. He scored thirty goals, though his breakthrough season ended with the jolting playoff loss to Buffalo.

Shutt returned home after the final game, went to the garage and sat in the dark by himself in his 1956 Bentley. He drank a case of beer. He listened to the radio. He thought about the season. He ignored a younger brother and three friends who were visiting and would not listen to his wife's pleas to come inside. At sunrise, he went to bed and slept all day. "God, I hate to lose," he said later.

Shutt's production jumped to forty-five goals in his fourth season, and when it hit sixty people began to say he was a superstar, something he found disconcerting. "I'm individually not a good player," he told journalist Earl McRae. "I can't stickhandle through a whole team like Pete Mahovlich or skate circles around people like Guy Lafleur. What I do well is, I adapt to whoever I play with, their style, their timing. I'm usually in the right place at the right time. It's not being in front of the net that's important. Anyone can get in front of the net. It's knowing when to be there, when to pounce."

Shutt produced better than a point a game during the 1977 playoffs. Centreman Lemaire was just as good. Lafleur averaged nearly two points per outing and won the Conn Smythe Trophy. The line piled up sixty-three points in fourteen playoff games, which was just one of the reasons why the Canadiens were formidable that spring. They beat the St. Louis Blues in four, the New York Islanders in six and the Boston Bruins in four to win the Stanley Cup—their twentieth.

The Canadiens came back with almost the same roster in 1977–78. Murray Wilson missed most of the season with a back injury, but that created an opening for Pierre Mondou, a twenty-two-year-old centre who played seventy-one games and scored nineteen goals. At the end of November, Pollock traded Peter Mahovlich to Pittsburgh for Pierre Larouche. Mahovlich was a disgruntled veteran. He had been bumped to the second line, had quarrelled with Bowman and his playing time had been reduced. Larouche was a pure offensive talent. He was just twenty-two, had already enjoyed a fifty-three-goal season, but arrived as a project to be turned into an all-round player.

Bowman and Pollock focused on improvements at the margins because the core of the team kept getting stronger. By the time the Canadiens began their pursuit of a third consecutive Cup, two other players—Bob Gainey and Larry Robinson—had acquired the confidence and ability to dominate a game.

Gainey was then in his fifth full season, and his career scoring record read like this: three goals as a rookie, then seventeen, fifteen and fourteen, and in 1977–78 he would contribute another fifteen. Yet he never spent a night watching from the press box. He rarely missed a shift and usually played as many minutes per game as more offensively gifted players. "There's a lot of dirty work to be done if you're going to win any hockey game," he told a writer with *The Hockey News*, "and I'm one of the guys who goes out and does it. I'm a defensive forward and if I do my job right no one scores so no one notices me."

Bowman certainly recognized Gainey's value. "The success of the

Canadiens, for all their great scorers, always has been built around defense, around a low goals-against average," Bowman told the same *Hockey News* writer. "The team almost always has had goaltenders in contention for the Vézina Trophy. To do this, you not only have to have good goaltenders and good defenseman, but forwards who forecheck and backcheck and play good defense and kill penalties, and Bob is just about the best of these."

Robinson, meanwhile, had become a key part of the defence, as well as the offence. A farmer's son from the eastern Ontario hamlet of Marvelville, he had played just one season of major junior hockey with the Kitchener Rangers before becoming a Canadiens prospect. He was a strong skater. He could pass the puck or carry it, and he had a hard, if often erratic, shot. His most obvious asset was his size. Robinson stood six foot three and could play a big man's game. He had no fear of fighting and he could hit hard enough to demolish an opponent and rattle an entire team.

At the start of his career, Robinson faced a dilemma: What type of player would he be—one whose game was based on physical intimidation, or one who played with skill and finesse? Several seasons elapsed before the answer became clear. The Canadiens sent him to Halifax after his initial training camp and recalled him midway through his second winter. In his first three full seasons in Montreal, he accumulated 127 points, but, according to Dryden, something was missing. He was neither the offensive force nor the physical menace his size suggested he might be.

All that changed after the 1976 Stanley Cup final against the Flyers and the Canada Cup international tournament held in the fall of that year. Robinson intimidated the Flyers with his physical play and unnerved the slick Europeans with his offensive ability. A new Robinson emerged from those experiences: a defenceman who possessed a unique blend of brawn and beauty.

"All the pieces had finally fallen into place," Dryden wrote. "He had found his game . . . a game of strength and agility, a commanding mix of offence and defence, his size a lingering reminder of violence. In the next few years, more than just an outstanding player, Robinson became a presence."

With their best players in their prime, and first-rate backups at each position, the Canadiens did not falter or wobble in 1977–78. They won fifty-nine games and lost only ten. They finished with 129 points, eighteen more than their nearest rival, the Islanders. They roared past Detroit in five games and Toronto in four. The Bruins put up a fight in the final, winning two of the first four contests, but were outscored by a total of eight–two in games five and six.

Robinson led all playoff scorers in assists with seventeen and tied Lafleur in points with twenty-one, a performance that earned him the Conn Smythe Trophy. Later that spring, at the NHL's post-season awards ceremony, Lafleur collected the Art Ross Trophy and the Hart. Dryden and his backup, Michel Larocque, won the Vézina. They shared the podium that evening with Gainey, the first recipient of the Frank J. Selke Trophy as the NHL's top defensive forward. He had beaten some very good players to win it—Craig Ramsay and Don Luce of Buffalo, Bobby Clarke of Philadelphia and Don Marcotte of Boston—and he was justifiably proud of the achievement.

But it was Bowman who put Gainey's contribution in perspective. "The Bob Gaineys are the guts of this team or any good team," he said. "I'm more aware than anyone else how well the stars of this team play and we would not win without them. But you do not win three straight Stanley Cups, as we have done, without a lot of players who are not in the spotlight playing well, and Bob is one of those, maybe the best one."

The Canadiens began pursuing a fourth Cup when training camp opened that fall, but Bowman was in a sour mood and his disposition had nothing to do with the talent on the ice. Montreal's powerful nucleus remained intact—Dryden, Robinson, Savard, Lapointe, Lafleur, Shutt, Lemaire and Gainey were all back. And there were good, new prospects to strengthen the supporting cast: Brian Engblom, who had spent most of the previous three seasons with the Nova Scotia Voyageurs, as well as Rod Langway, Mark Napier and Cam Connor, all of whom were drafted by the Canadiens but had turned pro with WHA teams.

On paper at least, the Canadiens were more than a match for their most serious rivals, the Boston Bruins, Philadelphia Flyers and New York Islanders, a fine young team built around goaltender Billy Smith, defenceman Denis Potvin and forwards Bryan Trottier and Mike Bossy. Bowman was blessed with a wealth of talent, but he had been shaken by developments off the ice. Edgar and Peter Bronfman, owners of the Canadiens since 1971, had sold the team to Molson Breweries of Canada for twenty million dollars. The deal closed in early August, and by the end of that month Sam Pollock had resigned.

Bowman coveted Pollock's job, but some powerful voices within the organization were aligned against him. Jean Béliveau's, for one. In his memoir, *My Life in Hockey,* the former star wrote: "Scotty had proved himself behind the bench. The trouble was, he'd proved himself behind the scenes as well. Whenever Scotty took issue with a player for any reason at all, he'd run upstairs to Sam's office and demand an instant trade. Bringing all his experience and knowledge to bear, Sam would calm him down.

"Sometimes, Scotty would barge in while I was meeting with Sam, whereupon I'd personally witness these unfortunate harangues. I made my mind up that if this guy was ever in the running for general manager, or any other position within the organization in which he'd have the final say on personnel matters, the Canadiens were going to be in trouble."

Morgan McCammon, president of Molson Breweries and of the team, sided with Béliveau, as did Pollock, a fact that was deeply hurtful to Bowman because the two men had been close for over three decades. "Sam and I have been together since I was playing midget hockey in Verdun in 1947, except for those five years in St. Louis," Bowman told *The Gazette*'s Tim Burke. "I never considered him a boss. We discussed everything, but he never, ever told Claude [Ruel] or me how to use the players. . . . He did all the signing and trading. Our roles were ideally intermingled."

The Canadiens settled instead on team executive Irving Grundman—a "quiet, reflective man," according to Béliveau, "who carefully considered all the possibilities and weighed every option before rendering an opinion." Grundman was a fifty-year-old Montrealer, the son of a butcher and, as the novelist Mordecai Richler once wrote, "When he was a kid he was up at 5:00 a.m. to pluck chickens in his father's shop." He won a seat on the Montreal city council and became a business associate of the Bronfmans. They had been partners in a chain of bowling alleys in Quebec and two other provinces. When the Bronfmans acquired the Canadiens, they made Grundman president of the Forum and put him in charge of the business side of the operation.

But Grundman became Pollock's protege and devoted himself to learning how to manage a hockey team. "I'm a graduate of the Sam Pollock school of hockey," he told a reporter shortly after his appointment. "Sam taught me all that I learned in hockey.

"Sam and I spent an average of five or six hours a day together during that five-year period. I observed him closely. I have attended meetings with him and we have had meetings of our own. I feel I have had a crash course in those five or six hours per day. It is probably the equivalent to a normal association of fifteen years."

Grundman's managerial talents were scarcely tested in 1978–79. He had inherited one of the best teams ever assembled, and his players kept on winning—though not quite at the same pace as in previous seasons. The Canadians won fifty-two, lost seventeen and tied eleven. They earned 115 points, one fewer than the Islanders, who finished first. In the play-offs, Montreal swept Toronto in four games and eliminated Boston in overtime in the seventh game (the Canadiens' first series in four seasons to go to the limit). They lost the opening game of the final against the New York Rangers, but won the next four. The fifth contest was played at the Forum, the first time since 1968 that the Canadiens had won a championship on home ice.

"By the third period, the crowd was in a frenzy of anticipation," *The Gazette* reported. "With the Canadiens in full control, roars of applause and foot-stomping thundered down from the upper decks at each hard check or good shot. With six minutes left . . . the delirious fans burst into spontaneous cheering."

The post-game revelry in the dressing room was more subdued than it had been in the past. The veterans had become accustomed to such triumphs, but not the newcomers. Langway, Engblom, Napier and a few others, all of them enjoying their first Cup, made plenty of noise, along with the veteran Yvon Lambert. He stood at the entrance to the room, spraying visitors with Champagne. "All right!" he bellowed when Pierre Trudeau showed up. "*Bienvenue!*" Lambert emptied a bottle of bubbly over Trudeau and then held up another king-sized bottle and offered him a drink as newspaper photographers snapped pictures of the prime minister taking a hearty swig.

The victory celebration culminated in another mammoth parade through downtown. Montreal was like no other city in North America when it came to these collective outbursts of love and admiration. No other city had had so many, and no other citizenry threw itself into them with such joy and enthusiasm. People stood shoulder to shoulder, ten or maybe even twelve deep—who could count? They stood from storefronts to curbs and spilled into the streets so that, viewed from overhead, the floats and vehicles carrying the players resembled small vessels plying a sea of radiant humanity.

People watched from rooftops, from second-storey windows, from lampposts and mailboxes until the last vehicles, carrying the bottom end of the lineup—the Black Aces, the players who practised with the team but spent most games in the press box—had passed, and then the vast throngs began to disperse. They went to Westmount and Notre-Dame-de-Grâce, to Pointe-Claire and Beaconsfield and suburbs further west, to Longueuil and Boucherville and elsewhere on the south shore, to Laval and Le Gardeur beyond the northern edge of the island and to the old east-end neighbourhoods of Plateau Mont-Royal, Maisonneuve and Hochelaga and they talked, not of the triumph just past, but of the one hoped for next spring.

The team of the late seventies appeared poised to win its fifth straight Cup. A duplication of the achievement of the Canadiens of the fifties seemed within its grasp. And then something completely unexpected happened: the organization began to bleed. An exodus of talent occurred.

Al MacNeil left after eight years with the Nova Scotia Voyageurs to become head coach of the Atlanta Flames. Bowman was next to go. He had never accepted Grundman's appointment, and he resigned to take over as coach and general manager of the Buffalo Sabres. Jacques Lemaire, a player of remarkable consistency, who had averaged nearly a point a game during his twelve seasons, retired at age thirty-three to become playing coach of a team in Switzerland. Ken Dryden, who had virtually owned the Vézina Trophy during his eight seasons, the way Doug Harvey once held the James Norris Trophy, retired for good at age thirty-two. Finally, Yvan Cournoyer, who had missed most of the previous season recuperating from back surgery, announced that he, too, was through. And the well-tutored but untested Grundman took up his managerial duties in earnest—with a platterful of problems in front of him and almost nothing in the way of experience or instincts to guide him.

1980-1993
THE LAST HURRAH

THE MONTH OF JUNE CAME AND WENT. July passed, and August as well. Training camp was just around the corner, and Irving Grundman had still not named a successor to Scotty Bowman. There were any number of interesting candidates available: Jacques Laperrière, Dickie Moore, Phil Goyette and Gilles Tremblay, to name a few. Grundman made his decision over the Labour Day weekend while walking by a lake near the village of L'Estérel in the Laurentians, and announced it at a Tuesday morning press conference at the Forum. The new coach of the Montreal Canadiens was Bernie Geoffrion.

Bernie Geoffrion? The choice immediately raised a host of questions among the assembled crowd of reporters. Hadn't he developed ulcers after half a season behind the bench of the New York Rangers in 1968–69? Hadn't health problems forced him to quit after two and a half seasons as coach of the Atlanta Flames? Hadn't he held a soft job with the Flames since then? How would he go from there to the hottest seat in hockey?

Geoffrion was the colour man on the Flames radio broadcasts. In the off-season, he joined the community relations department. He golfed and worked the banquet circuit, selling hockey in Georgia, and he was a hit wherever he went, a charmer and a joker with an accent that was part French-Canadian and part southern drawl.

Geoffrion's creased and craggy face was deeply tanned when he took his place in front of a bank of microphones, TV cameras and doubtful journalists that day in September 1979. His hair was a mass of tight, frizzed curls. He wore wire-rimmed glasses. He wanted Montrealers to know how happy he was, at age forty-eight, to be coming home. "It is a big dream," he said. "I never thought that one day after twelve years of not living in Montreal that I would be the coach of the Canadiens. I intend to finish my days here with the *bleu, blanc, rouge.*"

There was no doubting his good intentions. But what about his health, the reporters wondered. And what about the pressure of coaching in Montreal? "I'm sick and tired of answering questions about my health and whether I'll be able to stand the pressure," he snapped at one of his questioners. "Don't ask about my health anymore. How's your health?"

It was a feisty performance, but few were swayed. "Will Boomer laugh in the gallows tree?" was a headline in the next day's *Gazette*. And it wasn't long before Geoffrion was in trouble, not with the public or Montreal's prickly pundits, but his players. He was far too casual for a team accustomed to Bowman's iron rule.

Pre-game meetings under Bowman had begun at 6:30 sharp. They ran twenty to thirty minutes, during which Bowman thoroughly prepped his players. When they stepped onto the ice, they knew who was hot and who was slumping, who killed penalties and who did what on the power play, and where the soft spots were in goal, on defence and up front.

"Boomer set a record for the shortest pre-game meetings in club history," Larry Robinson wrote in his memoir *Robinson for the Defence*. "Most started at 6:30. Most ended by 6:32. His favourite line was, 'I don't have to tell you guys what to do; go out there and do your jobs.'"

Geoffrion lost control very quickly. The veterans questioned his decisions, while the others stopped listening. In late November, the Canadiens went into a skid that lasted nearly three weeks. "Canadiens lose yet another," a newspaper headline declared on December 12. "Road skid now six games." The Islanders had thumped the Canadiens, and the next morning Geoffrion failed to show up for practice. "Has anybody seen the coach?" Pierre Larouche asked his teammates in the dressing room after the workout.

"Has he quit?" Steve Shutt inquired of a reporter.

Claude Ruel, Geoffrion's assistant, insisted nothing was amiss. "Everybody needs a rest in this business," he said.

In fact, the coach was meeting with Grundman. They talked for two hours before lunch and six afterward. Geoffrion wanted out, but Grundman would not accept his resignation, and finally Geoffrion became exasperated, his voice rising until it was audible in the corridor outside, where a newspaper photographer, Michael Dugas, sat patiently waiting for the two men to emerge. Dugas pressed his ear to the wall. He grabbed a piece of scrap paper from his camera bag and began scribbling furiously.

"I'm sick and tired of them," Geoffrion bellowed. "They're not acting like professional athletes. Why should I get sick over a bunch of guys who won't listen to me? Guys coming in at two or three in the morning, laughing and joking around?

"I'm not going to stick around and let everyone in Montreal blame me for what's happening . . . because it's not my fault. I tell them if they don't feel one hundred per cent, then don't play. Then, after the game, if they play lousy, they complain about sore ankles.

"Larouche, walking through the airport the other night smoking a cigar, acting like we'd won the Stanley Cup when we lost the game. I thought Savard would help me, but he's more interested in his horses.

"I had a dream to coach this team. That dream is a nightmare now. I don't care if you pay me a million dollars. I will not stay."

Eventually, Grundman walked Geoffrion to the door and Dugas got his picture—and a front-page story to boot. Geoffrion was gone and Ruel was back, reluctantly. The Canadiens were thirty games into the season, having won fifteen, lost nine and tied six, good enough for third overall. But they were not the team they had been, and the problems went well beyond coaching.

"We are doing so many things wrong," Bob Gainey told a *Gazette* reporter, "that it's got to the point where nothing is certain anymore. We can't be sure of beating an eighth- or ninth-place team. What we're in is the bottom of a string that started last year.

"Looking back, people remember we won the Stanley Cup again so they think we whistled through another year. But we didn't whistle. We dropped fourteen points on the previous year. We snuck out with the Cup. We were lucky enough to have the momentum of the previous three years to carry us. We ran the tank empty last year and now it's showing up."

The Canadiens performed inconsistently for the better part of two months after Geoffrion's departure, but ended the season with a twenty-two-game unbeaten streak. They finished third overall with 107 points. Ruel relied so heavily on his top twelve players, according to Robinson, that they were either injured or exhausted when the playoffs began.

Nevertheless, the Canadiens rolled over the Hartford Whalers three straight in the opening round then met a more skilled and determined opponent in the Minnesota North Stars. The Stars stunned the Canadiens and their fans by winning the first two games at the Forum. Montreal rebounded with three straight victories, but faltered in the sixth, which sent the teams back to the Forum for game seven. They were tied at two with a minute and twenty-six seconds to go in the third when Minnesota's Al MacAdam tipped in a pass from Bobby Smith and toppled a Canadiens dynasty.

Montrealers absorbed the loss, and the end of another run of championships, with grace and without recrimination. The Canadiens had lost before and always recovered. Aging stars had retired or been traded, promising young players replaced them and the Canadiens regained their strength and their power and became champions again.

This time, everyone expected the renewal would begin at the June draft. The Canadiens had the number one pick overall, and there were two potential stars to choose from: Doug Wickenheiser of the Regina Pats and Denis Savard of the Montreal Juniors. This put Grundman in a bind, one that was nicely captured by a headline in *La Presse*: "*La tête indique Wickenheiser, le coeur Savard*"—the head says Wickenheiser, the heart Savard.

Scouts in Montreal and around the league favoured the prospect from the west—a big, strong centre who had scored eighty-nine goals and added eighty-one assists that year. The fans and the French-language media were set on Savard, a Montrealer and a centre who had been lighting up local rinks with his offensive wizardry since he was seven years old. He was small by NHL standards, but was a dervish on ice and had finished his amateur career by racking up 455 points in three dazzling seasons in the Quebec major junior league.

The 1980 draft was held at the Forum, the first time the league had opted for an arena. Delegations from each of the NHL's twenty-one teams sat at tables placed on the playing surface. The players, their families, friends and agents sat in clusters in the lower bowl of the stadium. When the proceedings began, Grundman went with his head: he chose Wickenheiser, who joined him and Claude Ruel on stage. The young man pulled on the famous red jersey and the three of them posed for a photo, shoulder to shoulder and smiles on their faces.

Savard was selected third. He donned another red sweater, one with black and white stripes and a warrior in profile on the chest. He had become a Chicago Black Hawk, a fact that would haunt Canadiens fans for years to come.

Denis Savard began his professional career with a flourish. In his first game, before a raucous, standing-room only crowd in Chicago Stadium, he set up three goals against the Buffalo Sabres. He played in seventy-six of the team's eighty games in 1980–81 and piled up seventy-five points (twenty-eight goals and forty-seven assists). He may well have won the Calder Trophy as rookie of the year were it not for the arrival of another brilliant newcomer, Peter Stastny of the Quebec Nordiques.

Wickenheiser, by comparison, was in the lineup one night and up in the press box the next. He appeared in only forty-one games, scored seven goals and added eight assists. The more charitable of the team's fans could argue that the Canadiens were just bringing him along slowly, as they had done with Yvan Cournoyer, Steve Shutt and many prospects over the years. Others were already grumbling. He's no Savard, they said, or, He's just not good enough to play a regular shift.

There were other troublesome developments that winter, specifically a rash of injuries and feuds between Claude Ruel and some of his veterans. Guy Lapointe, one of the team's great defenceman in the 1970s, missed more than forty games with pulled muscles, charley horses and other ailments. After returning to the lineup late in the year, he spent a night in the press box and another on the bench and responded by calling Ruel a hypocrite, among other things. Goaltender Michel Larocque, Dryden's backup for eight seaons, wound up third on the depth chart behind Denis Herron and Richard Sevigny and demanded a trade. Guy Lafleur spent time on the injury list on eight occasions. He appeared in fifty-one games and scored only twenty-seven goals, the first time since 1973–74 that he had failed to connect for fifty or more.

Lafleur's personal life made headlines that season as well. There were rumours of marital discord, and a highly publicized dispute with provincial tax authorities. There was a brush with death after a night at the clubs. Lafleur was on his way home, speeding west on an empty expressway when he nodded off. His vehicle, a rented luxury car, crashed into a fence and struck a signpost, which flew through the windshield, through the steering wheel, embedded itself in the back seat and nicked Lafleur's right earlobe.

Despite all the turmoil, the Canadiens were on a roll when March turned to April and the playoffs loomed. They had lost just once in their last twenty-seven games at home, and for the seventh consecutive season earned a hundred points or more.

They began their pursuit of the Stanley Cup in a best-of-five preliminary round against the fourteenth-place Edmonton Oilers. The night before the opener, Glen Sather and his assistant coach, Bruce MacGregor, had dinner with Red Fisher, sports editor of the Montreal *Gazette*. "It's a great experience for the kids . . . playing the Canadiens," Sather confided, "but I would have preferred to play another team in the first round. I think we could have beaten teams like Los Angeles and Buffalo."

Sather's "kids" were Wayne Gretzky, Glenn Anderson, Jari Kurri, Paul Coffey, Kevin Lowe and Mark Messier. They formed the core of the youngest team in the NHL, and all were still eligible to play junior. The kids, as it turned out, were not intimidated by Montreal and its mystique, but some of the Canadiens, notably goalie Richard Sevingy, badly underestimated their youthful opposition. "Lafleur will put Gretzky in his back pocket," Sevigny boasted to a reporter.

In game one, Gretzky earned five assists, a playoff record, while Lafleur could not escape the dogged checking of Dave Hunter and managed just two shots on net. The Oilers won six–two. They beat the Canadiens three–one the following night and completed the sweep at home. Fisher deemed it the biggest upset in his three decades on the sports beat. "I have covered nearly every major event this business has to offer," he wrote, "but no team has played better against greater odds than this team of wild, hungry and marvellous Oilers."

Four days after that defeat, Claude Ruel resigned, and Irving Grundman named a successor shortly before the June draft. The new man was Bob Berry, a thirty-seven-year-old native of Mount Royal who had excelled in his youth at hockey, football and baseball. Berry had made his name locally as the star left winger with the Sir George Williams University hockey team, then played two seasons in the minors with affiliates of the Canadiens. He reached the NHL with the Los Angeles Kings and lasted seven years before finishing his career as playing coach of the of the AHL's Springfield Indians. In 1978–79, he was back in the NHL as coach of the Kings and had been offered a contract extension when the Canadiens job became available.

Grundman chose Berry over a number of high-profile candidates, and the decision appeared sound. The Canadiens broke the hundred-point barrier in 1981–82, finished third overall and by the end of the season Red Fisher was touting Berry as coach of the year. "What he did in a very short time was earn the respect of his personnel without making huge waves," Fisher wrote. "No arm waving. No public outbursts. The team comes first, the individual—no matter who it happened to be—was somewhere further down the list."

Then came the playoffs. Berry's Canadiens met the tenth-place Quebec Nordiques. The teams were twenty-seven points apart in the standings, but in games against each other they were dead even: three wins, three losses, two ties. Furthermore, a scorching rivalry had developed between them.

Both sides were competing for the loyalty of French-Canadian fans. To make matters worse, the media in the two cities engaged in a debate over which better represented francophone Quebec: the Canadiens, who were managed and coached by anglophones, or the Nordiques, whose coach, Michel Bergeron, general manager, Maurice Filion and president, Marcel Aubut, were all French-speaking Quebecers. Mario Tremblay would later describe matches between the Canadiens and Nordiques as "the most savage games I ever played in. After some of them, I felt like I needed a wheelchair."

The first playoff encounter between the teams resembled warfare more than sport. There were scuffles and skirmishes, hits meant to hurt and to intimidate, sticks wielded as weapons and, in the fourth encounter, a brawl involving every player on the ice—goaltenders excepted. It lasted twenty minutes and led to the assessment of 149 minutes in penalties and two game misconducts.

The Canadiens were ferocious at times, but lacked the start-to-finish fierceness necessary to win the series. After a whirlwind opening game, a five–one victory, they lost the next two. They thrashed the Nordiques in the fourth, then chased them for most of the fifth. They tied the game midway through the third, and the score remained even after sixty minutes. Twenty-two seconds into overtime, Quebec's Dale Hunter completed a two-on-one rush by slipping the puck past rookie netminder Rick Wamsley and Montreal's season was over.

The team's fans were bewildered and distraught as they left the Forum or turned off their TV sets. How had it come to this again? *The Gazette*'s Tim Burke concluded that the Canadiens had overachieved during the regular season, "moulding, through hard labour, a superior club from average players, untested rookies and big stars who are two or three years past their peak."

But something else was also happening. As Bob Gainey, then the captain, expressed it, "We can't put on our sweaters anymore and expect to win." The mystique of the Canadiens, their aura of invincibility, had rested on three pillars: excellence on the ice, behind the bench and in the front office. That mystique had been undermined by the playoff losses to the North Stars, Oilers and Nordiques and by three coaching changes in as many seasons. It endured another blow in September 1982, when Grundman made the biggest trade of his managerial career.

The Canadiens sent four players to the Washington Capitals: the defence pair of Rod Langway and Brian Engblom, as well as forwards Doug Jarvis and Craig Laughlin. In return, they received centreman Ryan Walter and defenceman Rick Green. Grundman had been forced to deal Langway, a twenty-five-year-old American who had threatened to quit if he were not traded. Langway was disgruntled with Quebec's high taxes, which would become a serious liability for the Canadiens in years to come, and he disliked having to file tax returns in Canada and the United States.

Rick Green, a former number one draft pick and six-year veteran, was seen as fair value for Langway. Similarly, most commentators regarded Jarvis for Walter as a sound exchange. The twenty-seven-year-old Jarvis remained one of the league's premier defensive forwards while Walter, another number one draft pick, was twenty-four and had played four full seasons in Washington. Laughlin, a graduate of the U.S. college system who had played two seasons with the Nova Scotia Voyageurs and thirty-six games as a Canadien, was regarded as a throw-in merely to complete the deal.

Engblom was the player who didn't fit. He was twenty-seven. He had been on three of the four Cup-winning teams of the late 1970s and had made the second All-Star team the previous season, but the Canadiens had received nothing for him. "What was Irving thinking," Fisher asked rhetorically in a column, "when he agreed to relinquish Engblom, who had been the Canadiens' best defenceman, by far, during the last two seasons?

"Has the Canadiens' organization retrogressed," he continued, "to the point where it must now deal with a team that hasn't made the playoffs since entering the league in 1974?"

The passage of time did nothing to alter that judgment. Langway was awarded the James Norris Trophy after his first season in Washington, where the Capitals improved by twenty-eight points over the previous year and made their inaugural appearance in the playoffs. The Canadiens dropped by eleven points and earned fewer than a hundred points for the first time since 1973–74. And again, the post-season was a nightmare. The Canadians met Scotty Bowman's Buffalo Sabres in the opening round. The Sabres were a stronger team and they had a hot goaltender in Robert Sauvé. The Canadiens could not create good chances and were shut out in back-to-back games, an indignity they had not experienced since the 1961 playoffs. They broke their scoreless streak in the third game, but still lost four–two. "The charter carrying the Canadiens home to another long, hot summer has landed," *The Gazette*'s Burke wrote, "and the pain of this final loss . . . is still written on the faces young and old."

The defeat weighed most heavily on Grundman. He went from the airport to the Forum and sat in his office from two o'clock till four-thirty in the morning, asking himself what had gone wrong. Later that day, journalists put the same question to him. "I really don't have any answers," he replied. "I know this. There'll be a lot of heat from people in the media, but what else is new?"

The Canadiens lost on a Sunday evening, and on Wednesday team president Ronald Corey informed Grundman that he was through. So was Ron Caron, the director of player personnel, who had devoted nearly three decades to the Canadiens. Howard Grundman, Irving's son and the director of hockey administration, resigned. Finally, Corey told Berry that he would be scouting next season, not coaching, and the biggest front office purge in the seventy-four-year history of the Canadiens was complete.

Molson Breweries had appointed Ronald Corey early in the 1982–83 season to halt the slide that was occurring under Grundman. The new president had acted decisively by cleaning house. His next challenge was to find the right person to lead the Canadiens back to their accustomed place at or near the summit, and he received plenty of help from the French-language media.

La Presse columnist Réjean Tremblay was the first to lend a hand. In his opinion, the new manager had to be French-Canadian, and the best candidate was Serge Savard. *La Presse* consulted its readers, and their top choice was Jacques Lemaire, followed by Savard. The French-language dailies continued this drumbeat almost daily until the morning of April 29, when the Canadiens held a press conference at the Forum and introduced Savard as their new managing director. Corey disclosed that he had never really considered anyone else and added, "In my mind, Serge Savard will be with the Canadiens for the next twenty years."

Half a dozen players, including Savard's former teammates Larry Robinson, Steve Shutt and Mario Tremblay, were present for the announcement, and all gathered for photos afterward. Claude Ruel and Jacques Laperrière were there, and so were Toe Blake and Jean Béliveau. Savard reached for one of his beloved big cigars, Béliveau obliged with a light and the photographers merrily snapped away.

It was a triumphant moment for the thirty-seven-year-old defenceman, one of the best of his generation. Savard had been a Canadien for fourteen seasons and played for eight Cup winners. He had won the Conn Smythe Trophy, twice played for Team Canada and on four occasions represented the Canadiens in the all-star game. In his final two seasons with the team, he was the captain, though his once-luminous skills had slipped and the Forum crowds had jeered him. When the Canadiens were losing to the Oilers in April 1981, the fans let loose every time he touched the puck. Afterward, a distraught Savard pulled off his sweater, sat on a bench in the dressing room and wept.

That summer, he retired, but his old friend John Ferguson, manager of the Winnipeg Jets, coaxed him back and he played two seasons for the Jets before heeding Corey's call and returning to Montreal. "This is one of the happiest days of my life," he said after his appointment was announced.

But his first season was filled with turmoil and upheaval. Savard offered the coaching job to Lemaire, who had established his credentials the previous season with the Longueuil Chevaliers of the Quebec Major Junior Hockey League. The Chevaliers, who represented a suburban community on the south shore opposite Montreal, were a new team, and the players were mostly castoffs and rejects from other organizations. Lemaire turned them into winners who almost walked off with the league championship.

"He has developed the concept of collective play and completely changed our vision of hockey," said Jean-Jacques Daigneault, a defenceman who would go on to a lengthy NHL career. "Nobody is more important than the team. The only thing that counts is the success of the team."

Lemaire told Réjean Tremblay: "I know that I can coach. And when I say that, I mean at any level." But he turned down the head coaching job and signed on as an assistant instead. So Savard reinstated Bob Berry.

Early in the season, Savard traded forwards Mark Napier and Keith Acton to the Minnesota North Stars for Bobby Smith, the type of big, powerful centre the Canadiens had been looking for when they drafted Doug Wickenheiser. Shortly before Christmas, he sent Wickenheiser and two others to the St. Louis Blues for Perry Turnbull, a thirty-goal scorer for three straight seasons who failed to produce for the Canadiens.

The goaltenders, Rick Wamsley and Richard Sevigny, were unreliable. The defence suffered a major blow when Rick Green injured his wrist and was lost for the season, and a second when the league imposed a season-long suspension on Ric Nattress. The capable second-year defenceman had been arrested in August 1982 for possessing marijuana and hashish, while he was a member of the Nova Scotia Voyageurs, and a year later was fined $150 by a court in Brantford, Ontario. League president John Ziegler eventually reduced the suspension to thirty games and Nattress was back in the lineup in December.

The offence sagged as well. One forward after another succumbed to injury, and once-fearsome superstars Guy Lafleur and Steve Shutt were fading and disgruntled.

In the second half of the season, Shutt returned from an injury and dressed for two road games, but Berry left him on the bench—"as though he no longer existed," according to *La Presse*. Lafleur, the most brilliant player in the game in the 1970s and a fifty-goal scorer for six consecutive seasons, now struggled to reach thirty. Always quiet and introspective, he appeared sullen and distant and seemed not to care about his game or the team.

"Lafleur spent long afternoons at the Ritz drinking cognac and Scotch," Georges-Hebert Germain wrote in his 1990 biography *Guy Lafleur: L'Ombre et la Lumière*. "He would be seen, when evening arrived, at the chic and expensive discotheques on Crescent Street. He would arrive for practices and games at the last minute . . . infinitely calm, detached and perfectly indifferent.

"From time to time, in a formidable burst of energy, he would shake off his torpor and play great hockey. Then he would lapse into a sort of lethargy. And Berry left him on the bench more and more often and for longer and longer stretches."

By mid-February, the Canadiens were headed for their first losing season in thirty years and Berry was having a poorer year than most of his players. He was going through a painful and difficult divorce. The media had begun to speculate on how long he would last behind the bench. Journalists observed Berry between periods, standing in the corridor outside the dressing room, chain-smoking and looking nervous. Several times, he made critical comments in post-game interviews.

"I can't understand how we can play so lousy," he said at one point. And in another moment of exasperation, he complained, "Never in my seven years of coaching have I seen a team as tough to motivate."

But the players weren't listening and by late February the team had slipped to fourth in its division. Savard fired Berry and promoted Lemaire. Initially, the coaching change scarcely made a difference. The Canadiens finished eleventh overall and posted their worst record—thirty-five wins, forty losses and five ties—since 1950–51. "It was a team in complete disarray," Red Fisher wrote, " . . . an abysmal season in every way."

But the Canadiens redeemed themselves with a remarkable playoff run. They began by beating Boston in three straight games, even though the Bruins had finished twenty-nine points ahead of them. They atoned for an earlier playoff loss to the Quebec Nordiques by beating their provincial rival in six. In the semifinal round, they met the defending champion New York Islanders, who were chasing a fifth straight Stanley Cup. They won the first two games before losing the next four.

It had been a team effort and it started with the new man behind the bench, as captain Bob Gainey noted: "Jacques has a great appreciation of both individual talent and the talent of a team. For the last few years we've kept talking about needing more talent here, more talent there. It's been my belief all along that we had sufficient individual talent. The trouble was we were not playing to our capacity as a team. Jacques is the one who has brought team talent to the top."

Lemaire had gotten the most out of everyone, except for his old line-mate Lafleur. By the end, he was more a passenger than a participant, a fourth-line winger who played a few minutes a night, took an occasional turn on the power play and some nights barely saw the ice in the third period. The newspapers had taken to noting that he hadn't scored in the final fourteen games of the regular season, hadn't score in the playoffs and hadn't, in fact, notched a post-season goal since April 10, 1982.

"Guy Lafleur is the least of my worries," Savard said in a post-season interview. "He is under contract for two more years and he is not going to be traded. Guy Lafleur is not a problem."

On October 9, 1984—the day before they began their seventy-fifth season—the Canadiens held a meet-and-greet session for the fans. The event drew ten thousand. There were a few short speeches. The players were introduced, then all left the stage to mingle with the faithful. All but Guy Lafleur, who had to remain behind or risk being overwhelmed by well-wishers. He stood at the edge of the raised platform, wearing his Canadiens sweater, leaning forward slightly and signing autographs for a tightly packed throng of young men, most with their arms outstretched as though desperate to lay a hand on the pant leg of the player whose other-worldly speed and unbelievable moves had once left them spellbound. "Good year, bad year, fifty goals or twenty-seven," *La Presse* reported the next day, "Guy Lafleur is still the most popular of the *Glorieux*."

As he stood there that day, awash in the affections of the fans, Lafleur felt certain he had another good year in him. He had trained hard that summer: he had jogged, played tennis, made appearances here and there with the Canadiens softball team—demonstrating considerable skill as a hitter. He had fielded endless questions about his season-ending scoring slump and he faced more queries at camp, though he was tired of talking about the problem and wanted to focus on the future.

"I would like to score between forty and fifty goals," he said after the first session of the fall. "I believe I am capable of reaching that plateau."

Lafleur scored once in the pre-season, and the Forum crowd gave him a stirring ovation. He put one past Philadelphia's Pelle Lindbergh in game three of the regular season and was named the game's third star. Two nights later, though, he performed poorly in a close contest against the Los Angeles Kings and Jacques Lemaire left him on the bench for most of the third period. In the final minutes, a familiar chant drifted down from the upper levels of the Forum: "*Guy! Guy! Guy!*"

But Lafleur never moved and afterward stomped into the dressing room, grim-faced, angry and "smoking like a chimney," as one journalist put it. "It's like school," he snapped at the reporters clustered around him. "The teacher is always right, never the student. Here the coach is always right. Me, I'm only a player."

The crowd of journalists sought out Lemaire and one asked if he had heard the fans' chanting. "Of course," Lemaire replied. "A coach would have to be deaf not to hear it." But Lemaire would not be swayed by the passions of the crowd. "If I made my decisions based on names on the sweaters, we would have lost tonight," he said.

Lemaire had a sunny disposition. He usually had a smile on his face. But he was hard as nails when he had to be. He was prepared to fight a battle that others in the organization had avoided. Lafleur was no longer the magical player he had been in the late 1970s. He still had speed and a blazing shot, but he wasn't scoring. Only once in the previous four seasons had he connected for thirty goals. He had slipped, but he refused to accept this.

Instead, he had blamed Claude Ruel and Bob Berry for his troubles. He had threatened to sit out training camp in September 1982 unless the Canadiens renegotiated his contract. He had complained about his ice time, his role on the power play and his centres—he had gone through several of them: Pierre Larouche, Pierre Mondou, Keith Acton, Doug Wickenheiser, Ryan Walter and Guy Carbonneau.

Lafleur insisted that the scoring chances were coming, so the goals couldn't be far behind. By the fall of 1984, however, Lemaire and Serge Savard had decided that Lafleur would have to accept a lesser role on the team or he would have to go. Soon, others had reached the same conclusion.

"Slowly, inexorably, Guy Lafleur has put himself in his proper place: one of excuses, alibis and false pretexts," Guy Létourneau of *La Presse* wrote in late October. "He can no longer blame Claude Ruel. He can no longer blame Bob Berry. He can no longer blame the team of Corey and Savard. He can't blame Jacques Lemaire, who has proved he can win without him.

"He can no longer demand a trade: his value on the market is too low: one goal in thirty-two games. Who wants such a scorer, who takes himself for a star and commands the salary of a fifty-goal man?"

Public opinion turned as well. On a Friday afternoon in mid-November, former Canadiens defenceman Pierre Bouchard, then the host of an open-line sports show on radio station CKAC, asked his listeners which of the players should be traded. Lafleur was one of the names the fans cited most often.

Lafleur's ordeal brought him anguish and sleepless nights. It eroded his motivation and his desire to continue. It hurt his pride. Lafleur played his last game as a Montreal Canadien on November 24, 1984, a Saturday. Afterward, the team left for Boston and a Sunday evening encounter with the Bruins. Lafleur remained behind, onstensibly to rest his injured groin. On Monday, he appeared at a press conference at the Forum with Savard and Ronald Corey at his side and announced that he was retiring.

He had scored just twice in nineteen games, a dismal end to a glorious career that had lasted fourteen seasons. At his peak, he had been swift, nimble and brilliant, and one of the most prolific shooters the sport had ever known: a five-hundred-goal scorer, a fifty-goal scorer in six straight seasons, three times the NHL scoring champion, twice the league's most valuable player and once the winner of the Conn Smythe Trophy.

Lafleur was just thirty-three, but looked older and wore a pained and haunted expression as he gripped the podium and spoke into the thicket of microphones before him. He assured everyone—his teammates, who were back from Boston, the team officials and one of the largest gatherings of media in club history—that he would not regret his decision. "I am happy it is all over," he said. "My nightmare is finished."

Red Fisher was having a lousy summer. He'd spent a good part of it fighting an illness. He had been laid low by an opponent he couldn't see, or punch, as he put it, and now he had been compelled to drag himself out of a sick bed and travel downtown to the Forum on a hot, sticky afternoon in July 1985. The Canadiens had an announcement to make, and the news floored Fisher, along with just about every one else in the jostling crowd around him: Jacques Lemaire was resigning as coach to become director of hockey personnel. His assistant, Jean Perron, would replace him.

"What in thunderation is going on up there?" Fisher wrote later that afternoon. "Does it make a smidgeon of sense that someone who made remarkable progress in his first full season as head coach would decide he no longer wants to be coach?"

Even the players were perplexed. Larry Robinson received the news a few hours before the media were summoned. "I had no inkling," the big defence-man confessed to a reporter. "But knowing Jacques the way I do, I suppose that's not unusual. Jacques is very good at keeping things to himself."

Everyone agreed that the Canadiens were losing an excellent coach. Lemaire had taken over when the team was at its lowest point in three decades and produced better results than anyone since Scotty Bowman. He had guided the Canadiens to the conference final in 1984, then led them to first place in the Adams Division and sixth overall in 1984–85. The Canadiens had gone on to beat the Bruins in the first round before losing to Quebec in a heart-stopping series that ended when Peter Stastny scored in overtime in game seven.

"He knew our potential, got us close to it most of the time and made us consistent," Bob Gainey explained. "He did that by being able to evaluate teams and players better than some I've played for and working from that.

"Before Jacques, the Canadiens were always known as a fast-skating, forechecking team, even when we didn't have the speed and were unsuc-cessful. Jacques changed that. Instead of creating mistakes, we waited for the other team to make them because we didn't have the speed we once did."

Lemaire disliked the relentless pressure that came with the job. Win or lose, he couldn't relax after a game. He was always thinking about the next opponent. He had rarely talked to reporters during his playing days, but now had to endure a daily barrage of questions about every coaching deci-sion, every important play, every misstep by a player. Most of all, he was tormented by the lack of private space in his life. He was the face of the Canadiens in a way he had never been as a player. People recognized him everywhere. Someone was always wishing him well, congratulating him or inquiring about the team.

Lemaire wanted out, and Perron made that possible. He was a capable assistant and could provide the stability the Canadiens sorely needed after the upheavals of the past five years. Perron was thirty-eight and a native of St-Isidore-d'Auckland, a village near the U.S. border, 160 kilometres southeast of Montreal. He was the twentieth coach of the Canadiens and his credentials were unlike those of any of his predecessors.

He had never played pro hockey. Instead, he had studied physical education at the University of Sherbrooke, earned bachelor's and master's degrees there and a Ph.D. at the University of Michigan. Afterward, he coached the University of Moncton Blue Eagles hockey team for ten years and twice won national championships. He left Moncton to become an assistant with the club that represented Canada at the 1984 Olympics. When the Games were over, the pros came calling.

Perron received offers from St. Louis and Quebec, but chose the Canadiens. He was prepared to start in the minors; instead, Lemaire made him an assistant. His role during games was to observe from the press box and relay information to Jacques Laperrière, who handled the defence. Perron expected to play a secondary role for another season, perhaps longer. But on the morning of July 29, Serge Savard summoned him to a meeting at the Forum, informed him that Lemaire was quitting and offered him the job. Perron said he wasn't ready, that he needed time behind the bench to become better acquainted with the players.

"Ah, come on, Jean, you're ready," Savard replied. "If you want the job you've got it right now. Let's get on with it."

That afternoon, the Canadiens announced their new head coach. A few days later, Perron left on a fishing trip and, as he subsequently told broadcaster Dick Irvin: "I can remember sitting there and I started to shake. My line was in the water and it was shaking and I was saying, 'Christ, what did you do? What kind of a decision was that?'"

Questions, questions. Everybody had questions about the Canadiens at the outset of the 1985–86 season. Would the rookie coach flourish or wilt? Who would start in goal? Steve Penney, who had been the number one netminder the previous season? His backup, Doug Soetaert? Or the brash rookie, Patrick Roy? And what to expect of the offence, with its four new faces: Brian Skrudland, Kjell Dahlin, Sergio Momesso and Stéphane Richer, whom some observers saw as the next Guy Lafleur.

Two things seemed certain, according to hockey's punditocracy. First, the Canadiens possessed one of the league's best defence corps in Larry Robinson, Rick Green, Craig Ludwig, Tom Kurvers, Chris Chelios and Petr Svoboda. Second, the fans could put their dreams of a Stanley Cup championship on hold for another year. As Ronald King wrote in *La Presse*, "Let it be said right now that the chances of seeing a parade on Ste-Catherine Street next June are remote."

For most of the season, the Canadiens seemed destined to disappoint yet again. Thirteen rookies and a total of thirty-four players wore the colours. Injuries forced Perron to juggle his lineup frequently. The younger players proved inconsistent and were shuffled back and forth from the bench to the press box, or from Montreal to the minors.

"Nobody knew which Montreal Canadiens team would show up on any given night," Larry Robinson recalled later in his autobiography. "We could go into Philadelphia or Long Island and whip the Flyers and the Islanders, then . . . lose home games to Minnesota or Los Angeles."

A collapse was inevitable, and it happened in March. The team began the month atop the Adams Division with a four-point lead over the Quebec Nordiques. A six-game losing streak changed that. The Canadiens fell seven points back of the Nordiques and were in danger of missing the playoffs.

Perron resorted to stern measures. He ordered the younger players to stay out of the trendy nightspots of Montreal's Crescent Street. He held punishing ninety-minute workouts that consisted of little more than heavy skating drills. Some of the veterans resented this, and Robinson sounded off publicly.

"Is he telling us we're out of shape after seventy-three games of the regular season?" he fumed in an interview with Red Fisher. "Losing games is a problem so we've got problems. We've got a lot of problems. And the only way to solve problems is to get some discipline on the ice."

Rumours surfaced in the media that Serge Savard would fire Perron and reinstate Jacques Lemaire. Savard quickly killed that idea. In St. Louis, he summoned his veterans—Robinson, Bob Gainey, Bobby Smith, Mats Naslund, Ryan Walter, Lucien Deblois and Chris Nilan—to a meeting. Perron was staying, he told them, so they had better get moving.

The Canadiens survived their late-season swoon and finished second in their division and seventh overall, but questions remained. The team was still carrying three goalies. The fans, as well as some of the players wondered: Which one would start the post-season? Penney, who had fallen to third on the depth chart? Soetaert, who had earned three shutouts in just twenty-three appearances? Or Roy, the twenty-year-old native of Quebec City and graduate of the Granby Bisons who had played forty-seven games, more than the other two combined? Many nights, Roy had been spectacular, but too often, according to Robinson, he allowed soft goals that "sucked the air out of the team."

But Perron had seen enough to make up his mind. "I started putting Patrick into tough situations, especially on the road," he recalled later. "We played one game in Long Island and, let me tell you, he won it for us. When we approached the playoffs, I said, 'This is the kid I've got to have in net.' I could see that he was so much better than the other two guys."

The Canadiens met the Bruins in the opening round, a best-of-five, and Roy proved himself from the opening faceoff. The Bruins nearly ran the Canadiens out of the rink in the first twenty minutes of the series. They outshot Montreal fifteen-three, but the score was tied at one as the teams headed for their dressing rooms. The Canadiens won that night and swept the Bruins in three—the nineteenth time they had eliminated Boston in twenty-one post-season meetings. "I'm convinced that Roy's work in the first period of the first game kept us alive," Guy Carbonneau said when the series was over.

The Canadiens played the Hartford Whalers next in a best-of-seven that went the distance—including a final game decided in overtime. The rookie goalie earned more praise after that series. "Patrick has given us the best goaltending we've had in my fourteen years here," Robinson declared. Then Montreal rolled over the New York Rangers in five to reach the final for the first time since 1979—though this club scarcely resembled the great ones of the past, as Richard Hétu noted in *La Presse*. "This is not a team of big scorers," Hétu wrote. "There are not many big names. There are only players who are willing to sacrifice themselves for one another and who continue to surprise themselves."

Roy was one of the big surprises that spring. Right winger Claude Lemieux was the other. He had scored fifty-two goals and added fifty-eight assists in his final season with the Verdun Junior Canadiens and was expected to make the Canadiens in the fall of 1985. But he spent too much time hovering on the edge of the play, waiting for loose pucks, rather than fighting for possession and making things happen. Savard saw him as an opportunist and sent him to Sherbrooke. After a winter in the AHL, Lemieux returned to the Canadiens with five games left in the season and was a different player, as Red Fisher noted following his first outing. "Lemieux was . . . splendid," Fisher wrote, "dealing ten hard, clean body checks and helping create three good scoring opportunities for himself."

He was even better in the post-season. The Canadiens played fifteen games to advance to the final. Lemieux scored nine goals, three of them game-winners, including the overtime marker that ended the Whalers' season. It was an extraordinary performance in more ways than one. As Réjean Tremblay pointed out in *La Presse,* the Canadiens were getting exceptional value for their money in Lemieux. He had contributed mightily to a playoff run that generated approximately two million dollars in revenue for the Canadiens, but he had earned thirty thousand dollars for the season, less than public relations director Claude Mouton.

The Canadiens had a week off before opening against the Campbell Conference champions, the Calgary Flames. The series began in Calgary, and the Canadiens were no match for the Flames that night. They lost five–two. Forty-eight hours later, they redeemed themselves. The score was tied at two after sixty minutes. Perron put out his checking line— Brian Skrudland at centre, Mike McPhee on the left, Lemieux on the right—to start the overtime period.

Skrudland won the draw. The teams skirmished in the neutral zone, and McPhee wound up with the puck. He dashed over the blue line. Skrudland was with him. Only one Calgary defenceman was back. McPhee faked a shot, then slid the puck across the ice to Skrudland, who tapped it past goaltender Mike Vernon. Nine seconds had elapsed—the fastest overtime goal in Stanley Cup history.

The Canadiens won the next two contests, both at the Forum. Roy recorded his first post-season shutout in game four and Lemieux scored the only goal, his tenth of the playoffs and fourth winner. The Canadiens held a commanding lead as they flew to Calgary for the fifth game of the series, which was to be played on a Saturday night.

The Canadiens won that game and with it their twenty-third Stanley Cup. League president John Ziegler presented the trophy to Bob Gainey, who hoisted it over his head and led his teammates on a victory lap. By the time the players headed for the dressing room, the celebrations had begun in Montreal. Thousands of fans converged on downtown and things quickly spun out of control.

The trouble began, according to the police, near the intersection of Ste-Catherine and Crescent streets. Drunken young people left the bars and nightclubs to join the revelry. They began smashing windows and unleashed a whirlwind of violence and destruction. Cars were overturned. Stores were stripped of merchandise. Police, caught off guard, were unable to maintain order. By the time the riot had subsided, the mob had caused a million dollars' worth of damage.

A second, huge crowd converged on the airport in Dorval. At midnight, some ten thousand people were inside the terminal and standing in the road-ways outside. Most stayed all night. The team's charter landed shortly before 7 a.m. and the weary, somewhat bewildered players made their way through a path cleared by police officers.

There were those who questioned the legitimacy of the 1986 Cup because the Canadiens won that year without beating Edmonton's mighty Oilers, the reigning champs and owners of hockey's most dazzling lineup. Such second-guessing proved short-sighted. Serge Savard's Canadiens were one of the league's best teams for the next several seasons. They finished fifth overall in 1986–87 and beat Boston and Quebec in the playoffs to the reach the Stanley Cup semifinal, where they lost to Philadelphia in six.

The following season, 1987–88, they won forty-five games, earned 103 points and finished second, two points behind Calgary.

The Canadiens were blessed with veteran leadership in Bob Gainey, Larry Robinson and Bobby Smith. They had a good core of established players in Mats Naslund, Ryan Walter, Guy Carbonneau and the defence-man Rick Green. The roster included some of the NHL's brightest young talent in goaltender Patrick Roy, defencemen Chris Chelios and Petr Svoboda, and forwards Claude Lemieux and Shayne Corson. And they had the makings of a marquee goal scorer in Stéphane Richer, a handsome and richly talented kid from small-town Quebec who occasionally lifted the Forum fans to their feet, applauding wildly and filling the old building with roars of "RI-cher! RI-cher! RI-cher!"

The Canadiens had drafted Richer in the second round, twenty-ninth overall, in 1984. He was big enough—six foot two, 215 pounds—to with-stand the rigours of the NHL. He was a powerful skater who possessed a blistering shot that reminded commentators of Bobby Hull and Guy Lafleur. As Savard once said of him, "Anytime he was on the ice the puck could wind up in the net."

But for all his physical attributes, Richer was a puzzling young athlete. One night, he would dominate the game and dazzle teammates and fans alike. The next night, he might appear detached and indifferent. Or, as Yves Létourneau put it in *La Presse,* "Stéphane can make himself discreet to the point of being invisible."

Richer scored twenty-one goals as a rookie in 1985–86, and as a sopho-more earned a mid-season trip to the minors that shook his confidence and made him think about quitting. Midway through his third season, 1987–88, he led the team with twenty-five goals. He seemed to hibernate for the month of January, but began hammering pucks past opposition goalies in February and finished the month with forty goals, at which point a Montreal car dealer offered him the use of a Corvette—and another promised a Jaguar—if he scored fifty.

He seemed a cinch to succeed after striking for four goals against Los Angeles on March 6, including the winner, a scorching forty-foot blast that froze Kings goaltender Rollie Melanson. "Can that kid fire 'em?" Robinson said afterward. "Hoo boy . . . can he fire 'em. I always thought Guy Lafleur could shoot harder than anybody I've seen, but this kid shoots harder."

A few nights later, Richer injured his right hand. He sat out five games and gave up on getting fifty, but returned for the final weekend of the regular season, a home-and-home series against Buffalo. Richer went into the Saturday game with forty-five. He scored three times that night, and by the third period the crowd chanted his name every time he stepped on the ice. Twenty-four hours later, he struck for his forty-ninth and fiftieth and, at age twenty-one, became the fifth Canadien to score fifty, and the youngest.

Savard had built a contender, but there was one big problem: Jean Perron could not control the players. This became apparent during the second half of the 1987–88 season. In late January, after a four–one loss at home to the St. Louis Blues, who were nineteen points behind the Canadiens, Perron moved the next day's practice back from noon to 9 a.m. Robinson responded by berating the coach. He criticized Perron's use of players and his inability to adjust to the Blues' game plan that night.

"I suppose he's gonna get tough now," Robinson told Red Fisher. "Okay. He wants respect from the players, but in order to get respect you've got to respect them."

The dust from Robinson's outburst had barely settled when Savard traded Chris Nilan. A Boston native and a nine-year veteran, Nilan had long been at odds with Perron. He was a robust player with an exuberant personality, which made him popular with his teammates and the fans. He had, as *The Gazette*'s Tim Burke put it, a "naughty, little boy's grin and an open-hearted manner," and from day one was "full of holler and mischief in and out of the dressing room, establishing a rapport with everyone he encountered."

For several seasons, he, Gainey and Carbonneau had formed one of the league's top defensive lines. He was also Montreal's enforcer. "He became the club's fearless protector for almost a decade," Burke wrote, "up there with Sprague Cleghorn, Émile Bouchard and John Ferguson as the top 'policemen' in the history of the Canadiens."

But he couldn't get along with Perron. There had been several blow-ups. After he suffered a knee injury, his ice time had been reduced, and his attitude changed for the worse. Savard finally sent him to the Rangers and delivered the news while the team was in Buffalo preparing for a game against the Sabres. One by one, the players came by his room to wish him well. Gainey and Carbonneau were the last to leave. "Both players spent several moments in the room, talking quietly," Fisher reported. "Gainey and Nilan hugged each other when it was time to leave."

A more pointed clash, this one between Perron and Lemieux, occurred during a game in mid-March at the Forum. Lemieux was upset with his ice time and the two exchanged words on the bench during the second period. At the intermission, they continued the discussion in Perron's office. Lemieux returned to the dressing room two minutes before start of the third and kicked an ashtray on his way. Perron followed and, in a loud, angry voice, told him: "Get undressed. You're not going back on the ice."

Lemieux erupted. He smashed one stick over his knee and then several others, all the while hurling obscenities at Perron. After the game, Savard suspended Lemieux indefinitely, and he stayed home while his teammates flew to Minnesota for a contest against the North Stars. Lemieux rejoined the team for its next outing in Winnipeg, and a strange thing happened when he walked into the dressing room.

Brian Skrudland stood and began clapping. Chris Chelios and Bobby Smith joined him. Larry Robinson, Guy Carbonneau and Patrick Roy rose next, and then the rest of the players were on their feet, all applauding enthusiastically.

"We love you, Claude!" Chelios shouted.

"Way to go, big guy," Skrudland said.

"Awright Claude," Roy added.

After the Lemieux–Perron blow-up, players and coach set aside their differences. They were, after all, serious contenders for the Cup. They had won ten straight games, starting in mid-February, and lost only two of their last twenty. They eliminated Hartford in six and won the opening game of the second-round series against Boston. Then they lost four straight and a question immediately arose: Would Perron be back next season?

Savard addressed the issue at a press conference on April 28, two days after the team's elimination. He was unequivocal: he was sticking with Perron. But the script quickly began to unravel.

Mario Tremblay, a hockey commentator on radio and TV, disclosed between periods on *La Soirée de Hockey,* the French-language equivalent of *Hockey Night in Canada,* that Perron had resigned. His source, he said, was "solid, solid, solid."

When the story broke, Savard was in Chicoutimi, five hours northeast of Montreal by car, watching a Memorial Cup game with Pat Burns, coach of the Sherbrooke Canadiens, Montreal's AHL affiliate. Twenty or more hockey writers converged on them at the end of the first and began firing questions. "I don't know if it's true," Savard said, sounding surprised. "I just heard it from you guys."

Perron and his wife were on vacation in Guadeloupe, a French-speaking archipelago in the eastern Caribbean, but he soon let it be known he wasn't quitting. He returned to Montreal on May 14, a Saturday. A radio reporter, Jean Gagnon, was on the same plane. "I have not submitted my resignation," he told Gagnon. "I have never had any intention of doing that. I am a career coach. I'm committed to coaching the Canadiens."

At ten o'clock Monday morning, Perron and Savard met in the general manager's second-floor office at the Forum. They talked for over two hours. They differed on how to run the team. Savard said he'd have to think about whether to extend Perron's contract, which expired June 30. Perron's position was untenable. He resigned, and the Canadiens announced his decision that afternoon.

"He knew the game," Savard would say some years later. "He worked hard. But he lacked the ability to project authority."

The Canadiens held a press conference on June 1 to announce Perron's replacement. It lasted ninety minutes and, according to Gilles Blanchard of *La Presse,* the word "respect" came up on ten occasions. Savard used it. So did assistant coach Jacques Laperrière, and it was top of mind with the new man himself, thirty-six-year-old Pat Burns. "I have always been respected by my players," Burns said. "I have never experienced major discipline problems. I'm a coach who is very close to his players. I can also be very tough. There's always a line you don't cross."

Burns was accustomed to dealing with people who had no respect for the rules or for authority. He was an ex-cop. He had grown up in the working-class district of St-Henri, a few miles west of the Forum and a few blocks from an aged and enormous Imperial Tobacco factory where his Irish-Canadian father and French-Canadian mother had worked for years—and where most of his five siblings, all older, had put in time as well. Burns didn't because his father died when he was fifteen and his mother moved to Ottawa to live with one of her daughters. There, Burns played some junior hockey, and at age eighteen became a cadet with the city's police department and whizzed around the streets of the capital on a scooter, issuing tickets for parking violations. The following year, he moved across the Ottawa River to Gatineau, joined the force there and stayed for fifteen. He pursued miscreants of every stripe—thieves, burglars and murderers, among others—and in his off-hours developed a knack for coaching.

Burns worked with bantams and midgets, spent four seasons with the Hull Olympiques of the Quebec Major Junior Hockey League and one with Sherbrooke. When he was introduced to the Montreal media, Burns insisted he was a coach, not a cop, but acknowledged that some of his law-enforcement skills had served him well in hockey.

"I have interrogated so many liars and hypocrites, so many thieves and cheats that I can smell a lie," he said. "You walk into a dressing room and you can spot the bad guys, the jerks. You know who's lying."

This was precisely what the Canadiens needed, according to Réjean Tremblay of *La Presse*. "The young toughs of the Canadiens, Corson, Chelios, Lemieux and company are going to meet their match," he wrote. "They will speak of respect, but we all know that it's fear that will provoke a change in their attitude."

The young toughs, as Tremblay called them, tested Burns early. In the first month of the season, he had a run-in with enforcer John Kordic. He sat Lemieux in the third game of the season. Stéphane Richer missed a curfew and spent an evening watching from the press box. The team won four, lost seven and tied one in October, and the talk on the open-line shows and elsewhere was that Burns would be gone by Christmas.

But he received some timely help from the veterans—Bob Gainey, Larry Robinson, Rick Green, Bobby Smith and Mats Naslund. They showed up at his office after practice on the last day of October and closed the door. Burns feared a mutiny until Gainey spoke. "We know what you're trying to do and we like it," he said. "We need some law and order around here and want to help."

"Geez, that's great," Burns replied.

What Gainey had in mind was a players-only meeting. The team left for Hartford later that day. After arriving at the hotel, Burns turned over his suite to Gainey, who summoned his teammates. They met for three hours, and their discussion proved to be a turning point. The Canadiens beat the Whalers the following evening and did not lose two straight until late January.

They completed the season with a twenty-nine-game unbeaten streak at home, a new team record. They earned 115 points, two back of first-place Calgary, and Burns was named coach of the year. In the playoffs, they eliminated Hartford, Boston and Philadelphia and advanced to the Stanley Cup final against the Flames for the second time in four seasons.

The Canadiens started poorly. They lost the first game, and one of the young toughs—Lemieux—wound up being the main attraction. He collided with Calgary's Jamie Macoun, fell to the ice and writhed as though in great pain. Burns had seen this routine before—taking a dive to draw a penalty—and refused to send out trainer Gaetan Lefebvre. Lemieux skated to the bench unassisted, but afterward in the rubdown room berated Lefebvre. Shayne Corson intervened. He accused Lemieux of disrupting the team, and the following morning Savard had a private talk with his wayward forward. Both refused comment afterward, but Lemieux sat out the next two starts.

The Canadiens won both, then the Flames earned back-to-back victories, one in Montreal, the other at home, and they pushed the Canadiens to the brink. The sixth game was played at the Forum, and the commentators invoked history to provide perspective and give the Canadiens an edge. "Seven times Montreal has faced elimination in a Stanley Cup final at the Forum," *The Gazette*'s Michael Farber wrote. "Seven times Montreal has won the game."

History was no help on this occasion. The Flames prevailed and the standing-room-only crowd watched quietly as the visitors hooted, hollered, hugged one another and made a circuit of the Forum ice holding the stately, silver Cup aloft. The fans were just as subdued as they filed out of the Forum onto Ste-Catherine Street and Atwater Avenue.

The city administration, mindful of the post-game victory riot of 1986, had posted a hundred police officers and thirty cruisers around the Forum. They arrested three people for disturbing the peace, but that was it. The party that night took place in Calgary. Twenty-five thousand fans, mostly young people in Flames jerseys, took over Eleventh Avenue, also known as "Electric Avenue," a nightclub strip. They howled and high-fived friends and strangers alike, but otherwise behaved responsibly and police were not required to make a single arrest.

Bob Gainey's last act as captain occurred on July 18, 1989. He sat at a table in the media room at the Forum with Serge Savard to his right, wife Cathy to his left and a large crowd of teammates, team officials and journalists before him. He spoke in English and French, switching effortlessly from to the other, performing with his customary poise and distinction, as one writer put it, and announced that after sixteen bruising and sometimes punishing seasons, he was through.

"The people of Montreal are known, and rightly so, as the strongest and most knowledgeable fans," he said. "I tried to perform for them every night I played and I'll carry with me many great memories."

Savard spoke warmly of his former teammate. He cited his many accomplishments: the Stanley Cup championships, the individual awards, the all-star nominations and the appearances with Team Canada. "If I can describe Bob Gainey in one word," Savard said, "it would be determination. He once played with two separated shoulders and no one even knew about it. In his prime he was one of the most feared players in the league. He is one of the greats in the history of the Canadiens hockey club."

Pat Burns spoke of the future and the challenge ahead. "You don't replace Bob Gainey," Burns said. "You put someone else out there, but you don't replace him."

Larry Robinson had the character, the experience and the stature to step into the breach, but his contract had expired and he signed one week later with the Los Angeles Kings. There was no clear and obvious successor when the players returned in the fall and were asked to choose the next captain. Three rounds of voting produced a stalemate—nine votes for Guy Carbonneau, nine for Chris Chelios. Savard solved the problem by making them co-captains who would wear the C on alternate nights.

Carbonneau, then twenty-nine, had skated alongside Gainey almost from the time he joined the Canadiens in 1982. He had won the Frank J. Selke Trophy the previous two seasons and had absorbed some of Gainey's subdued intensity, his formidable determination and his ability to shoulder responsibility and lead by example. The twenty-seven-year-old Chelios had played six full seasons and had won the James Norris Trophy, and fans and pundits alike assumed he would be the cornerstone of the defence for years to come.

His conduct off the ice was an issue. "He's a free-spirited guy who does what he likes," Gary Suter, the Calgary Flames defenceman and a former teammate of Chelios's at the University of Wisconsin, told a feature writer for the Montreal *Gazette*. "I can't tell you much more than that because I don't want to get him in any trouble." Canadiens defenceman Petr Svoboda told the same writer: "He likes to have fun both on and off the ice. We're doing a lot of good things together, some things you can't mention. This is for the newspaper, eh? "

His off-ice antics spawned a swirl of gossip and rumour (tales of an affair with the wife of a Canadiens executive, alleged dalliances with starstruck, underage teens, a fracas with a streetwalker). Reporters chased every story, and Savard always reached with trepidation for his morning paper, half expecting that he would see his co-captain's picture on the front page beneath a large, shocking headline and alongside a scandalous story. But none of the rumblings were ever substantiated.

Chelios did make headlines as co-captain, but they were all related to hockey. Early in the season, he signed a new, five-year deal that made him the league's highest-paid defenceman at $775,000 annually. Then, in mid-February, he injured his knee and was out of the lineup till early April. And on the final day of June 1990, the news was that Chelios had been traded to Chicago.

He was shocked. So was Burns. The Canadiens had never dealt one of their best players, let alone a team captain, in his prime. A rumour, never proved, soon circulated to the effect that team president Ronald Corey had forced his general manager to deal Chelios because he had tired of the player's off-ice behaviour and the ever-present risk that he would embarrass the organization.

Savard has always maintained that he alone made the decision. The team doctors had advised him that Chelios's injured knee would likely shorten his career. As well, the Canadiens needed a centre in the mould of Jean Béliveau, Henri Richard or Jacques Lemaire who could play with the team's two top wingers, Stéphane Richer and Shayne Corson.

There was good reason to believe that they had found their man in Chicago's Denis Savard. He was only twenty-nine, a year older than Chelios. He was a highlight-reel player who had accumulated just over a thousand points in ten seasons as a Blackhawk. He was thrilled to be return-ing to Montreal, where he grew up. A few days after the trade, he toured the Canadiens dressing room, met Béliveau and left the building feeling, as he put it, "like a kid who just had his dreams come true."

"The divorce is final," a headline in the sports section of *La Presse* declared on September 4, 1990. The "divorce," as the newspaper called it, involved the team's troublesome winger Claude Lemieux, who had informed Serge Savard that spring that he wanted out.

Lemieux had plenty of talent, but he could be testy, unpredictable and hard to handle. At every stage of his career, he had fought with his coaches, as columnist Michael Farber pointed out: "Lemieux battled Yvon Lambert when he played junior in Verdun, ultimately undermining Lambert's job. While in the American Hockey League at Sherbrooke, Lemieux had run-ins with Pierre Creamer. And he and Jean Perron despised each other in Montreal."

He was no fonder of Burns, and the feeling was mutual. Under the circumstances, Savard made what seemed a sensible trade, dealing

Lemieux to the New Jersey Devils for Sylvain Turgeon, a twenty-five-year-old native of Noranda, Quebec, and a high-scoring left winger who had twice enjoyed forty-goal seasons. But Turgeon was recovering from back surgery and played just nineteen games in 1990–91, collecting twelve points.

The Denis Savard trade did not turn out as expected, either. He signed a three-year deal that paid him $1.25 million annually, making him the team's first millionaire player, but contributed only fifty-nine points in his first winter as a Canadien—a poor effort for a player who had averaged 101 points in ten seasons as a Blackhawk.* The fans were prepared to reserve judgment. Even great players had off years. Perhaps Savard would display his usual razzle-dazzle next season.

But they were completely out of patience with Stéphane Richer. What they had seen in Richer—twice a fifty-goal scorer by age twenty-four—was the Canadiens' next great offensive star, the next in a line that could be traced back sixty years to Howie Morenz. What they wanted was what all those other players had given consistently: excellence night in and night out, season after season. That, and not mere talent, was the mark of greatness. What they got from Richer was inconsistency. He would be fabulous one game, invisible the next. He had scored fifty in 1987–88 and exactly half that the following season. He had struck for fifty-one in 1989–90, and then what? Another poor year. By mid-February 1991, some sixty games into the schedule, he had just twenty goals and the fans were ticked. They booed every time he touched the puck.

Richer's worst moment occurred on Fan Appreciation Day, a Sunday in February when the Canadiens opened the Forum to the public to watch the team practise. Every seat in the building was full, and most of the occupants were children. When they saw Richer step on the ice, the kids

---

* The spelling of the team's nickname has been a source of some controversy. Over the course of the club's first sixty years, "Black Hawks" was the generally accepted version, although "Blackhawks" appeared occasionally in team publications. Prior to the 1986–87 season the team formally adopted the latter, "closed" spelling.

began to boo, and the jeering grew in volume. It became, in the words of one writer, "a chorus of boos so hearty that it shook the foundations of the venerable Forum."

The reporters covering the team saw Richer as a likeable but tormented young man. They tried to explain, and sometimes protect, him. Bertrand Raymond of *Le Journal de Montréal* disclosed that the Canadiens had paid for psychological counselling for three seasons. Réjean Tremblay of *La Presse* wrote that Richer was prone to mood swings and had "a destructive adolescent side," and asked the fans to give him time to mature. Michael Farber wrote, "The only way he can possibly pull himself out of this tailspin is if he clears his head, which means he is allowed to go about his work—if not to raucous cheers—at least discreet silence."

But trouble seemed to follow him. He tried consulting astrologers and foolishly acknowledged in an interview, "All three told me the same thing, either I'm loved or not loved. They told me this is peculiar to Geminis." And try as he might, things kept going wrong. After a blunder cost the team a game against the Bruins, he confessed, "I wanted to have a good game and redeem myself, but another brick fell on my head."

By the time the season was over, Savard had seen enough. At training camp in September 1991, he sent Richer to the Devils for Kirk Muller, a trade that would come to be seen as one of the best in franchise history.

Through all the turmoil and upheaval, Serge Savard never lost confidence in his law-and-order coach, Pat Burns. The two men worked well together. They became close friends. And a few days before Christmas 1991, Savard rewarded Burns with a new three-year deal worth $1.05 million, even though there was a year remaining on his existing contract.

By then, Burns was one of Montreal's most visible personalities, as broadcaster Dick Irvin noted in *Behind the Bench*, his 1993 book about coaching in the NHL. "He appeared in TV commercials and had his own radio show," Irvin wrote. "His face and words dominated the wall-to-wall media coverage the team received in both languages. Pat Burns was a regular every night on the early and late TV news."

He was a natural for the role. He was outgoing, talkative and comfortable in front of the cameras. But by his fourth season, he had tired of the media attention and the daily deluge of questions and, according to Irvin, it showed. "The face on the TV screen wasn't smiling very often," he wrote. "And he usually sounded as sour as he looked."

Things became really grim after the Bruins swept the Canadiens four straight in the playoffs—the third consecutive year that Boston had eliminated Montreal in the post-season. The public, already disenchanted with the team's defence-first approach, blamed Burns for the defeat, and some of the players, having tired of their coach as well, said so publicly after their season ended.

One May morning, Burns picked up the morning papers and found himself described by defenceman Éric Desjardins as less than human. Another player, who was not identified, complained that Burns was beginning to behave like the unpredictable and tyrannical Mike Keenan, a comment that could only have come from Denis Savard, who had played for Keenan in Chicago.

A few days later, Burns left for a vacation in Jamaica. He stayed a week, during which he thought about his future and decided to resign, a decision Serge Savard accepted with regret. "I had no intention of firing Pat Burns," he said when he announced the coach's departure. "I wanted Pat to coach here as long as I live. He was doing a good job. He was ready to go. But if he can't function, he made the right move."

That was the crux of it, as Burns acknowledged. "When you're criticized openly, like I have been for the last two weeks," he said, "it's hard to take. It would have been difficult to come back in September."

The search for a successor immediately became a public spectacle, one that played out in the sports pages and on open-line radio shows. There were two candidates: the fiery Michel Bergeron, who openly declared his interest, and the well-travelled Jacques Demers, who allowed his agent, Don Meehan, to inform Serge Savard of his interest. Both were well-known francophone Quebecers with solid credentials. They had NHL experience (Bergeron with the Quebec Nordiques and New York Rangers, Demers with the St. Louis Blues and Detroit Red Wings) and they were fluently bilingual.

Callers to the open-line shows debated their merits. Newspaper columnists touted one or the other. Savard had no desire to inflame things any further. He insisted on thorough medical examinations, knowing that Bergeron had suffered a heart attack the previous year. With the advice of the physicians in hand, he was able to cite health concerns as his reason for passing on Bergeron.

On June 11, 1992, Savard introduced Demers at a press conference at the Forum and, as Dick Irvin wrote in *Behind the Bench*, "The crush of reporters, microphones, cameras and TV lights . . . made you wonder if World War Three had just been declared." But this was a happy occasion for the organization, and a joyous homecoming for the forty-eight-year-old Montrealer who had just been named coach of the Canadiens.

It was the end of an odyssey that had begun on the streets of Montreal when Demers was a teenager, a high school dropout who could scarcely read or write, who worked as a Coca-Cola delivery man and coached hockey evenings and weekends. First peewees, then bantams, midgets and Tier II juniors—the St-Léonard Cougars for half a winter and the Châteauguay Wings for two seasons that produced consecutive championships in the Montreal Metropolitan Junior Hockey League.

And then, in 1972, opportunity knocked. Marcel Pronovost, the former Detroit Red Wings defenceman, had been named head coach of the WHA's Chicago Cougars. He hired Demers as an assistant. Demers lasted three seasons in Chicago, until the Cougars folded, then he moved on to the Indianapolis Racers. After they went under as well, he landed with another WHA team, the Cincinnati Stingers, who were running a promotion to boost season-ticket sales—to the three thousand mark—when he was hired.

In 1978–79, the WHA's final season, Demers coached the Quebec Nordiques. The Nordiques joined the NHL the following year and Demers was ecstatic, but not for long. He knocked the team's star forward in a coffee shop conversation with a Quebec City reporter, his comments made headlines and Demers was out, banished to Fredericton of the American Hockey League.

He was stuck there two seasons, winning coach-of-the-year honours once, before another opportunity arrived. The St. Louis Blues hired him. The Blues were in a shambles—they were as disorganized and financially shaky as the WHA clubs Demers had coached, but he lasted four years and in the spring of 1986 took the team to the Stanley Cup semifinals—a series that boiled down to a two–one loss at the hands of the Calgary Flames in game seven.

Then he moved again, this time to the Detroit Red Wings. The Wings were at one of the lowest points in a history that had spanned six decades. They hadn't posted a winning record since 1972–73, and in 1985–86 they finished last with forty points. Opponents called them the Dead Things. In Demers's first season, the Wings improved by thirty-eight points and Demers guided them to the Stanley Cup semifinals and was named coach of the year. They reached the semifinals the following spring as well. Then the Wings slipped. They lost in the first round, then missed the playoffs in 1989–90. Demers was dismissed.

His next stop was the broadcast booth, providing colour commentary for Quebec Nordiques games. He did that for two seasons before Savard hired him to run the Canadiens. "I'm a Montrealer," he declared proudly the first time he addressed the city's hockey media. "I grew up dreaming about the Canadiens. When Serge Savard called me, I thought, 'What a feeling.'"

By opening night of the 1992–93 season, seven members of the previous year's team were gone, most notably Shayne Corson, a street fighter and barroom brawler whose late-night, off-ice scraps had repeatedly embarrassed the organization. Savard traded him to Edmonton along with two other players for Vincent Damphousse, another Montrealer who was delighted to be coming home.

Damphousse was twenty-five. He had spent six years in the league, five of them with Toronto. He was a goal scorer and a playmaker, had led the Leafs in points once and had been the Oilers' most productive forward in his single season with them. Damphousse asked Edmonton general manager Glen Sather for a trade for personal reasons. "I was going through a divorce," he would later disclose. "In a week I got traded[,] I signed my contract and my divorce papers. It was like a piano fell off my shoulders. I was free to play. I was ecstatic."

The off-season changes generated considerable optimism among the fans. Nearly two thirds of the 752 people who responded to a Montreal *Gazette* poll predicted the Canadiens would finish first in their division. Almost half picked Damphousse to lead the team in scoring. One third said the Canadiens would win the Stanley Cup.

They were right about Damphousse, who accumulated a career-high ninety-seven points, but wrong about the divisional standings. Boston took top spot, Quebec was second, Montreal third. And after two playoff outings against the Nordiques, and a pair of losses, nobody was betting on the Canadiens to win the Cup.

The Canadiens saved their season with an overtime win in the third game, then won the next three, including another in overtime, to eliminate the Nordiques. They beat the Buffalo Sabres four straight, although three of those wins came in overtime. They ran their unbeaten streak to eleven with three consecutive victories over the New York Islanders in the semifinal series. They faltered in the fourth contest, but buried the Islanders at home in the fifth to reach the final for the first time since 1989.

With time expiring in game five, the Forum crowd stood and roared and, as *The Gazette*'s Michael Farber wrote, "Years of frustration seemed to vanish with every second on the clock." The players stood as well, waiting to go over the boards, but one of them, Denis Savard, turned, embraced the team's athletic therapist, Gaetan Lefebvre, and wept.

"Savy. Savy," Lefebvre said, "you're crying."

"Gates," Savard replied, "it's my first time."

Later, in the dressing room, Savard said: "I've dreamed of this . . . since the playoffs began. It's come to me in my sleep. It started after we beat Quebec. I've dreamed it a lot since then. I've been thinking about this every day."

Savard and his teammates had a week to prepare while the Toronto Maple Leafs and Los Angeles Kings waged a tight semifinal which the Kings finally won. During that time, the city was surprisingly quiet. "There are no visual clues here," Farber wrote on the day the final opened. "Nothing screaming THIS IS IT. If you didn't know better, you could hardly guess that the Canadiens and the Kings start the Stanley Cup final tonight."

That changed as the series progressed and the likelihood of a Montreal victory grew. The Kings won the opener and were up by a goal with under two minutes to go in the second contest. They were trying to run out the clock when Jacques Demers summoned referee Kerry Fraser and asked him to measure the blade of Marty McSorley's stick. Fraser waved the Los Angeles defenceman to the timekeeper's bench, set a ruler against the toe and heel of the blade, found that the warp exceeded the legal limit and assessed a minor penalty.

Demers pulled Patrick Roy, and the Canadiens played with six skaters to the Kings' four. Thirty seconds later, defenceman Éric Desjardins fired a rising shot from the point. It beat Kelly Hrudey and the game was tied two–two. Fifteen seconds into overtime, Desjardins scored his third of the night and the series was even.

Game three, played at the Great Western Forum in the Los Angeles suburb of Inglewood, drew a sellout crowd that included many famous faces—Ronald and Nancy Reagan, tennis star Andre Agassi and actors Nicholas Cage, Michelle Pfeiffer and Goldie Hawn, among others. The Canadiens led three–nothing early in the second, but squandered that comfortable edge and the teams were tied at the end of the third. Overtime lasted a mere thirty-four seconds. John LeClair snapped the puck past Hrudey during a goalmouth scramble and the Canadiens went up two–one in the series.

Game four was also played in California, but the Canadiens opened the doors of the Forum and eighteen thousand fans bought tickets to watch the game on the big TV screens above centre ice. They witnessed a sizzling contest. Again, Montreal took the lead, but the Kings pulled even. Neither side could break the deadlock in regulation time, and nearly fifteen minutes of the fourth period had elapsed before LeClair scored and the Canadiens had won their tenth consecutive overtime game.

In the dressing room, there was disbelief. "I'm numb," said captain Guy Carbonneau. "I don't know what to think, whether to laugh, be serious or be happy. Happy I guess because we're leading the series three–one."

Back home, there was delirium. Fans poured out of the Forum and onto Ste-Catherine Street and spontaneously celebrated. Others left bars or their homes to join in. Clusters of police officers stood on almost every corner to keep the peace. Pedestrians chanted or screamed, "We're number one!" Motorists honked their horns. Traffic was snarled for twenty blocks. But all this was a mere warmup. The real victory party occurred two nights later, after the Canadiens had spanked the Kings four–one and captured the Stanley Cup for the twenty-fourth time in the trophy's hundred-year history.

The players circled the ice, took turns hoisting the Cup aloft before a jubilant and adoring crowd, then retired to the dressing room. There, they hooted and howled. They guzzled Champagne straight from the bottle or sprayed one another with it, and they shared their triumph with parents, siblings and friends who packed the room and spilled out into the corridor.

Outside the Forum, a massive celebration was occurring, though it quickly turned ugly. Ste-Catherine Street was jammed with motorists and pedestrians. Youthful fans walked over cars and trucks. They smashed windshields and the plate-glass windows of storefronts. They ransacked a hundred shops, set six fires and damaged forty-seven police vehicles, fifteen buses and three subway cars.

Police Chief Alain St-Germain later told the news media that he had six hundred officers on duty when the game ended at around 10:20 p.m., and by midnight four hundred reinforcements had been deployed. They made 115 arrests; 168 people were injured, including 49 officers. The Insurance Bureau of Canada estimated the damage at ten million dollars.

"My store looks like a tornado hit it—Hurricane Jean Doré," one exasperated merchant said, referring to the mayor of the day.

Montrealers cleaned up the mess and officially celebrated their latest Stanley Cup with the customary parade, although this one was shorter than most and followed a different route. It began at Parc Lafontaine on Sherbrooke Street East and proceeded west on Sherbrooke for about three kilometres. The players rode on flatbed trucks as opposed to the convertibles used in 1986, which put them above the crowd and out of reach. A hundred thousand people attended, according to official estimates, and twelve hundred police officers lined the route.

But this crowd was well behaved. People packed the sidewalks and spilled onto the street. They watched from rooftops and balconies, from trees and light standards. As the parade passed through the downtown core, a deluge of confetti and strips of newspaper fell from hotel balconies, apartment buildings and office towers. It was a joyous day for the faithful, both young and old. "Ecstatic, overjoyed, words can't express how happy I am," a twenty-four-year-old fan told a Montreal *Gazette* reporter.

"This is unbelievable," added fifty-nine-year-old Michel Gagné, who had driven five hours from Jonquière just for the parade. "This team deserves it."

"Now that No. 24 has come home to Montreal, can No. 25 be far behind?" Red Fisher asked in a post-Cup column. "Do the Canadiens build on what they have? Is this the start of something big? The answer: no."

Those were prophetic words, but on that June day few among the team's legions of diehard fans were listening. They had waited seven years—far too long for those who had witnessed or remembered the glory years of the fifties, sixties and seventies. They went home hoping they would not be forced to endure another seven-year drought.

But the NHL was changing, and conditions would make it much more difficult to produce repeat champions, let alone dynasties. Two new teams would begin play that fall, the Ottawa Senators and Tampa Bay Lightning. Also on the horizon were new divisional alignments and a revamped playoff structure.

Other changes were less obvious, but no less important. The era of the mega-salaries had begun. Players were more assertive and likely to be driven by their own interests rather than loyalty to an organization, even one with an illustrious history.

1993-2001
WIN, TABERNAC!

THREE MONTHS TO THE DAY after they won the Stanley Cup, the players were back in Montreal to start training camp. They swapped stories about the usual summer diversions—golf, weddings and family vacations—and regaled each other with accounts of the twenty-four hours they were allotted to share the Cup with family and friends. Patrick Roy had hosted a party at his Quebec City home and dropped the trophy into the swimming pool, only to discover that forty-seven pounds of silver wouldn't float. Stéphane Lebeau had invited 150 people to a buffet dinner in the suburban south-shore community of Varennes, about twenty kilometres east of Montreal, and 250 showed up. Brian Bellows told of how he'd taken the Cup to a backyard wedding reception in St. Catharines, Ontario, and turned the inevitable photo session into a fundraiser for a local hospital. He'd charged five dollars per picture and collected twelve hundred in two hours.

In the small towns of Quebec, people had reacted with wonder and awe. "They couldn't believe that the Cup was right there in their communities," said Bernard Brisset, the team's vice-president of communications. "It was like the holy grail to them. They wondered where the security was. But who'd want to run off with the holy grail?"

Training camp signalled the end of the revelry and the start of the Canadiens' defence of their latest championship. Nobody expected it would be easy. "It's going to be tougher to repeat than to win it," captain Guy Carbonneau admitted. Coach Jacques Demers added, "It's difficult to repeat if you don't have a powerhouse, which we don't."

The Canadiens had won with four solid lines, six good defencemen and a superstar goalie. In their pre-season predictions, most of the pundits picked them to finish second or third in their division. They placed third, as it happened, and drew the Boston Bruins in the first round. "Let the party begin," a Montreal newspaper declared on the morning of game one, since the Bruins were seen as a better proposition than the more formidable Pittsburgh Penguins or New Jersey Devils.

Two weeks later, Boston had eliminated the Canadiens in seven games, and Montrealers were singing a different tune. Outraged fans lit up the phone-in shows and the media called for blood. "Who pays the price for this embarrassment?" Red Fisher asked in his post-season analysis. "Who put out? Who didn't? Who stays? Who goes?"

Patrick Roy was merely ordinary, for once, but there was a legitimate reason for that. He had developed appendicitis and missed game three, a six–two loss, because he was in hospital. Nobody was blaming Carbonneau or the perpetually hard-working Kirk Muller. But Vincent Damphousse, the team's most gifted forward, had disappeared. And a whole lot of others had failed to display the desire and tenacity necessary to succeed in the playoffs. "We didn't seem to have that look in our eyes," Demers said. "We could see that some of the guys who let us down in March would likely let us down in April—and it happened."

A few days later, a public-relations fiasco cut short the post-mortems. Roy, Carbonneau and Damphousse were playing a round of golf. Normand Pichette, a photographer with *Le Journal de Montréal,* a tabloid newspaper, tagged along at a distance, snapping pictures with a high-power telephoto lens. The following morning, the newspaper devoted its entire front page to the golfing truants: Roy on the left, Damphousse on the right and Carbonneau in the centre with his middle finger raised.

The Canadiens captain tried to laugh off the matter, saying that he was merely testing the wind. He pleaded his right to privacy during the off-season. In the end, he issued an apology to assure the fans that his gesture was not aimed at them. Most people dismissed the matter as a lapse of judgment and forgot about it until late August, when the Canadiens announced that they had traded their captain to the St. Louis Blues for an unproven player named Jim Montgomery, a twenty-five-year-old Montrealer with sixty-seven NHL games and twenty points to his credit.

Serge Savard insisted the trade was strictly business and had nothing to do with the finger flap, or the fact that he and Carbonneau had been trying to renegotiate his contract. Carbonneau was thirty-four, a twelve-year veteran who was earning $750,000 a year. He had also undergone surgery on both knees. Savard said he made the deal while Carbonneau still had value in the market and he likened the unheralded, unknown Montgomery to an undervalued asset.

"It's like buying stock at $4," Savard said. "You think it will go up to eight in a year's time. Montgomery's got a chance to become a good third- or second-line player."

Others weren't buying that. "They made a big mistake," right winger Mike Keane said in an interview from his home in Winnipeg. "He'll be sorely missed. He was always the guy who kept it together when things got edgy, we were losing or there were conflicts between players."

Réjean Tremblay let loose with an impassioned rant in *La Presse:*

"Tradition, they say!

"The colours, they claim!

"Loyalty, they chant!

"Bullshit!

"Carbo wasn't a superstar," Tremblay added. "But he was the real thing. Tough, stubborn, proud, capable of speaking his mind."

A dispute between the owners and players over a new collective bargaining agreement delayed the start of the 1994–95 season nearly four months. By the time the Canadiens opened their abbreviated, forty-eight-game schedule on January 21 against the Rangers in New York, Kirk Muller had been named captain. He had more than enough heart for the job and soon Jacques Demers was saying, "This is Kirk Muller's team."

But Muller didn't generate much offence and neither did his teammates, a state of affairs that led to another major trade three weeks into the season. This time, Serge Savard earned rave reviews. He sent defenceman Éric Desjardins and forwards John LeClair and Gilbert Dionne to Philadelphia in exchange for Mark Recchi, a handsome, curly-haired triggerman originally from Kamloops, British Columbia. In five full NHL seasons with Pittsburgh and Philadelphia, Recchi had scored 206 goals. "Check the numbers and drool," *The Gazette*'s Jack Todd wrote. "When was the last time the Canadiens could ice a player who has scored fifty-three goals and seventy assists in one season? Yeah, I know. His name was Guy."

The trade should have made the Canadiens "swift, tough and dangerous," as Todd put it, but things didn't go according to plan. Recchi contributed better than a point per game, which wasn't enough to reverse the team's sinking fortunes. The Canadiens were good at home, but terrible on the road, and by early April they were desperate to make the playoffs. This led to one more big trade—and the departure of yet another captain. Savard dealt Muller, defenceman Mathieu Schneider and centre Craig Darby to the New York Islanders in exchange for Vladimir Malakhov, who brought size and muscle, and Pierre Turgeon, a twenty-five-year-old centre from Rouyn-Noranda who had twice scored more than a hundred points in a season.

In his Montreal debut, a home game against the Nordiques, Turgeon played on a line with Recchi and Vincent Damphousse. He scored once, assisted on another and led the Canadiens to a six–five win. The fans stood and wildly applauded his efforts. He was named first star and Demers had visions of something big. "These guys," he said of Turgeon, Recchi and Damphousse, "are capable of combining for 300 points, well at least 270 points a season."

But they could not make the Canadiens a contender that spring. Internal conflicts, some of them between French- and English-speaking players, others between those paid millions and those earning a lot less, undermined the unity of the team, and for the first time in twenty-five years, Montreal missed the playoffs.

———

The Canadiens opened the 1995–96 season by retiring the number that their great goaltender Jacques Plante had worn with distinction for ten seasons. Plante's predecessor, Gerry McNeil, and his successor, Gump Worsley, participated in the on-ice tribute and Michel Plante represented his father, who had died of cancer in February 1986.

After a brief commemoration in words and images, Plante's sweater and his number 1 joined those of Howie Morenz, Maurice Richard, Jean Béliveau, Guy Lafleur, Doug Harvey and Henri Richard, all of which had been set aside, never to be worn again. Then the Canadiens played an awful game. They lost seven–one to the Philadelphia Flyers, their worst opening-night defeat since 1922–23. According to one commentator, "The crowd of 17,646 booed until the rafters shook."

The Canadiens played their next two games on the road against Sun Belt expansion teams—the Florida Panthers and the Tampa Bay Lightning. They scored a goal in each contest, lost both, and when they landed at Dorval Airport a surly mob of TV and radio reporters hurled questions and demanded answers.

The public was just as unhappy. Jerry Trudel, host of a sports phone-in show on radio station CKAC, summed up the mood when he told a fellow journalist: "The fans are made as hell. They want Jacques Demers fired and Patrick Roy traded. It's so emotional. I've never seen this after only three games. But the three games remind people of last season. Tolerance is zero."

That was evident when the Stanley Cup champion New Jersey Devils paid a Saturday night visit to the Forum. The Canadiens outplayed the champs and outshot them by a margin of more than two to one, yet suffered their fourth straight loss. Some people wore paper bags over their heads. Others stayed home. There were empty seats in the reds, the most expensive in the building. The crowd booed each of New Jersey's four goals and during the third period they jeered each time the home side touched the puck. "Suddenly," *The Gazette*'s Pat Hickey wrote, "it's embarrassing to be a Canadiens fan."

Team president Ronald Corey witnessed the debacle from his customary seat right behind the Canadiens bench and he had seen enough. The following Tuesday afternoon, he purged his front office for the second time since taking the job thirteen years earlier. He fired Serge Savard, dumped his assistant, André Boudrias, and scout Carol Vadnais and demoted Demers to an unspecified position.

All of this occurred amid the second referendum over the future of Quebec. The story bumped the campaign from the top of the day's newscasts, and that evening Parti Québécois leader Jacques Parizeau interrupted a speech before a thousand supporters in Gatineau to announce: "My friends, we witnessed a catastrophe tonight. It is one that has taken place with the Canadiens."

Corey had reacted hastily to a crisis of the moment, and in so doing left himself no time to conduct an extensive search for either a new coach or general manager. There were games to play and decisions to be made. So Corey turned to the team's past—or, as Red Fisher put it, "Le Club de Hockey Canadien president Ronald Corey has taken a short skate from his second-floor Forum office to the Old-Timers Room to find the new blood he needs to lead his floundering team to a better tomorrow."

Corey hired Réjean Houle as his general manager. Houle chose former teammate Mario Tremblay as his coach, and Tremblay insisted on adding Yvan Cournoyer to a roster of assistants that included ex-Canadiens Jacques Laperrière and Steve Shutt. The triumvirate of new faces had played for the team for a total of thirty-seven seasons. They had won twenty Stanley Cups, but Houle, Tremblay and Cournoyer had not a day's experience in the positions they now held.

The Canadiens' president was taking a huge gamble, especially with Houle, who had spent the previous decade in the communications department of the Molson-O'Keefe Brewery, owner of the Canadiens. Corey explained his decision this way: "He got good experience at Molson. He went to school there. He knows the media. He knows the Canadiens. I know him so well. He's here every week. He's like a member of the family. He's so close to us and the players."

That did little to satisfy the skeptics, and few were as hostile as Réjean

Tremblay. "Peanut as general manager of the Canadiens—after a decade spent selling beer," he wrote, using the nickname Houle had acquired in his playing days. "Peanut, the big boss of the *Glorieux,* responsible for the revival of the team, in charge of dealing with old foxes like Cliff Fletcher, Harry Sinden, Bob Pulford and company, who know hockey like the backs of their hands.

"What did Ronald Corey want when he fired Serge Savard? A cheer-leader who could galvanize the demoralized troops. A man as experienced as Serge Savard has been replaced by a director of communications for Molson who has never managed anything in his life other than a softball team."

Tremblay received a more favourable reception. He was one of those former players who had the CH tattooed on his heart, according to Corey. He had made the team in 1974 as a reckless eighteen-year-old. He played with the same furious abandon for twelve seasons until his shoulders, knees and other parts would not endure any more punishment. Emotion had kept him in the game, and it also kept him out. He operated at such a fevered pitch that Scotty Bowman rarely used him at crucial moments. Tremblay had become a colourful and engaging hockey commentator on TV and radio after his career ended, but was thrilled to be back in the game. And the fans welcomed him warmly on his first appearance as coach.

"When he took his place behind the bench," *La Presse* reported, "a sheet of paper in his hands to keep the lines straight, he received a tremendous ovation. The people showed that they had forgotten Jacques Demers, one of the most popular coaches in the history of the Canadiens."

The Toronto Maple Leafs were the visitors that night, and the Canadiens beat them with a goal in the last second of play. Over the next five weeks, they won twelve games. They enjoyed a winning streak of six games and another of five, then lost three straight at the end of November. Tremblay's direct and intense approach inspired the players after their disastrous start. The mini-slump prompted some observers to wonder whether he would be equally effective when the team was losing.

The answer became clear on December 2, a Saturday, when Montreal hosted the Detroit Red Wings, one of the league's best teams. The game was a colossal mismatch—a horror show, one commentator called it.

Another said the Canadiens resembled a minor league club. The Wings smothered their offence. They shredded the defence with speed, hustle and dazzling passing. They made a great goaltender, Patrick Roy, look like an amateur. The Wings fired twenty-six shots at him and scored nine times.

With every save, the crowd jeered, and Roy responded by throwing his arms in the air in mock triumph. He was livid by the time he was relieved midway through the second. He stomped into the corridor at the end of the bench. He shed his stick, gloves and mask and then had to walk the length of the bench to reach the stool reserved for the backup. On the way, he confronted Corey, who was seated in his customary box seat. "This is my last game in Montreal," he snapped. He glared at Tremblay, who stood with arms crossed, eyes blazing and lips tight, and then growled, "Do you understand?"

A television cameraman, stationed above the bench, captured everything. A clip of Roy's outburst—his face contorted and his finger jabbing at Corey—played on newscasts across the country that night and the following morning. On Sunday afternoon, Houle announced to a stunned media that Patrick Roy was through as a Canadien and would be traded.

Roy later apologized to the fans. He explained that he had felt abandoned and humiliated by his coach. "If I had had one word of comfort from Mario Tremblay, if I had felt he wanted to help me, I would not have spoken to Ronald Corey."

Tremblay insisted that he never intended to humiliate Roy. "Maybe I should have pulled him after the first period when the score was five–one," he reasoned, "but I didn't because I felt we were still in the game. When the score went to seven–one in the second, I was hoping it would stay that way until the end of the period, when I could tell him in the dressing room that I was putting Pat Jablonski in for the third. Instead, boom, boom. Two more goals and now I had to get him out."

A novice coach's miscalculation had cost the Canadiens their only superstar. In his ten seasons, Roy had led the team to two Stanley Cups, was awarded the Conn Smythe Trophy twice and the Vézina three times. He insisted that he be traded to a contender, and the Canadiens accommodated by moving him to the Colorado Avalanche—who had been the Quebec Nordiques until moving to Denver the previous summer.

The Canadiens received goaltender Jocelyn Thibault, a twenty-year-old Montreal native who had grown up idolizing and mimicking Roy. Thibault had only played fifty-seven NHL games over three seasons. He was still an emerging talent, and so the Canadiens were spared direct comparisons with their departed star.

The deal also included three forwards. The Canadiens moved their captain, Mike Keane, in exchange for right winger Martin Rucinsky, a Czech, and left winger Andrei Kovalenko, a Russian. "We'll just have to sit back and see how this works out," Houle said. "A trade like this, you never know, eh."

One thing was clear, though: the Canadiens were a team in turmoil. They had traded three captains (Carbonneau, Muller and Keane) in the space of eighteen months. A total of twenty-two veterans had been dealt, cut or left the organization as free agents. Only four players remained from the 1993 Stanley Cup team.

Haste and desperation had replaced the patience and clever design that had produced so many championships. The organization had drifted away from its past, more by accident than design, and now a complete break was imminent. The Canadiens were about to vacate the Forum, their home since 1926. They were moving to the brand new, $265 million Molson Centre, a state-of-the-art building from the ice-level dressing rooms and training facilities to the twenty-eight-ton octagonal scoreboard suspended over centre ice.

The Canadiens won their final game at the Forum, played on a Monday night, March 11, 1996, against the Dallas Stars. Both teams were fighting for playoff spots, but neither looked particularly good, which didn't matter much. The big, happy crowd, the fifty-six former Canadiens in attendance, nearly half of them Hall of Famers, and the 160 journalists from across the continent were there to celebrate the past.

Maurice Richard, Jean Béliveau and Guy Lafleur performed a ceremonial opening faceoff, dropping the puck between the sticks of captain Pierre Turgeon and former captain Guy Carbonneau, who was playing for the

Stars. The anthems were next. Montreal opera singer André Ouellet performed "The Star-Spangled Banner." Then everyone in the building lifted their eyes from ice level to the scoreboard where there appeared the image of the late Roger Doucet, the barrel-chested baritone who had sung the anthems at televised home games from 1971 until shortly before his death in 1981. A recording of Doucet singing "O Canada" issued forth from the public-address system like thunder rolling off a mountain.

A second celebration took place after the game. Broadcasters Richard Garneau and Dick Irvin served as emcees. They introduced the Hall of Famers, and each took his place on the red carpets laid on the ice: Scotty Bowman, Sam Pollock, Hartland Molson, Guy Lapointe, Steve Shutt, Bob Gainey, Guy Lafleur, Jacques Laperrière, Serge Savard, Jacques Lemaire, Ken Dryden, Frank Mahovlich, Yvan Cournoyer, Gump Worsley, Henri Richard, Jean Béliveau, Tom Johnson, Ken Reardon and Émile Bouchard.

The fans cheered and cheered and the applause delayed the calling of some of the names, but that was a mere warmup for the ovation that began when the final former Canadien was announced and the Rocket emerged from the stands and walked onto the ice for the second time that evening. The entire crowd stood clapping, whistling and chanting—"Rocket! Rocket!"—for nearly ten minutes.

The evening ended with a dramatization of the team motto, "To you with failing hands we throw the torch. Be yours to hold it high"—lines lifted half a century earlier from John McCrae's First World War poem "In Flanders Fields" and inscribed on the wall of the dressing room. Bouchard held a torch aloft first. At age seventy-five, he was the eldest of the eight captains present, and he passed it to his successor, the Rocket, who relayed it to Béliveau, and from there it went down the line to Henri Richard, Cournoyer, Gainey (then coach of the Dallas Stars), Carbonneau and Turgeon.

When the torch was extinguished, the players and ex-players left the ice, the fans left the building and the Forum ceased to be a hockey rink after 3,229 regular-season games and fourteen Stanley Cup-winning contests— twelve by the Canadiens, two by the Maroons. The closing ceremony was the start of a week of activities that included an auction of the contents of the Forum, a parade to the new building witnessed by a crowd estimated at fifty thousand and an evening of entertainment dedicated to raising the team's Stanley Cup banners.

The Canadiens officially opened the Molson Centre with a Saturday evening game on March 16 against the Rangers. A sellout crowd of 21,273 attended. Prior to the opening faceoff, Turgeon stepped onto the ice holding the torch aloft, and touched the ice with it. Ronald Corey cut a ceremonial ribbon at centre ice. Banners bearing the retired numbers of Jacques Plante, Doug Harvey, Jean Béliveau, Howie Morenz, Maurice Richard, Guy Lafleur and Henri Richard were raised to the rafters to hang among the Cup banners.

Prime Minister Jean Chrétien and Quebec Premier Lucien Bouchard, who were bitter political rivals, stood side by side and took turns addressing the crowd. Mayor Pierre Bourque came closer than either senior politician to explaining his city's near-mystical bond with the country's national pastime. "Montreal is rediscovering its soul, its past, its present and its future in this celebration of hockey," he said. "The Canadiens carry the name of our city all over the world . . . and hockey brings us together."

The Canadiens won that night and they captured their next three games. They then reverted to the inconsistency that had distinguished their play all year. They qualified for the playoffs in the final week of the schedule, won the first two games of their series against the Rangers, but lost the next four. By that point, all the goodwill generated by the move to the new building had evaporated.

The public was not happy, and captain Pierre Turgeon, who had accumulated ninety-six points during the season, bore the brunt of the criticism. The fans booed him and took shots at him on open-line radio. The media commentary was harsh and unsparing. Turgeon, they said, had taken the series off. He didn't look like a captain or act like one. He only been given the C because Corey wanted a francophone to carry the torch from the Forum to the Molson Centre. Turgeon looked like the Phantom of the Opera, only the Phantom was more dangerous.

That playoff defeat cast a long shadow over the Canadiens. Saku Koivu was the team's best centre in the series. A short, quiet, fair-haired Finn, Koivu was just twenty-one and had two full seasons behind him. At training camp that fall, he was tagged to become the number one centre. Vincent Damphousse anchored the second line and Turgeon was bumped to the third. Turgeon had been the top centre on every team he played for and could not accept the demotion. Prior to opening night, he asked for a trade.

Turgeon played his last game as a Canadien on October 29, 1996. He skated most of that evening as the left winger on the first line, a position he had never played. The Canadiens lost five–four to the Phoenix Coyotes but their captain set up all four goals.

The following afternoon, the team was flying to Detroit to start a road trip. Turgeon was one of the first to arrive. The coaching staff showed up a few minutes later, took him aside and told him he'd been traded to St. Louis along with two other players for Murray Baron, a big, tough defenceman, and Shayne Corson, a former Canadien who played a very physical game. Turgeon immediately left the terminal. Outside the door, he bumped into communications director Donald Beauchamp.

"Where are you going?" Beauchamp asked.

"Don't tell anybody," Turgeon replied, "but I've just been traded to the St. Louis Blues."

"Oh sure," Beauchamp said. "Tell me another one."

For the fourth time in twenty-six months, the Canadiens had unloaded their captain and had to appoint a new one, Damphousse in this case. They had dealt one of the league's slickest offensive centres and a gentleman whose personality and demeanour reminded many people of Jean Béliveau. "This trade makes us a bigger, tougher team," Réjean Houle explained. "It's a trade for the second half of the season and the playoffs."

Mario Tremblay added: "Shayne is a player I've always liked. He will give us character on the road. These two will bring us the chemistry we've been missing."

Some people weren't buying that. "Players like Pierre Turgeon are part of an infinitely small minority," Réjean Tremblay wrote. "There are only so many who can collect a hundred points a season year after year. When you get such a player you make him happy and let him produce. You don't put him on the third line with pluggers who can't score."

The Turgeon deal was the first upheaval in a tumultuous season. In early November, Tremblay had a confrontation with enforcer Donald Brashear, and four days later Brashear was traded. Baron was dealt to Phoenix at the trading deadline for an even tougher defenceman, Dave Manson. Goaltender Jocelyn Thibault ran hot and cold, and it was apparent that he would not be another Patrick Roy.

The team was hopelessly inconsistent. They would beat a strong opponent one night and lose to a weak one the next; win on the road and lose at home. In the eyes of many, Tremblay was the problem. He was too emotional to be effective. "Behind the bench, he is a bundle of nervous tics," *The Gazette*'s Jack Todd observed. "He adjusts his jacket which never seems to fit quite right. He fiddles with his tie, fiddles with his shirt, puts his hands in his pockets, takes them out again, shouts at the ref, folds his arms, unfolds them again, chews gum, paces."

The Canadiens snuck into the playoffs on the final day of the season, earning the right to meet the conference-leading New Jersey Devils. They fell behind three–nothing, in part because of shaky goaltending, and Tremblay took a big gamble in game four. He started José Théodore, an unknown and scarcely tested twenty-year-old netminder. There were several hundred empty seats in the Molson Centre that night, and scalpers were dumping tickets, but the crowd witnessed a near miraculous performance from the handsome, dark-haired goalie who grew up in the suburban Montreal community of Ste-Julie.

The teams were tied at three after sixty minutes, and they played two full periods of overtime before Patrice Brisebois scored seven and a half minutes into the third. Théodore stopped fifty-six shots, including twenty-eight in the extra sessions. He was just as good in the fifth game. "If young Théodore had not been brilliant, above all in the first period," *La Presse* reported, "the Canadiens would have been eliminated after twenty minutes."

As it was, it took more than 107 minutes, but the Devils defeated the Canadiens and the faithful immediately demanded change. Four days later, they got it. Tremblay resigned. He announced his departure at a press conference and came close to tears more than once.

"I sat at home with my wife and two daughters on Sunday [after the Canadiens had lost] and I didn't see any happiness in their faces," he said. "I told myself I have to do something."

Tremblay also lashed out at his media tormentors. "I know there are some people here who want to see me on my knees," he said. "There were some things written that were just mean. That was not right. But at least I can leave with my integrity."

Tremblay's resignation was front-page news across the province. Even Premier Lucien Bouchard was called upon to comment as he left the National Assembly in Quebec City. "Sports sometimes is as tough as politics," Bouchard said. "I would like to say to Mario Tremblay that he can leave with his head up. I wish him luck."

Réjean Houle interviewed a dozen candidates before settling on a successor. The twenty-fifth coach of the Canadiens was Alain Vigneault, thirty-six, a native of Hull, Quebec, a former defenceman and the son of a doctor. He had played forty-two games with the St. Louis Blues in the early 1980s, coached Tier II junior in Trois-Rivières and major junior in Hull and Beauport (a suburb of Quebec City) and had served as an assistant for three seasons with the Ottawa Senators.

Vigneault chose Dave King as his top assistant. King was forty-nine, a westerner and a career coach. He had started in junior and university, had been in charge of the Canadian men's Olympic hockey team for eleven years and the Calgary Flames for three.

Houle introduced the new men at a press conference May 26, 1997, at the Molson Centre. Around a hundred media representatives attended. Most didn't know Vigneault. He appeared bright, youthful and enthusiastic, though to the crowd of journalists he was just another coach, the ninth the Canadiens had announced since Scotty Bowman left the organization eighteen years earlier. One every two years—an average befitting an expansion team, not the oldest, most famous club in pro hockey.

But Vigneault exceeded expectations in his first season. The Canadiens improved by ten points and finished 1997–98 with a winning record. They upset the division-winning Pittsburgh Penguins in the first round of the playoffs—their first post-season triumph since the Cup run of 1993. In round two against the Buffalo Sabres, they ran into a wall named Dominik Hašek. The Buffalo goaltender allowed just ten goals on 158 shots and the Sabres swept the Canadiens in four.

By then, there were wounded everywhere in the Montreal dressing room. Among the forwards, Saku Koivu had a broken hand, Shayne Corson and Benoît Brunet had separated shoulders and Martin Rucinsky a sprained ankle; on the blue line, Igor Ulanov had a fractured foot and Stéphane Quintal a bruised ankle; goaltender Andy Moog had a painful gash on one knee. The players had performed gallantly. Vigneault had coaxed the best out of them and, for the first time in several seasons, the Canadiens appeared to be an improved club.

Instead, they continued to slide. Thirteen members of the team had played out their contracts and six of them were absent when training camp opened in September: defencemen Patrice Brisebois and Vladimir Malakhov and forwards Saku Koivu, Brian Savage, Martin Ručinský and Mark Recchi. Salary disclosure had come to the NHL. Everybody knew how much everybody else was making, and the unsigned Canadiens were trying to keep pace with their peers.

Houle signed his holdouts, but the deals cost a bundle—$33,175,000 over three years, and those were U.S. dollars. As salaries rose, so did expectations. The fans rightly expected results. They didn't get them. The Canadiens had their worst season in nearly half a century. They finished last in their division and missed the playoffs. Ručinský, who was earning well over two million a year, led the team with seventeen goals, the first time since 1940–41 that the Canadiens did not have a twenty-goal scorer. Koivu, who was being paid nearly $3,500,000 accumulated a team-high forty-four points.

The Canadiens' balance sheet was also a mess. Molson Companies Ltd. announced that spring that its sports and entertainment division—which essentially consisted of the Canadiens and the Molson Centre—had lost

$3,800,000 in the year ended March 31, 1999. Free agency and rising salaries were driving costs through the roof. The low value of the Canadian dollar compounded the problem. The team earned its revenues in Canada, but paid its players in U.S. dollars. Then there was the tax burden. The City of Montreal charged the Molson Centre $9,600,000 annually in property, business and water taxes—more than the combined bill of the NHL's twenty-one American clubs. Once, hockey decisions alone—draft choices, trades and the capabilities of those hired to coach and manage—had determined how the team performed. Now, an onerous tax burden and unfavourable economics were undermining the organization's ability to compete.

It was enough to make Molson reconsider its involvement in pro hockey, as chief executive officer James Arnett disclosed in a newspaper interview. The Canadiens were not "some sort of sacrosanct asset," he said, adding that the board was "prepared to make decisions based on rational economic criteria. They're not just going to keep the team for romantic reasons."

Molson was not planning to make any personnel changes, but the turmoil caused one high-profile casualty: at the end of May, team president Ronald Corey resigned, a move that no one anticipated. Corey was sixty. He had held the position for seventeen years, had won two Stanley Cups, built the Molson Centre and presided over the move from the Forum. But the job was affecting his health. During a late-season stop in Phoenix, he awoke gasping for air in the middle of the night. The next morning, he flew home to seek medical attention. He saw several doctors and was diagnosed with asthma.

"I have had many good years with this team and some tough ones," he told a packed press conference held to announce his departure. "Like Canadiens fans everywhere, I harbour a passion for this team that never diminishes."

Corey's successor was just as passionate. Pierre Boivin, a forty-three-year-old, McGill-educated Montrealer, attended his first Canadiens game with his grandfather at the age of six in October 1959. He had been a fan ever since, but never imagined that one day he would be running the organization. Boivin had spent his career in the sporting goods industry. He started with a part-time job in a ski and cycle shop while attending college, at age twenty-five founded a company called Norvinca Sports, which became the largest sporting goods distributor in Canada and went on to become chief executive officer of Montreal-based Canstar Inc., owner of the Cooper and Bauer brands and the biggest manufacturer of hockey equipment in the world. Nike Inc. bought Canstar in 1995, and Boivin remained in the top job till the spring of 1999.

Molson's James Arnett introduced Boivin at a press conference on September 2. Arnett also made a surprise announcement: the Molson Centre was for sale, though not the Canadiens. It was part of a broader strategy of selling assets outside the company's core businesses of brewing and hockey.

The slight, energetic Boivin, stylish in dark-rimmed glasses and a smartly tailored suit, was stepping into a difficult job made more complicated by Molson's now-tentative ownership. But he impressed his audience that day. He was sincere and committed and deftly handled tough questions. He was also realistic. The Canadiens, he said, had to become competitive again before they could contend for the Stanley Cup.

Boivin waited until early in his second season before putting his stamp on the team. The Canadiens began horribly in 2000–01. A loss to the Washington Capitals on November 17 left them tied for last place in the thirty-team league. They had a single win in their previous ten games and only one on the road since opening night.

On November 18, a Saturday, they played the Maple Leafs at home. *Hockey Night in Canada* televised the game nationally. Montrealers booed their team as play began. Several thousand Toronto fans, attracted by the easy availability of inexpensive tickets, and most of them wearing or waving Leaf colours, cheered their side loudly. Jonas Höglund, a Canadiens castoff, scored four minutes in, again at the fifteen-minute mark and completed the hat trick midway through the second. Darcy Tucker, another ex-Canadien, scored as well. The Leafs ran the score to six–one and late in the third people began heading for the exits.

"With nineteen seconds left," Jack Todd wrote, "the big cheerless barn they call the Molson Centre was two-thirds empty. The Canadiens fans had gone home. From ice level to the rafters, all you could see was blue and white: Leaf jerseys, Leaf flags, Leaf banners. When the final horn sounded, there were raucous cheers, not boos. Cheers for the Leafs; no one was left to boo the Habs."

The Canadiens now owned last place. They were behind even the two new expansion teams, the Minnesota Wild and Columbus Blue Jackets. Boivin had hesitated to clean house because by this point Molson was trying to sell the team as well as the building and hoped to conclude a deal by year end. Boivin believed that, in principle, the new owner should approve any management changes. But the Canadiens had fallen into a black hole, as he put it.

Boivin called Réjean Houle at six o'clock on Monday morning and instructed him to come to his seventh-floor office at the Molson Centre. Houle was there within an hour and knew from the expression on the boss's face that he was through. "You can go home and have a coffee with Micheline," Boivin said, referring to Houle's wife. "Take some time to absorb what has happened. I will understand. Or you can stay with me and meet the others involved in this decision."

Houle stayed. Later that day, he met the media. He acknowledged his mistakes. He conceded that he had let Mario Tremblay push him into making bad trades. He shed tears, not for himself, but the team he loved. He was honest and brave and earned begrudging admiration, even from the newspaper columnists who had been so brutally critical. Houle was, as one of them put it, "a *Glorieux* to the end."

Boivin delivered the news to Alain Vigneault at 9 a.m. "Ah, oui," he replied and immediately left. He took the elevator to the coach's office in the basement, slipped out of his training suit and into street clothes and was gone.

The Canadiens were scheduled to play the Florida Panthers that night, and Boivin had announced replacements by game time. The new general manager was forty-seven-year-old André Savard, a retired player whose career had taken him from Boston to Buffalo to Quebec. He had worked as a Nordiques scout, assistant coach and head coach and had scouted and coached with the Ottawa Senators before joining the Canadiens the previous summer as director of player personnel.

Boivin promoted Michel Therrien, the head coach of the Canadiens' AHL affiliate, the Quebec Citadelles. Therrien, thirty-seven, was a Montrealer, a "little guy from the east end of the city," as *La Presse* put it. He had played junior in Longueuil under Jacques Lemaire, coached the Granby Prédateurs to a Memorial Cup championship in 1996 and led the Citadelles to the semifinals two years later. And Therrien had a new assistant beside him that night: Guy Carbonneau, who had retired from the Dallas Stars and had come to the Canadiens to work in the player personnel department.

The changes did not generate much enthusiasm or excitement. "Vigneault didn't win with the players he had," Red Fisher wrote, "and this new bunch can't win either with the tired blood they're inheriting."

He was right. The Canadiens lost their first game under the new coaching staff. Their record in December was one win, ten losses and two ties. In mid-January, *The Globe and Mail* asked three rival general managers what they would do if hired to rebuild the team. "It's like buying a house," one said. "You have to decide whether you want to renovate or blow it up. I think this house needs to be blown up."

By the end of the month, though, the team's woeful performance had been overtaken by off-ice developments that startled the country and shocked Montrealers. The Canadiens had a new owner: sixty-two-year-old George N. Gillett Jr., a native of Racine, Wisconsin, and a resident of Vail, Colorado. "Who would have believed it?" *Le Devoir* asked the day after the sale was announced. "The Montreal Canadiens, the mythical symbol of French Canada for nearly a hundred years, have been sold to an American businessman."

Molson had put the team up for sale the previous June. Within two hours, George Gillett had phoned Dan O'Neill, then the president of the brewery, to express his interest. The following day, he flew to Montreal for meetings and talks with Molson executives. Their negotiations faltered, and Gillett returned to Colorado.

Several NHL franchises were for sale, including the Florida Panthers, the team Gillett decided to pursue next. He had been friends for three decades with team president Bill Torrey and the two men spent several weeks working on a deal.

In Montreal, meanwhile, rumours circulated about potential buyers. Bell Canada Enterprises was reportedly interested. So was Bombardier. Some saw Jean Coutu, founder of the province-wide chain of pharmacies that operated under his name, as a possibility. There was even speculation that René Angélil, Céline Dion's husband and manager, was preparing a bid.

Gillett re-entered the picture on Christmas Day. O'Neill and his family were on a ski holiday in Colorado, and on the afternoon of December 25 the Molson executive stopped at Gillett's home to drop off a packet of documents pertaining to the Canadiens. Gillett asked him in. The two men retreated to his office. O'Neill was immediately struck by the boards on the wall—one for the Canadiens, another for the Panthers and others for the Phoenix Coyotes, New York Islanders and Ottawa Senators, all of which were also for sale. Gillett had listed potential buyers and the financial strengths and weaknesses of each franchise. The Montrealer and his host talked for three hours. By the time they sat down for Christmas dinner with their respective families, Gillett and O'Neill had reached an agreement on the core elements of a deal.

Lawyers and underlings for both sides began working on a detailed agreement in the new year. By late January, word of the impending deal leaked to the media and the newspapers quickly produced profiles of the prospective buyer. They were far from flattering. "Gillett's past inspires more questions than confidence," concluded a report in the Montreal *Gazette*.

Gillett's career spanned four decades. In 1966, at age thirty-four, he had become business manager and a minority partner in the Miami Dolphins of the National Football League. From 1968 to 1979, he owned the Harlem Globetrotters basketball team. But a personal bankruptcy in 1992 cast clouds of suspicion over him.

At the time, he controlled a business empire that consisted of an unusual mix of assets: ski resorts, TV stations and meat-packing plants. He had financed several acquisitions with so-called junk bonds—high-risk securities that carried above-prime interest rates and were popular among entrepreneurs who wanted to buy things with little or no money down.

Furthermore, Gillett had arranged financing through the New York investment firm Drexel Burnham Lambert, a company that went bankrupt itself after one of its star employees, Michael Milken, was convicted of insider trading and other offences and sentenced to a ten-year term.

Gillett's world crashed when the bonds came due. According to documents filed with regulatory authorities, Gillett Holdings Inc. defaulted on obligations worth $983 million. He was forced to declare personal bankruptcy as well. He owed just over $66 million, but his assets totalled only $18 million. The ordeal cost him the family home, the family dogs, his cars (a collection of antiques and exotics valued at over $5 million), his suits (all of them finely tailored from superior fabrics) and his shirts.

Gillett quickly recovered his garments from the trustee. He had such an odd-shaped body—a forty-six-inch chest, short torso and twenty-six-and-a-half-inch arms—that his shirts and jackets would fit very few men, as he jokingly told a Denver newspaper. Gillett also bounced back financially in a remarkably short period of time. He was discharged from bankruptcy on July 20, 1993, was reinstated as president and chief executive of Vail Resorts Inc. and over the next three years earned $6,600,000.

In 1996, he formed Booth Creek Ski Holdings Inc. with two financial partners, John Hancock Life Insurance Company and CIBC WG Argosy Merchant Fund, and acquired ski resorts in New Hampshire, California, Washington and Wyoming. He also reacquired the Packerland Packing Company of Green Bay, Wisconsin, which employed thrity-five hundred people and was one of the largest beef producers in the U.S.

O'Neill introduced Gillett as the new owner of the Canadiens on January 31, 2001. The two men shared a stage erected on the ice at the Molson Centre. Along with a typically large media crowd, the event attracted most of the current players as well as team legends Henri Richard, Yvan Cournoyer and Guy Lafleur. O'Neill promptly dealt with the question that weighed on most minds: Why an American?

"For your information," he said, "we did not secure a single offer from any Canadian company or Canadian individual."

He also made it clear that Molson had sold cheap. The building itself had been constructed at a cost of $265 million. *Forbes* magazine had recently valued the Canadiens at $191 million (U.S.). Gillett acquired the Molson Centre and eighty per cent of the Canadiens for $275 million (Canadian). "It's a huge, huge loss," O'Neill candidly acknowledged. "It's devastating, but that's the way it is."

The alternative was to continue absorbing annual losses—something a publicly traded company like Molson could not do. "He [Gillett] is a private individual," O'Neill said. "If he loses ten million a year on the team, that's his business. If we lose ten million, we have to explain it to our shareholders."

Gillett's objective that day was simply to make a positive first impression, and he succeeded in coming across as affable and down to earth. He answered, forthrightly it seemed, the inevitable questions about his bankruptcy. "I did make a mistake," he said at one point. "I have accepted responsibility. That mistake was not made eight years ago. It was made fourteen or fifteen years ago when I put together the capital structure. The businesses I owned were all operating in a highly profitable fashion. The bankruptcy was a capital structure bankruptcy, not a business management bankruptcy."

Gillett hit all the right notes. He put on a Canadiens jersey and posed with a hockey stick for the photographers and cameramen. He paid homage to the team's great tradition. He assured his audience that he would never move the Canadiens out of Montreal. He promised to leave the management of the franchise to the professionals. And he spoke glowingly of the club's prospects. "If this team is healthy, it's a playoff team," he said, "I've got to tell you this: these last few games have been absolutely fantastic. The last few weeks have been fantastic. The energy has been fantastic."

But words alone could not ease the profound misgivings of many Montrealers. "Gillett is getting a team whose value cannot be measured by punching numbers into a spreadsheet," *Gazette* columnist Mike Boone wrote. "He is buying a piece of our soul."

The Canadiens of 2000–01 were not a playoff team, despite the best wishes of the new owner. They finished with a losing record. For the third straight year they sat out the post-season. That meant a four-and-a-half-month summer. Injuries healed. Disappointments faded. Doubts disappeared and confident veterans reported for duty on the Labour Day weekend.

Before undergoing physicals, or donning skates and equipment, the players participated in a charity golf tournament, an annual event for team alumni, businesspeople and civic leaders that was sponsored by the Fondation du Club de Hockey Canadien pour l'Enfance. George Gillett was there that day, acting as the jovial host. He drove from hole to hole on a motorized cart. He launched the odd drive down a fairway. He posed for photos and dispensed as much goodwill as possible.

Only one veteran was absent: team captain Saku Koivu. His teammates learned why the following morning during a meeting at the Molson Centre: Koivu was a patient at Montreal General Hospital. He had experienced stomach pains and nausea on the flight from his home in Finland. He reported the problem to team doctor David Mulder and the physician had him admitted to Montreal General for tests. The results were not yet conclusive, but club officials were certain that Koivu was out for the season. They even feared that the illness might end his career.

One week later, prior to a 9 a.m. practice, Pierre Boivin, André Savard and Michel Therrien met with the players to inform them that Koivu had the form of cancer known as non-Hodgkin's lymphona. It was treatable, but the survival rate was only slightly better than fifty per cent. Doctors were to begin aggressive chemotherapy immediately.

Koivu was twenty-six. He had played six seasons. He was small for the NHL—just five foot ten and 180 pounds. But he was an inspirational player whom his teammates had chosen as their captain after the Canadiens traded Vincent Damphousse in March 1999. Now he was gravely ill.

"His fiancée called my wife one day," defenceman Craig Rivet later recalled. "Saku had just come back from his third shot of chemo. He hadn't eaten, hadn't moved all day, just lay in a dark room because the light hurt his eyes. Brian Savage and I thought we'd go over and get him up and take him for a walk outside. Once we got over there and saw the way he was, it hit home."

Koivu remained in this low state for weeks, but gradually rose from his sick bed, began to recover his strength and energy, began to go to the rink, even talked of returning to the lineup that season, though such a thing seemed as unbelievable as the illness itself. Players came back from injuries. But cancer? Yet by early March, he was skating. By the end of the month he was practising with the team. In the first week of April, he accompanied the Canadiens on a road trip. Then the doctors cleared him to play.

There were three games remaining. The Canadiens had won seven straight. They were fighting for a playoff spot. They had a new star in goaltender José Théodore, a hometown boy for all intents and purposes, and a French-Canadian. He was slight, and small by the standards of his profession, but handsome as a Hollywood leading man and Montrealers loved him. Many nights that winter they had filled the Bell Centre with chants of "Tay-o, Tay-o," the French pronunciation of Théo, his nickname.

But the evening of April 9, a Tuesday, belonged to Koivu. "Get set for tears tonight," a newspaper headline advised that day, and there were tears. The house lights went down. Flashing multicoloured lights and high-volume rock music greeted the players as they skated onto the ice. Montreal's starting five, Koivu among them, took their places along the blue line for "O Canada." Then the cheering began.

The fans filled every seat. They packed the luxury suites between the lower and upper bowls. And they were on their feet, chanting "Sa-ku, Sa-ku, Sa-ku." They drowned out the pre-game announcements and the national anthem. They produced more than a roar—one commentator likened it to wave after wave of thunder. The ovation lasted eight minutes. The starters for the Ottawa Senators, the visitors that night, abandoned their blue line and returned to the bench.

The Canadiens beat the Senators and clinched a playoff spot. Koivu was named the game's first star. And something else happened, according to some who were there. "That was the first time we felt that the building had a heart," recalls Marc de Foy, the longtime beat reporter for *Le Journal de Montréal*. "The fans cheered like they did for the Rocket the night they closed the Forum. Up in the press box, we looked at each other and said, 'This building has a heart.'"

Koivu's return was the start of a stirring spring. The underdog Canadiens eliminated the Boston Bruins in six games in the opening round of the playoffs. Koivu scored the winner in the third contest, while Théodore stole the last two by facing seventy-two shots and allowing one goal. The series ended before an ecstatic home crowd. "It started with 1:09 remaining," Red Fisher wrote, "men, women and children rising to their feet, stamping them into a thunderous, ear-splitting drum roll. Mouths were open, screaming with pure and soaring joy."

The next morning, on his way to the airport to catch a flight home to Colorado, George Gillett told Fisher's colleague Dave Stubbs: "My ears are still aching. I've never felt anything like it."

The team's amazing run was having an impact on the entire city, according to Pierre Boivin. "We often say that when the Canadiens win, people are smiling on the subway," he told Stubbs. "When they lose, people are miserable. I'm not trying to be arrogant, but as the Canadiens go, so goes the mood of Montrealers and certainly at playoff time. People have a bounce in their step. They're happy."

The Canadiens gave their fans another big lift in round two against the Carolina Hurricanes. They lost the opener, then won consecutive games and took a three–nothing lead into the final period of the fourth contest. Théodore was performing his customary acrobatics. The Canadiens' advantage appeared solid. They were twenty minutes away from taking control of the series. An appearance in the Stanley Cup semifinals seemed a strong possibility, and the Molson Centre crowd was chanting and cheering.

And then Carolina charged back. The Hurricanes scored once early in the third. The Canadiens took a penalty, Therrien disputed the call, leaning forward with one foot on the boards. He was livid and protested too vociferously, and referee Kerry Fraser assessed a bench minor. With a two-man advantage, the 'Canes scored again. They tied the game in the final minute and won it early in overtime.

The big crowd went from up to down, from a joyous roar to shocked silence. The Canadiens never recovered. They lost the next two—couldn't even come close to the Hurricanes—and their season was over.

But there was a postscript, and it was a happy one: Koivu won the Bill Masterton Trophy for perseverance and sportsmanship. Théodore was a bigger winner. He took the Vezina Trophy and the Hart, becoming the first

Canadien to win the latter since Guy Lafleur in 1978 and the first Montreal goaltender since Jacques Plante in 1962.

His breakthrough season earned José Théodore a new three-year contract worth $16,500,000 (U.S.)—the richest in team history. His performance inspired hope and optimism. For the first time since the departure of Patrick Roy, the Canadiens had a goaltender who could keep them in the game most every night.

Furthermore, the team's playoff performance raised expectations. The faithful believed that the free fall of the past decade was over. But in 2002–03 they endured what one commentator described as "a dismal, disappointing and, at times, desperate year." Théodore performed poorly. He and his teammates won only two of twelve in late December and early January and André Savard fired Therrien. His replacement was Claude Julien, head coach of Montreal's AHL affiliate, by this time the Hamilton Bulldogs. The shakeup changed little. The Canadiens finished with a losing record and missed the playoffs for the fourth time in five seasons.

That spring, Pierre Boivin and Savard sat down for what they would later describe as a heart-to-heart conversation about the future of the team. Savard had a plan, one based on good scouting, sound drafting and in-house development of young talent. But it would take several seasons to yield results, and the fans were now thoroughly exasperated. Season-ticket sales had been declining for several years, so had attendance. Some nights there were two to three thousand empty seats in the upper bowl of the team's big building, which had been renamed the Bell Centre. Something had to be done, and the two men came up with an idea that was unusual for the ruthless world of pro sport.

Savard agreed to relinquish his position. He also agreed to remain with the organization if the right person were available to take over as general manager. As it happened, Boivin had someone in mind: former Canadiens captain Bob Gainey.

Gainey was one of those rare individuals who had been successful as a player, a coach and a general manager. He had caught the attention of the hockey world in the spring of 1991—his first behind the bench—by taking the Minnesota North Stars from the back of the playoff pack to the Stanley Cup final, where they lost to Mario Lemieux and the Pittsburgh Penguins.

He stayed with the North Stars when they took up residence in the Sun Belt and became the Dallas Stars. He soon gave up the coaching job to focus on being general manager and by 1999 had produced a Stanley Cup championship. The following year, the Stars were back in the final, though this time they lost. Gainey resigned his position in January 2002, but served as a special consultant to the Stars for the sake of continuity and to ensure a smooth transition.

He was less than a year and a half removed from the pressure and demands of his former position and ready for a fresh challenge when Boivin called in the spring of 2003. On June 3, the Canadiens held a press conference at the Bell Centre to introduce Gainey as their new general manager and executive vice-president of hockey operations. George Gillett flew in for the occasion. Jean Béliveau had a front-row seat, next to Molson CEO Dan O'Neill and chairman Eric Molson. The overflow crowd of journalists peppered the new general manager with questions and he responded in his plain-spoken, honest manner that was devoid of hyperbole or bravado.

"Montreal provides me with a great challenge and a much different environment than the one I competed in for the last ten years," he said. "It's going to be different. It's going to be exciting. It's going to be testy. It's going to be fun."

His return produced something approaching rapture. The *Gazette* welcomed him back in an editorial. Red Fisher evoked memories for many Montrealers when he wrote: "No player I have covered in this business has ever worked harder, hit harder or played through so much pain. No player I have ever known has led better by example." Over at *La Presse*, Réjean Tremblay wrote: "André Savard was competent and credible. But Bob Gainey. It's another story. When Gainey speaks to the players, they listen. When he speaks to the coaches, they listen. When he speaks to other general managers, they listen. It's been a long time since that happened. Such a long time."

The radio stations opened their lines to callers and the newspapers took comments from readers on their websites, and fans from far and wide had their say. "Bob Gainey???" Christopher van Dyke of Vancouver wrote. "God loves the Montreal Canadiens after all!!! Thank you, God! We Hab fans have been in hell too long."

Gainey remained, as ever, the quiet man in the eye of the storm. The fans could dance, but he would work. He was prepared do whatever was necessary to rejuvenate a once-proud and powerful organization brought down by defeat and criticism. In late August, that meant selling tickets. He joined Boivin and a number of former Canadiens and they worked the phones. They called season-ticket holders who were reluctant to renew and urged them to stick with the team. Better times, they pledged, were just around the corner.

COMEBACK TIME

AT LEAST ONCE A GAME, when the Canadiens appear on *Hockey Night in Canada*, a cameraman somewhere in the Bell Centre trains his lens on the general manager's box, some seven storeys above the ice, and captures an image of Bob Gainey. Television viewers invariably see the hard, fixed face of an old warrior who appears steeped in thought and displeased with the spectacle unfolding below. His pained expression arises in part from personal discomfort (he has never become comfortable with his post-retirement role as spectator) and in part from the demands of watching the same group of young men perform sixty, seventy, even eighty times a year, watching and wondering, *How do I fix this?*

There were no quick or easy answers. Three seasons came and went—excluding 2004–05, the year the owners locked out the players—and the Canadiens made little discernible progress. Gainey twice watched his team start quickly and falter. The first time around, he fired his coach, Claude Julien, took over himself, steered the Canadiens to a playoff berth, then witnessed a variation on this drama the following year under his hand-picked successor, Guy Carbonneau. A slump began at Christmas. It became a free fall and the Canadiens tumbled from fourth of fifteen Eastern Conference teams to sixth, to eighth and out of the playoffs on the final weekend of the regular season.

Scarcely a month passed without an upheaval or a crisis, some emergency of the moment that had to be resolved. General managers get paid to make decisions, and Gainey makes them. He traded a popular hometown boy, goaltender José Théodore, after his play slipped—problems with his family seemed to be taking their toll—and the fans started to turn on him. He dealt another equally likeable Montrealer, forward Mike Ribeiro, for similar reasons. He played the peacemaker after the Russian winger Alex Kovalev told an interviewer in his homeland that Carbonneau didn't like Russians and that warring factions had split the dressing room, all of which made the Montreal papers and caused an uproar. During the summer, when tempers had cooled and passions had subsided, Gainey and Kovalev talked and closed the breach that had opened between the player and the team.

Every general manager faces similar challenges, and they always threaten to derail a long-term building program. But in Montreal, there are additional hurdles. Gainey inherited a mediocre team. In their worst year of the previous ten, the Canadiens had finished twenty-fourth in a league of thirty. Otherwise, they were in the middle, or they slipped into the bottom half of the standings, but not to the bottom. They were never truly bad, and in the age of the universal draft the worst are rewarded with top draft picks. Such organizations have the opportunity to select star-quality talent in their darkest years and a good supporting cast as they rise through the standings. The Ottawa Senators, Tampa Bay Lightning and Carolina Hurricanes all followed this path and became contenders or Stanley Cup champions. The Canadiens could not embark on such a journey. Their fans would not tolerate it. The media would be in revolt, not for the usual days or weeks, but for years.

The Canadiens are a team of champions, Hall of Famers, legends and gods. A brief stint in the basement—even to secure a number one draft pick—would be incompatible with the team's luminous past. It would dishonour a club that remains *Les Glorieux*—the great and glorious representatives of French Canada.

Gainey must also do without the best free agents. He has pursued them—Brendan Shanahan one summer, Daniel Brière the next—without success. His predecessors fared no better after chasing such players. Those who have come to Montreal through the draft or through trades will say that there is no better place to play. But those who have the ability to choose are put off, rightly or wrongly, by the language barrier, the high taxes, the long winters and the extraordinary demands of fans and media. So the Canadiens have been doubly cursed—by history and by circumstance.

And yet, as the Canadiens approached their centennial year—celebrated formally from January to December 2009—Gainey and his supporting cast (the assistant general manager, the director of player development, the coaches and the pro and amateur scouts) had shaken these twin curses. They had produced a team that was young, fast and exciting and good enough to finish first in the Eastern Conference during the 2007–08 season.

When they pulled even with the Ottawa Senators, sixty games into the campaign, there was jubilation from the bloggers, the callers to open-line radio shows and the fans who fill the Bell Centre for every home game. "Aahhhhhhhhh!" read an entry from a blogger named Grimsk, which appeared on the website of *La Presse*. "It is good to be a Canadiens fans. The snow seems to fall more softly this winter."

Another, who identified himself as Soniagreg, wrote: "Ah well, I'm laughing because my *blonde* [a québécois term for girlfriend] who has had no interest in hockey for such a long time, is always asking me now when the next match will be on the tely. Unbelievable, huh? Like the Canadiens all year, UNBELIEVABLE!!!!!"

Yes, it was good to be a Canadiens fan again. The team hadn't been so high in the standings at such an advanced point in the season since 1993. Montreal had achieved it with a youthful roster that many nights included ten players who were in their mid-twenties or younger. There was the goaltender, Carey Price; defencemen Mike Komisarek, Ryan O'Byrne and Josh Gorges; and forwards Tomáš Plekanec, Chris Higgins, Guillaume Latendresse, and the Kostitsyn brothers, Andrei and Sergei. Goaltender Jaroslav Halák joined the Canadiens from the Hamilton farm team for the run toward the playoffs.

And that wasn't the end of the talent pool. There were others on the

Bulldogs with the potential to make the NHL club, and promising draft choices still playing junior and college.

The Canadiens had recovered from the lost decade that began in the mid-1990s. They were back, and so were the fans—in record numbers. Television audiences were way up. Réseau des Sports, the French-language all-sports channel, broadcast each of the eighty-two regular-season games and routinely attracted a million viewers, up from 400,000 in the lean years. The Canadiens were setting attendance records as well. The Bell Centre seats 21,273—the largest capacity in the NHL. By the end of the 2007–08 regular season, it had been sold out for 141 straight games.

Season-ticket sales had climbed from a low of about 11,700 in 2002 to some 15,000. The 135 corporate suites located between the lower and upper bowls were fully leased. But more importantly, the Canadiens had attracted a new generation of youthful, energetic and enthusiastic fans.

Most were too young to have experienced the years of glory directly. They were won over by two things: cheap tickets and the Bell Centre experience. The Canadiens have wisely priced seats in the upper bowl at levels that are affordable for young families, teenagers and college and university students. One end has been designated the Saputo Family Zone, named for a food company that is one of the team's corporate sponsors. The crowd in that section often has a Saturday morning at the supermarket look to it. At the opposite end is the Molson Ex Zone, where the atmosphere there resembles pub night on campus.

The fans in these sections, hundreds of them wearing the team colours, supply spontaneity—something that is missing from too many contemporary stadiums. The upper bowl is where the booing begins when the Canadiens are performing poorly. The newest chant—the "Olé, olé-olé-olé" made famous by fans at soccer's World Cup—usually starts there and spreads to the rest of the building.

The Canadiens have rebuilt their fan base with a comprehensive and slickly executed marketing strategy. The organization's forty-five-member sales and marketing department has one overriding objective: to make every game an unforgettable outing. "We're selling a choice," says Ray Lalonde, the team's NBA-trained vice-president of marketing, who runs

an operation that includes ticket sales, consumer products and video production and editing, among other things. "The fans can stay home. They
can go to a movie. They can do many other things. We have to offer them
a valuable experience to convince them to spend $100 or $200 to see a
sports event that is televised. When they see the live product it has to be a
memorable moment."

The Canadiens rely on the same gimmicks and props as most other
NHL teams. During breaks in the action, they bombard the fans with music
meant to keep them and the players pumped. Or they use the scoreboard and
the electronic power ring that separates the upper and lower bowls to deliver
messages that prompt the crowd to cheer. But they do all this so well that
other teams now use the Canadiens as the benchmark against which they
measure themselves.

"We treat our game presentation like a Broadway show," says Lalonde.
"It's choreographed minute by minute and second by second and it begins
with the lead-up to the opening face off. We create the sense that this is the
start of a tremendous event."

This sort of thing can have real impact on the ebb and flow of a game.
"One of the ways you create home-ice advantage is through your game
presentation," says Pierre Boivin. "Over the years, with the right designers
and choreographers, we've ended up with an unbelievable production. It's
tight, it's sharp, it's loud, and it's energizing. We went from dead last in this
area to being the reference point. Our players let us know that they could
feel the difference. They could feel the energy in the building."

The Canadiens have also dug themselves out of the financial hole
that scared off every potential buyer in 2001 with the exception of George
N. Gillett Jr. Many Montrealers were downright skeptical when he took
over. Some were even hostile—an understandable reaction, Gillett acknowl-
edges. "This was one of the most dramatic things that ever happened in the
history of the franchise," he says.

But he has made believers of the skeptics. Gillett is an inherently
friendly man. He has a politician's knack for connecting with employees and
fans. "He walks around the building during games," says Eric Molson,
chairman of the brewing giant that retains a twenty per cent interest in the

team. "He talks to people. He knows the guys who cook the hot dogs in the concession stands."

"He reaches out to people," says Bertrand Raymond, a sports columnist for *Le Journal de Montréal* who has covered the team for four decades. "He'll sit in the stands with kids and older fans. He asks them what they like about the team. What he can do for them? That's changed the whole perception."

Gillett still lives in Vail, Colorado, but his son Foster serves as managing partner and is based in Montreal. The elder Gillett attends about twenty home games per season. He usually watches the first period and sometimes the second from seats close to the ice in the lower bowl. During intermissions, he's on the move. "I sample the food each game," he says. "My son does it when I'm not there. We make sure we're giving our customers proper value, both from the standpoint of size and quality."

Those are habits acquired during four decades in the sports and entertainment business. But Gillett keeps a sharp eye on the big picture. He knows how to make an organization more productive, efficient and profitable, and he has done that in Montreal. He has insisted that Boivin and his team develop a strategic plan, define the franchise's corporate values and stick to budgets. He has also put the front-office staff to work for Gillett Entertainment Group, which he describes as one of the four largest companies of its kind in North America.

Their job is to ensure that the Bell Centre is open and generating revenue as often as possible on the three hundred nights or more per year when there is no hockey. They now book dozens of events annually, including rock concerts, skating shows, circuses and motor sport competitions. The building has become one of the busiest arenas in the world for entertainment events—rivalled only by a similar venue in Manchester, England.

This side of the business has become so big that it routinely cuts into the Canadiens' practice time. As a result, the team is building a new training complex with two ice surfaces, retail space and a restaurant on the south shore of the St. Lawrence. But it has all been good for the bottom line and the future of the Canadiens. "The entertainment company is a major profit centre," Gillett says. "It supports the hockey side of the business."

The resurrection of hockey's greatest organization is complete in all but one essential. The faithful are awaiting that spring day when the leaves are out, when Mount Royal is green, when the St. Lawrence sparkles in the sunshine and the city holds a parade down Ste-Catherine Street or some other downtown thoroughfare and they can converge in their thousands and tens of thousands to celebrate—as only Montrealers can—the Canadiens' next championship, their twenty-fifth, and the return of the Stanley Cup after the longest absence in the history of the franchise.

ACKNOWLEDGEMENTS

The material for this book was drawn from many sources and I have been helped by many people.

I would like to thank those who granted interviews: the late Sam Pollock, Pierre Boivin, George N. Gillett Jr., Ray Lalonde, Elmer Lach, Dickie Moore, Émile Bouchard, Ray Getliffe, Dick Irvin Jr., Frank Selke Jr., Scotty Bowman, Dick Duff, Serge Savard, Jacques Demers, Guy Carbonneau, Craig Rivet, Claude Lemieux, Bobby Smith, Marc de Foy, Bertrand Raymond and Yvon Pedneault. Those who provided advice or guidance or access: Carl Lavigne, Donald Beauchamp, Réjean Houle and Dominick Saillant with the Canadiens, Pat Park of the Toronto Maple Leafs, Craig Cameron and Kevin Shea at the Hockey Hall of Fame; Alan Hustak of the Montreal *Gazette*, and Susan McGuire, formerly of the Atwater Library.

I am indebted to those who have written so ably and colourfully about the Montreal Canadiens: Red Fisher, Réjean Tremblay; Ken Dryden and Roch Carrier among the living; Elmer Ferguson, Jacques Beauchamp, Andy O'Brien and many others who are no longer with us.

I would like to thank Tim Rostron, Martha Kanya-Forstner, Maya

Mavjee and the rest of the Doubleday Canada team; also Lloyd Davis, Steve Hopkins, Lenard Kotylo and Ron Leger.

A special thanks to my friend Bob Gainey, whose generosity and hospitality were invaluable.

As always, I am grateful for the support I have received at home from my wife, Helene, and children Jesse, Isabel and Patrick.

BIBLIOGRAPHY

Barrette, Rosaire. *Leo Dandurand, Sportsman*. Le Droit; Ottawa, 1952.

Béliveau, Jean, with Goyens, Chris and Turowetz, Allan. *My Life in Hockey*. McClelland & Stewart; Toronto, 1994.

Bernier, Serge. *Canadian Military Heritage: Volume III; 1872–2000*. Art Global; Montreal, 2000.

Black, François. *Habitants et Glorieux: Les Canadiens de 1909 a 1960*. Sport Mille Îles; Laval, Que. 1997.

Brown, William. *The Montreal Maroons: The Forgotten Stanley Cup Champions*. Vehicule Press; Montreal, 1999.

————. *Doug: The Doug Harvey Story*. Vehicule Press; Montreal, 2002.

Bruneau, Pierre, and Normand, Léandre. *La Glorieuse Histoire des Canadiens*. Les Éditions de l'Homme; Montreal, 2003.

Dryden, Ken. *The Game: A Thoughtful and Provocative Look at a Life in Hockey*. Macmillan of Canada; Toronto, 1983.

Frayne, Trent. *The Mad Men of Hockey*. McClelland and Stewart; Toronto, 1974.

Geoffrion, Bernard, and Fischler, Stan. *Boom-Boom: The Life and Times of Bernard Geoffrion*. McGraw-Hill Ryerson, Whitby, Ont. 1997.

Goyens, Chrys, and Turowetz, Allan. *Lions of Winter*. Prentice-Hall Canada; Scarborough, Ont., 1986.

Granatstein, J. L. *Canada's Army: Waging War and Keeping the Peace*. University of Toronto Press; Toronto, 2002.

Guay, Donald. *L' Histoire du Hockey au Quebec: Origine et développement d'un phénomène culturel*. Les Éditions JCL; Chicoutimi, Que. 1990.

Hewitt, Foster. *Hockey Night in Canada: The Maple Leafs' Story*. Ryerson Press; Toronto, 1953.

Hunter, Douglas. *Scotty Bowman: A Life in Hockey*. Penguin Books Canada; Toronto, 1998.

Irvin, Dick. *The Habs: An Oral History of the Montreal Canadiens, 1940–1980*. McClelland and Stewart; Toronto, 1991.

———. *Behind the Bench: Coaches Talk about Life in the NHL*. McClelland and Stewart; Toronto, 1993.

Kiple, Kenneth F., ed. *Plague, Pox & Pestilence: Disease in History*. Phoenix Illustrated; London, 1997.

Mahovlich, Ted. *The Big M: The Frank Mahovlich Story*. HarperCollins, Toronto, 1999.

McAllister, Ron. *Hockey Stars . . . today and yesterday*. McClelland and Stewart; Toronto, 1950.

McNeill, William H. *Plagues and Peoples*. Anchor Books; Garden City, N.J., 1977.

O'Brien, Andy. *Fire-Wagon Hockey: The Story of the Montreal Canadiens*. Ryerson Press; Toronto, 1967.

Oldstone, Michael B.A. *Viruses, Plagues & History*. Oxford University Press; New York, 1998.

Ouellete, Rolland. *Les 100 Plus Grands Québécois du Hockey*. Les Éditions internationales Alain Stanké; 2000.

Plante, Raymond. *Jacques Plante: Behind the Mask*. XYZ Publishing; Lantzville, B.C., 2001.

Richler, Mordecai. *Dispatches From the Sporting Life*. Alfred A. Knopf; Toronto, 2002.

Robinson, Dean. *Howie Morenz: Hockey's First Superstar*. Boston Mills Press; Erin Mills, Ont., 1982.

Robinson, Larry, with Goyens, Chrys. *Robinson For The Defence*. McGraw-Hill Ryerson; Toronto, 1988.

Selke, Frank J., with H. Gordon Green. *Behind the Cheering*. McClelland and Stewart; Toronto, 1962.

Stanley, George F. G. *Canada's Soldiers: The Military History of an Unmilitary People*. Macmillan Canada; Toronto, 1974.

Ulmer, Michael. *Canadiens Captains: Nine Great Montreal Canadiens*. Macmillan of Canada; Toronto, 1996.

Whitehead, Eric. *Cyclone Taylor: A Hockey Legend*. Doubleday Canada; Toronto, 1977.

Young, Scott and Astrid. *O'Brien: From Water Boy to One Million a Year*. Ryerson Press; Toronto, 1967.

WEBSITES

www.canadiens.com
www.habsinsideout.com
www.bibleoflacrosse.com
www.garywill.com/wrestling
www.hickoksports.com
www.hockeydb.com
www.losthockey.com
www.sihrhockey.org
www.wrestlingclassic.com

NEWSPAPERS AND MAGAZINES

La Patrie
La Presse
Montréal-Matin
Le Devoir
The Gazette, Montreal
Montreal Star

Montreal Herald
Montreal Standard
Boston Globe
Toronto *Telegram*
The Globe and Mail
Toronto Star
Cobalt Daily News
New York Times
The Hockey News
Saturday Night
Maclean's

IMAGE CREDITS

INDEX